BORROWED TIME

BORROWED
TIME

Ann Craddock

JANUS PUBLISHING COMPANY
London, England

First published in Great Britain 1994
by Janus Publishing Company
Duke House, 37 Duke Street
London W1M 5DF

British Library Cataloguing-in-Publication Data
A catalogue record for this book is available
from the British Library.

ISBN 1 85756 190 2

Phototypeset by Intype, London
Printed and bound in England by Antony Rowe Ltd, Chippenham,
Wiltshire

We look before and after,
    And pine for what is not:
Our sincerest laughter
    With much pain is fraught;
Our sweetest songs are those that
        tell of saddest thought.

Yet if we could scorn
    Hate, and pride and fear;
If we were things born
    Not to shed a tear,
I know not how thy joy we ever
        should come near.

P.B. Shelley, *To a Skylark*

Dedicated to a special friend who cared enough to help me through the hardest year of my life.

With gratitude to: Mr Kai-Chah Tan, and transplant team; Mr J Pain and cardio-vascular team; organ donor and his next of kin; Todd Ward, King's College Hospital, London; St Bartholomew's Hospital, City of London; Newham General Hospital; St Andrew's Hospital, Bromley-by-Bow; Dr Kambiz Boomla; Metropolitan Police Service, Limehouse and Isle of Dogs; District Nurse Lesley Goddard; Gail Priddey and Inform-Al; Nancy Banks-Smith; and the Revd Victor Stock, St Mary-le-Bow Church, City of London.

Without their support and involvement, this book would never have been written.

Contents

Prologue

This book is about a man who survived transplant surgery and its grave aftermaths before living courageously on *borrowed time* – and the surgeons and medical staff in London's hospitals who fought to give him that extra time.

Frank Craddock died of a cerebral aneurysm in February 1991. He is remembered by his many friends in the London Stock Exchange as a colourful character with a taste for fine whisky and Piccadilly cigarettes.

And he is remembered by those close to him, as well as doctors and nurses, as the man who survived major surgery in the wake of a liver transplant after being given only two hours to live. Here is a vivid picture of the day-to-day dedication of NHS surgeons and doctors charged with fighting for the lives of the desperately ill.

Vivid also is the author's portrait of Frank Craddock the man. There was nothing grey about Frank. He was expansive and larger than life – expensive in his tastes, extravagant by nature and habit, flamboyant in everything he did.

Ann Craddock is able to write at first hand only about the last eleven years of his life – years in which Frank's cavalier lifestyle was coming to an end – but we get huge glimpses of the man as he must have been in his heyday, not least because through all his latterday problems he never really lost the gleam in his eye and his own inimitable brand of what he called *Stock Exchange humour.*

Frank was the sort of man who could remain on excellent terms with all concerned after warning a New York waiter that the two men who had just entered the restaurant (erstwhile Stock Exchange colleagues) were likely to take anything that was movable and leave without paying the bill. He was able to get priority service in pubs and hotels while making real friends with those who were providing it. He was the life and soul of any gathering, loved by many, loathed by some and ignored by virtually none.

This was the reputation of the man whom Ann, his wife-to-be, met in 1980. It was a reputation which she found to be fully warranted and so this book is partly a celebration of Frank the man and partly a celebration of the doctors whose skill and dedication were to be so crucial to Frank in later years.

Frank's fortunes and lifestyle were gradually leading him towards severe health problems. His health took a turn for the worse in 1983 when he received the cruel news that his annual company contract was not to be renewed. Even before this blow, there had been grim signs that the battering to which Frank had been subjecting his internal organs for so long was having its effect. Frank's pride took a big dent with the news that his city career was all but at an end, but far from shunning his lifelong habits he turned to drink with a vengeance. So this book has its sombre moments. It tells of Frank's fierce but losing battle against alcoholism and his great battles against the illnesses which afflicted him as a result of alcoholism. And it records Frank's great fights for life in the wake of repeated major surgery.

The author spent many days and nights in hospital while Frank was there, and if any evidence were needed to uphold the excellence and dedication of those charged with saving lives at London's threatened hospitals – particularly Bart's – this book provides it.

Evidence for the cleanliness of the nurses' quarters and those of patients' relatives in some London hospitals is not to be found here, however. Far from it. And the author has some sharp words about the state of bathrooms and lavatories while she was there – even those used by transplant patients for whom infection might have been fatal. She also has a few similar words to say about the attitude of some militants in whose eyes political opposition to the government's NHS policies appeared to justify a situation in which cleaners, for example, did not bother to clean.

Frank's troubles had a profound effect upon Ann's life. He became dependent upon her practical and psychological support to a degree which threatened her own career. But the love they had for each other through good times and bad is so extraordinarily evident in every paragraph of this book that it will be an inspiration to anybody wishing to hear about the strength of true love – and the Christian faith which they shared – when times are hard.

And the author has a final reason for writing this book. Frank spent some of the last months of his life in the company of several people who had travelled the same alcoholic road. Many had not gone so far down the road as to have no better prospects than his own. Frank was determined to spend the last months of his life saying or doing anything he could which might cause such people to think again. This was his message:

Look at the mess I have made of myself. Learn by my mistakes and only do as I say, not as I have done. Life is an uphill struggle – it is easier to slide down than to climb to the top. Once you start to slip your energy is sapped and you will not have the strength for the struggle ahead. Come what may, even in adversity, remain your own man and stay in command of your own life, living it to the full. Be in command of your death and go when called for service by the great Architect in the sky, knowing that you are ready and are not hanging around for the satisfaction of mankind.

Part One

1980-November 1989

1.   The Man in the Crowd

The trains were crowded. Many had been cancelled and there was hardly room inside the crowded compartments to scratch your nose, for you were unable to raise your arms in the crush.

It was in such a train that we met. A conversation was started between us on the lines that if we were animals there would be a public uproar that the conditions were inhumane.

On the following morning, he got into my compartment again and sat by me. By the time we had reached Liverpool Street Station I had been asked to have a coffee with him before we left for our places of business.

He was employed in the International Stock Exchange and had the appearance of a city gentleman in every sense of the phrase. He wore an extremely smart and expensive-looking dark suit, an immaculate plain white shirt and silk tie held in place with a discreet Victorian horseshoe studded with tiny rubies. Over this he wore a dark cashmere coat with a velvet collar. He carried a long furled umbrella hanging by the handle over his arm. He could see his face in the shine on his quality black leather shoes. He was proud of his signet ring which he wore on the little finger of his left hand, for it bore the crest of the London Stock Exchange.

At five feet ten inches, he was too portly for people to appreciate his height. His hair did not have one strand out of place and there were only a few grey wisps amongst the brown. Frank had a mischievous twinkle in his otherwise sad eyes. It was obvious that he wanted to impress me and he looked totally out of place propped on a stool in a British Rail cafeteria. He had talked me into having dinner with him during the following week before we parted and went our separate ways.

I was a director of a company running 25 employment agencies in London. I had been married when I was too young to settle down and although the marriage had lasted 14 years, I had divorced my husband 12 years earlier. I had brought up two daughters and a son who were in their teens.

Much later, he told me that he had appreciated my sense of dress and thought that I was charming, confident, attractive and very feminine but with a protective barrier, an aura around myself which could make me appear aloof. He intended to break this down and reach the real and relaxed me.

I had two main weaknesses, the first being my love of travel. The second was my addiction to fashion and good clothes. The image I was projecting was one of a businesswoman always dressed for interview for I had to set an example both to my staff and to applicants for our vacancies. I could hardly tell people to conform to city standards on their interviews for employment if I were not dressed correctly myself.

Frequently I wined and dined personnel officers or company directors at lunch (many were from blue chip companies) and would visit their offices to give advice; and currently, as I was director of an agency called 'Career Girl', this was a nickname I had to accept and was a way of life that I had naturally adopted and enjoyed.

I could see the reflection of Frank in the window of Asprey's the jeweller in Bond Street as he stood outside the main door to the building where my second floor office was on the opposite side of the road. The chemistry between us was so right that I could feel my heartbeat quicken. Little did I realise what a change this man would make to my future as I joined him and the waiting taxi in which we went to a top hotel for drinks before going to an exclusive French restaurant for a gourmet meal. He did not stop talking. The conversation was mainly about his daughters and the horses he had bought for them to ride. It was obvious that he loved horses and that he was married but unhappily so. He did not try the 'My wife doesn't understand me' routine but I knew that, much as I was attracted to him, I was not going to go out with him again.

Flowers arrived at my office. For about a fortnight I received telephone calls at around four o'clock when trading had stopped on the trading floor of the Stock Exchange and he had returned to his office in London Wall, and then I think he finally got the message and stopped trying to contact me.

Two years later, after I had been working late, I walked past a smoking compartment of the train in Liverpool Street Station, not noticing that Frank was sitting on the seat in the corner enjoying a cigarette after the pressure of the day, trying to read the evening newspaper through his distinguishing half-frame tortoiseshell spectacles. Still with his head down, he raised his eyebrows, opening his eyes wider, and peered over the lenses to see me joining the train further along the platform. A longing stirred deep inside him. I got into the next compartment and started to read my evening newspaper.

The train left the station with Frank wondering how he was going to get into conversation with me again. He walked to the toilet at the end of the corridor and on his return I happened to look his way, just as he willed me so to do. We smiled at each other and he slid the door open and entered to speak to me. I was travelling alone so he could say what he wanted without being overheard. He tried to tell me that he was now separated, without making it obvious what he was doing in case he was rebuffed before we arrived at his destination. I gave him my card for I now had a new office in Bow Lane and a different telephone number so that he left me, happy in the knowledge that this was my way of inviting him to meet me again.

He appeared to walk with a lighter step as I waved to him, holding him in view for as long as I could as the train left Shenfield Station, carrying me further down the line. Previously I had felt the strain of the day, but now I was glowing with happiness.

I received flowers on the following morning carrying an invitation to dinner. There then followed a relationship which is both very beautiful and extremely sad but one which I look back on with no regrets.

Frank had been born in the East End of London and was the middle child of three. I understand that his father drove a bus, a job of which to be proud as he earned more money than any other man in the street and could keep his children well shod, never hungry with 'good basic food in their bellies', which was more than most of the other kids could boast. Frank talked of him changing gear without using the clutch, of alarming exploits on the skid pan with the bus at a maximum degree tilt and of his bravery in the London blitz. Frank's mother was employed by the post office in their 'fraud squad' in her later years. She had been involved with main- and sub-post offices where books appeared to have been cooked or money was missing, irregularities over state benefits, all internal problems and even stolen mail. The post office delayed her retirement or asked her to return to work for she was efficient at her job. Frank's father had died in hospital with a pittance in his pocket, this fact having such a profound influence on his son that Frank always carried a few hundred pounds on his person. Frank loved to talk about the war for he had spent it on the Bowes-Lyon estate, living in a farmhouse in the country. He had been allowed to help with the animals and developed a love for horses. Apparently he had actually loaded and passed the loaded gun to King George and spoken to Princess Elizabeth and Princess Margaret when they were riding, as if they were friends rather than nodding acquaintances: rather a delightful incident when a future queen had made a war evacuee feel so special. He adored the Queen Mother until his dying day, referring to her as 'Everyone's favourite Granny'.

One Christmas he had been given a complete riding outfit by the family and recounted the story to me with moist eyes. He had so many happy memories of this time and obviously found it difficult to return to London and come down to earth.

Frank had been head boy at his school. He returned to his school many years later and was proud that the headmaster knew him immediately. 'Crad' he had been called. Crad had broken a record in athletics and it still stood when he returned to the school. No one had been able to run the distance faster.

Frank's handwriting was copper plate in style. He took great care with the formation of each letter but hated writing letters. He found it difficult to express himself on paper. However, he was a wizard with figures and prided himself that he could work out details over shares faster than any computer. He loved anything to do with mathematics.

Frank had been snooker champion of the Stock Exchange and said that he could have been a professional. He had nevertheless been beaten by Joe Davis and was proud that he had been good enough to be his opponent. He also said that he could have been a professional ballroom dancer in his twenties.

Frank had enjoyed a wild nightlife in his youth, frequenting the London nightclubs with his mates. He was certainly one of the boys known as 'townies' at the time. He loved driving his Sunbeam Talbot in rallies. Life was one of gambling, song, wine, women and cars – the faster the last two were, the better. His mother always asked Frank if he had a 'French letter' in his pocket when he went out which shows that she was very liberated for that time. Yet she believed that sex was only for men. Women were not supposed to take too active a part in love-making nor enjoy the act but just lie back and think of England and the washing up.

On one occasion a Kirby grip had been left in Frank's bed as a prank by his brother and he often climbed into the house through an open window when returning in the early hours of the morning. Frank said little about his sister except that she was prim and proper, 'A proper little madam'. He gambled and placed bets at horse-races both for himself and for others. He called Joe Coral, the bookmaker, 'Uncle', for he knew him well enough to feel adopted. Frank was known as 'Frank Stock Exchange'. He was involved in many gambles in the Stock Exchange among the jobbers and brokers, gambling on such things as how many people would try to pick up a coin which was stuck with glue to the floor.

Frank was not really promotion material in spite of his knowledge and skill, for always he was brutally frank and outspokenly forthright and lacked diplomacy when dealing with his bosses. He had made partner level with a company but lost that when the company merged with another. Frank always supported the underdog in cases of unfairness, and he never let any friend down. He had a yellow Audi 100 when I met him and he still drove like a bat out of hell.

I always felt that I would not have liked Frank if I had met him when he was young for he must have been loud and very much one of the boys. He always loved fun and assessed a party by the amount of drink that had been available. Whether or not I would have liked him, I believe he had always been kind, caring and extremely generous.

Our relationship developed with a near daily meeting over a drink before we went to our own homes on the same train in the evening. Frank had his own seat in *The Stirling Castle* in London Wall. As soon as he appeared the landlord would pour a double, double whisky into a glass and place a jug of water beside it. Frank would then sit at his table in the corner and whilst waiting for me he would enjoy chatting with other city people. He always seemed to be the life and soul of the party. I have never drunk too much alcohol and usually joined him later when he always made me feel someone special. I think I was overdue for this fuss and attention at the time and I absorbed it like blotting paper encountering ink.

Frank, although sometimes coarse, had impeccable manners and a lovely old-fashioned attitude towards women. There was no such thing as 'Going Dutch'. He always walked on the kerb side of the pavement, opened doors, sat down after me and was extremely attentive to my needs. Other women were treated as the 'weaker sex' as well. He was verbose in his feelings that women should not be admitted to work on the Stock Exchange floor. Even as a woman, I noticed the way many of the female brokers appeared to give business to the person who wined and dined them in the most extravagant manner; and often, after supposedly conferring extramarital favours, they would appear carrying a new Gucci bag or some such item. Needless to say the male gossipers, who were ten times worse than the female ones, made comments, some of them far-fetched, about the women's activities. However, they were adamant that two of the women had 'set themselves up in business at the Great Eastern Hotel every Friday night.' I'm not aware that they had their facts right but the two people were known to arrive at work from a different direction every morning!

The males of the Stock Exchange had nicknames for nearly everybody. One woman, who had so much make-up on her face that it looked as if she needed to scrape it off every night, always wore far too much perfume so that you could smell her coming; she was known as 'Smelly Betty'. A 'little short arse' who always wore very high heels to make her look taller, and walked with her bottom stuck out as she had to lean forward for balance, was known as 'Superbum'.

It might seem cruel but was never actually meant to hurt anyone. There was still a unique feeling that although all were competitors in business they were the best of friends and would trust and help one another out of trouble. Everyone knew everyone else by sight. As I write, this spirit of camaraderie is changing for computers have taken over and the Stock

Exchange floor is virtually empty. Frank had been greatly saddened by Big Bang and Black Monday but had not been working for some time when the changes came into force. His comment was that he was 'better off out of it all'.

I had only been out with Frank twice since our second meeting on the train when I was struck down with the most excruciating pain in my abdomen. I was lying in bed in a pool of perspiration when my youngest daughter arrived home from a party. She insisted on telephoning for the doctor in spite of my protestations that it could wait until the morning. My GP came to the house and rang for an ambulance. I stubbornly dragged myself on to my feet for I told the ambulance driver that I would not be carried over my threshold until I was dead. I was admitted to Basildon Hospital immediately and kept under observation over the weekend. I was worried that now Frank had found me he might think that I was avoiding him but I was not allowed to get off the bed, and the trolley telephone was out of order.

Frank was to get to know my family in my absence for he phoned my home and spoke to Claire.

'You may not know me but I am a friend of your mother,' he had said, and Claire told him what had happened.

Frank's beautiful blue and white flower arrangement arrived as I was being prepared for theatre. It was immediately removed from me.

'Can I ask you to do something for me?' I asked the lady in the bed next to me.

'Of course, dear. What do you want me to do?'

'Please make sure that the flowers are near my bed so that when I come round from my op I can see them.' I would then know that I was not dreaming and Frank really was aware of me.

When I recovered consciousness I was in shock and did not notice the flowers were nowhere near. The nurses needed every bit of space near the bed to look after me. Later, the flowers were returned to my bedside. During evening visiting my eldest daughter Lydia and her husband were sitting at my side when I glanced down the ward and broke into a beaming smile which was returned by a worried Frank. I watched his characteristic rolling gait as he walked tall and straight to me.

Lydia and Frank 'hit it off' immediately and Chris had many interests and hobbies in common with him. A firm friendship was formed between the three of them which was never broken.

In a quiet moment when Lydia and I were alone she said, 'He is the man who took you out to dinner a couple of years ago, isn't he?'

'How on earth do you know that?' was my amazed reply, for I did not remember talking to anyone about that evening.

'Mummy, there was something very different about it. It showed in your face and I could feel it in the atmosphere around you as you told me where you had been.'

Frank and Chris returned to my bed to say that they were now going to leave me to rest. Lydia turned to Frank.

'Mummy will come home to us from the hospital so that I can look after her. If you want to come to see her you will be welcome at any time.' Frank visited me there frequently, after following Lydia's diabolical instructions and getting lost on his first attempt. (Lydia had once navigated from the north of England to Billericay in Essex and had arrived at Kings Cross in London instead!)

It wasn't until Christmas that Frank was to meet my son. Alan was serving in the Royal Air Force in Scotland but he was home on a rare but long leave. Alan was delighted to be at home as he had a local girlfriend. Frank was not well at the time and was suffering from bronchitis. He had been staying with me for a few days for he really needed someone to care for him. I, in my turn, needed to be needed.

Once, while we had been sitting in *The Stirling Castle*, I had been taken gently to one side by a middle-aged barmaid who had recently been mugged on her way home from the pub. Frank had shown great understanding and quietly arranged financial help for her. He was always affectionate towards people he liked and gave her a warm embrace. He was a hurt man suffering from a broken marriage who certainly needed his confidence boosted and to feel that someone believed in him. 'You won't leave him, will you?' She showed great concern. 'I've known him for years and he really does need you. At the moment he isn't fit enough to care for himself.' She was correct.

When Frank had been too poorly to get out of his rented house in London, I had gone to him and brought him home with me so that he could have the love and care which had been lacking from his own family.

Alan was not as quick to accept Frank. We believed that he was not sure that Frank's intentions were honourable. Frank and I were not sleeping together, having separate bedrooms. Alan was always protective towards me and had assumed responsibility ever since his grandfather had unwittingly said 'take care of Mummy' after my divorce. I had found him cuddling his teddy at the age of 12, crying that he could not make a living to support us all. As he grew up, we rarely agreed and argued over anything and everything. Alan goaded me and I used to fall for it, even though I knew that this was what he wanted me to do.

During a very sombre discussion between Alan and myself, Frank hoped to sort out the problem. It was the only time that I can remember him being diplomatic.

'You must know that I love your mother and want to marry her. (He had never proposed to me.) I want you to know that when that happens I will be the one to wear the trousers in the house and I will expect the household to understand. I know that your mother can drive you mad and that it hasn't been easy for you to put up with it all the time. But I will expect you to treat me as the head of the family and leave me to sort her out.' He had winked at me and hoped that he would not alienate Alan by showing he understood his frustrations, and that he wouldn't side with me always. Alan seemed to respond well to this conversation.

I felt that Alan needed to be a saint when Frank made him help with the erection of a new curtain rail on a stubborn solid wall, for Frank was useless at DIY. He would brush aside his incapacity in this area by saying things like: 'My father was brilliant with electrics. He used his brawn and not his brain'. I always told him, much to his disgust, that I would earn enough money to pay someone else to do my manual work for me.

That would have been alright if he hadn't always attempted to do the work first before giving up and calling in the expert and then interfering. I could hear the knocking, swearing and a few heated arguments before Frank decided to visit his two daughters on this Christmas Eve.

'Now leave it until I get back. Don't touch a thing whilst I am out!' Alan listened. Frank left the house. As soon as he had gone Alan got to work. He was in a hurry to complete the chore before Frank returned. It was easier to do the job alone without interference and lectures. 'Eureka, Mum, I've got the damn thing up. Where are the curtains? I'll hang them, too.'

I gave him the heavy full-length curtains. Having hung them Alan was delighted, for now he could go out. I went into the dining room and was pleased with the result but decided to draw them to see how they hung. As Alan watched I closed the curtains, which promptly fell on my head, curtain rail and all.

I laughed. Alan fumed. We had the biggest of our many rows. 'You were alright before you became a career woman. You were a proper mum then. But you stopped coming to sports day and school things. You have really changed,' he shouted at me. It was now that I believed I had learned why Alan had been taking his anger out on me.

'How do you think I would have been able to bring you all up if I had not had a responsible job?' I asked. 'How on earth could we have managed on the maintenance of £3.25 a week? And that was when I had been back to court for them to get it out of your father!'

He looked shocked. I had never involved my children in my marital problems and had never run their father down, although I felt that he had behaved like a bastard, particularly when he managed to ignore their upkeep, birthdays and Christmases. He wasn't 'out of sight, out of mind' to Alan, who had built a glossy picture of his father but hadn't seen him for years. Whenever reprimanded or just bored with living in a house of women, Alan as a child would say he would rather live with his father and although this was hurtful, I'd tell him that I would help him pack his case which was nearly as big as he was. Sometimes he would leave the house but he never went further than the corner of the lane without finding some excuse as to why he wouldn't go then but wait until tomorrow. Thank goodness that tomorrow never comes.

'Do you think I wanted to work?' I shouted. 'I would have loved to be a proper mum. It's been a nightmare for me too.'

I stormed into the lounge and turned on the radio so that I could listen to the carol service from King's College Chapel in Cambridge, the city of my birth and childhood years. I knew that my ex-husband would be listening to this programme wherever he was in the world. What was he thinking now he had a new wife and daughter? Did he ever think of his other children? Quietly, Alan put his head around the door. He smiled kindly as he produced a tray with the steaming tea pot, cups and milk in a jug. A plate held my home-made mincepies.

'I thought you might feel like this,' he said, as he placed the tray on the coffee table. 'I never knew, Mum. I never knew a thing. I never bothered to think.' He was obviously speaking from his heart and meant every word. 'You'd better be mum,' he said, as he indicated to me to pour the tea. 'You haven't done a bad job of being my mum so far.' He put his arm around me and we became good friends from that moment and although he continued to tease and provoke me, it has always ended in fun without animosity. The choir were still singing like angels on the radio but for the first time I was oblivious of them for the whole of the service. I had the best Christmas present that I could receive. My son was with me in flesh and spirit.

Frank returned to find the curtain on the floor and plaster crumbs sprinkled over them. He turned crossly to Alan.

'I told you to leave things alone.'

'Don't have a go at him,' was my reply, as I gently touched his arm. 'He's repaired something much more important. The curtains can wait.' And the curtains did wait until the money which Frank had earned was paid to someone else for the work.

Claire's meeting with Frank did not go as well for they were equally stubborn. Claire was my youngest child and had stayed at home with me after the others had left. We had had good times together for I was more affluent than I had ever been before. She had had me to herself. I think she was jealous of a man taking me over.

One day she shut herself in her bedroom accidentally. The door handle came off in her hand and she couldn't get out. She was frightened but Frank did not appreciate her fear.

'You silly cow,' he said, laughingly, as he went to help her.

'I won't be spoken to like that; who do you think you are?' She was nearly in hysterics. 'I hate you.'

Eventually I calmed the pair of them and Frank did get Claire out of the room. She would not thank him and he would not let the matter rest. I felt that it was six of one and half a dozen of the other. How I wanted to bang their heads together. Could they not understand that they could both have my love? Claire found it very difficult with a man in the house for she could not remember experiencing this before. She certainly did not appreciate Frank's sense of humour for a long time.

Frank knew he was drinking too much. He asked me to pour his drinks and only give him half his normal amount. He went to see my doctor and collapsed in the waiting room. The doctor examined him and said that unless I looked after him he had better go to hospital as his lungs were bad with bronchitis.

I said I would keep him at home if the doctor would continue to see him. The doctor said that he must cut down on his drinking and showed me photographs of the puffy, bloated faces of alcoholics. He was obviously trying to tell me something.

Frank had been brought up in a family which enjoyed drinking. He had taken a profession which was pressurised and one in which he had to socialise. He always had a glass of fluid near him but it was not always alcoholic. He had not wanted to go home, feeling that he was not welcome nor loved, so he stayed in the city propping up the bar for as long as possible every weekday evening. He found it very difficult to sleep and on being refused more sleeping tablets some years previously had taken to his nightcap on which he had come to depend. He always found reasons to celebrate or console himself. Frank truly believed that I would be able to help him control his drinking and I truly believed that I would be able to help him in his battle. Frank was also a heavy smoker. He loved food and could afford to eat well and often.

Frank had been active in his youth and had been a physical training instructor in his army call-up days. However, his only sport was golf now and even that was being dropped since he had hurt his finger by cutting a tendon and nerve. He was putting on far too much weight.

I understood that he had suffered with high blood pressure for some time and had recovered from a blood clot in his eye which had meant that his eyes had aged too.

Making up for these troubled characteristics was one of the greatest personalities I had ever met. He was witty and kind. I loved being in his company. We were certainly compatible in every way.

Frank stayed with me for a fortnight, spending Christmas with my family, before he returned to his lonely home in London. He met my parents for the first time and there seemed to be acceptance and approval from both sides. Frank had a sense of humour identical to my father and indeed they seemed to hold the same opinions over matters in general.

2. Together

'I wish I had met Frank years ago,' was my father's comment before he departed for home in Dorset. They were both stubborn and forthright, rocks on whom I could depend. The only difference seemed to be that my father hardly touched alcohol. I had been brought up in a family which only partook on special occasions and was rather naïve over people with drink problems.

I had always said that when Claire left school I would move into London to live for I was tired of commuting a total of 70 miles each day in crowded and dirty trains which were often late or cancelled. The journey was becoming very expensive. Claire started training as a nurse in University College Hospital four days before her 18th birthday in the summer. I easily sold my home in Billericay although the property market was in the doldrums, and purchased a tall, narrow house in a private square in derelict but developing docklands, overlooking the river Thames at a time when Canary Wharf was a mere twinkle in the eye of the architect. It seemed pointless for Frank to be paying rent and living by himself with me paying a mortgage and also living alone. We knew that we would eventually be living together as husband and wife so it seemed sensible, though unnatural, for Frank to live with me. He was spending most of his time with me and was never in his own home anyway.

'I can't ponce off a woman,' he said to me.

'You won't be doing that if we use your money as investment. My investment will be the house,' I replied. 'Anyway, it doesn't matter whose money it is if we are going to share everything in the future.' He accepted this but I do not believe that he was ever really at ease over the arrangement and was quick to jump down my throat if I ever said 'my house' in a conversation.

Our living together was totally against my own judgement for I had always tried to live morally and set the standards of behaviour for my family. I could imagine the comments.

'What a turn up for the book!'

With Frank by my side it did not matter.

I had yet to meet his own family. I had resigned as a director of the company and set up my own business in the city (Ann Warrington Secretarial Careers), having allowed myself to be talked into this by Frank and his friends. It was to provide me with a tremendous challenge.

'You've made a lot of money for other people,' he said. 'Start making some for yourself. You have me to lean on now if you get into any difficulties.'

I also felt that Frank was jealous of any other man I was working with and as I had been the only woman on the board of directors, he hadn't really approved, but had been wise enough not to say anything about his feelings.

It was strange when we set up home together for I had been on my own for so long that I had to adapt to living with another. I could no longer have my own way all the time and it was irritating to find petty things such as the toilet rolls unwinding from the nearest side instead of against the wall, and having to roast my potatoes after they had been cut into small segments so that they would absorb the fat and be squashier, when I loved them large and crisp.

Frank insisted on always carving the joint which pleased me, for my father had been the same. He would not allow me to touch his lethal carving knife, which he had obtained from a butcher friend. He was proud of his prowess with carving and of his educated knowledge of meat, telling me where it had been on the animal and the direction of the grain, and he always insisted that 'Meat needs to have a bit of fat otherwise it has not come off a healthy animal.'

As far as I was concerned, he was welcome to the fat. I wouldn't eat it. I stopped buying the meat and left this shopping to him. It was not unknown for him to take the carving knife from the chef in a carvery and carve both his and my meat. He had the type of personality which did not upset the chef, who usually ended by looking at the remains of the joint with satisfaction for it was probably in better shape than it had been before the incident. Discreetly, Frank would put a note in his hand for a tip and the chef would beam his thanks.

Returning to the restaurant, we would be recognised and treated well. 'Let's start as we mean to go on,' he ordered. 'You will not pour the drinks in this house. That's my job. I will not interfere in the kitchen.' He frequently did voice his opinion in the kitchen, however, and I frequently had to dilute my drink.

He had to be 'the man of the house' and be seen to be 'wearing the trousers.' He called himself 'the boss's boss' in jest to my staff. Frank would not use public transport and arranged that a car would collect us in the morning and drive us into the city leaving him in Threadneedle Street for the Stock Exchange and me in Copthall Avenue and later in London Wall when I transferred my business to a different address.

At that time as the roads in the docks were private, we were not allowed access to the shortest route to the business. However, daily we would slow down at Gate 7 where the security guard would check the passengers.

Frank would be sitting in the back of the car reading the pink *Financial Times*. He would glance up, peer over his half-frame glasses and proffer an acknowledging nod. The security guard in return touched his cap and waved us through. It was only on trying to drive the route alone and being refused admittance that I appreciated his command of respect and his arrogant cheek.

I only knew Frank to use the underground on one occasion. That was when we visited Wormwood Scrubs for a pantomime as guests of a group of prison visitors from the city and they chose that mode of transport, the attraction to all being duty free drinks at the bar afterwards. On his one bus ride he helped an 'old dear' with her heavy shopping and held the bus up as he climbed on again to the annoyance of other passengers and the driver. He travelled on a riverbus once but was never interested in the Docklands Light Railway.

Frank did not appreciate the theatre and never went to the cinema. He bravely tolerated my love of music and grew to appreciate a greater variety than was provided by the honky-tonk piano. His father 'could tinkle the ivories of the old Joanna like the best of them, provided there was a pint of ale on top of it.' Renditions of *Danny Boy* would reduce him to tears, reminding him of those days; and so would *Abide with Me*, for as a schoolboy he had played a football match at Wembley. He loved listening to *Sing Something Simple* on a Sunday afternoon and would join in the singing at home. Firm favourites were Chas and Dave and their East End style but he also grew to love and make us hush and listen to *Nabbuco – The Chorus of the Hebrew Slaves*. We adopted 'All I ask of You' from *Phantom of the Opera* as our song although later on he seemed to substitute this with another.

To a degree, he was still one of the lads. He had a wicked sense of humour which he said was 'Stock Exchange style'. Whatever it was, I certainly appreciated it, and we used to bait each other by keeping it going. Frank seemed to be at ease with everyone except children. Somehow they took his confidence away. Yet my grandchildren were fascinated by him and loved him. Stuart had been playing 'Let's Pretend' and was mimicking Frank. He pretended to puff on a cigarette and kept raising his pretend glass to his lips. Frank laughed with us but was secretly rather taken aback that this was the image he was creating.

The children used to dare each other to sit in Frank's armchair but as soon as they heard Frank coming, the brave one would scuttle out of the chair and far enough away not to get into trouble. When Stuart was staying with us he rushed downstairs with Frank when he heard him in the morning. Frank was used to being quiet at this time so Stuart was sent to get in bed with me for cuddles.

'Where's Uncle Frank?' I asked the lad.

'Uncle Frank is gathering his thoughts,' was the serious reply. That early morning period of time will always be known as 'Uncle Frank's gathering thought time.'

Frank would not tolerate fools. He lacked patience with people but when he was trying to complete a task he would take endless time in order to complete it perfectly. He had patience with himself. He was not keen to take orders but was good at issuing them.

He rarely kept his opinions to himself but could get away with anything without causing offence, except on one occasion when he managed to pass the blame to someone else.

We were in a party of city folk on a rare visit to the Bank of England. As we gathered together in the foyer and were checked for security purposes Frank was unable to control himself and, although silencing it, allowed a smelly silent fart to escape. As the pungent aroma wafted in front of us all, the dignitaries were trying to look as if their noses did not smell or that they had sinusitis.

Frank looked at me and said simply and with disgust, 'Ann!' Everyone was made to feel that I was the guilty person and they all moved a few feet away from me. I did not know whether to laugh or be cross with him.

There was an occasion when he had invited his friend Ken to stay with us after they had been to a charity boxing evening, and they arrived home around midnight giggling like young schoolboys who had been mischievous. I had gone to bed and decided to stay there, leaving them to their fun. Apparently Ken had won a bottle of rather good red wine which he had opened but not finished at the dinner. He had corked it and put it into his briefcase with his change of clothes for the next day. Unfortunately the wine had leaked over his clothes; so they hung them over the radiator in the bedroom to dry out. Next morning Frank lent a pair of socks and underpants to Ken. Ken was wearing the shirt which he had worn the day before. They went to the Stock Exchange.

When Ken went to urinate, answering the call of nature, and was standing with other brokers doing the same, he could not find the Y in the Y-pants for Frank had previously sewn it up. Poor Ken had to drop his trousers and underpants to stand and relieve himself in desperation, firstly thinking that he had dressed with them on back to front, to the amusement of his colleagues.

When he approached the box where Frank was working he received a cheer from the rest of the jobbers who had been out to buy him a pair of pants.

'You sod,' said an embarrassed if not amused Ken. What he did not know was that Frank had found his underpants so uncomfortable that he had stitched up every pair he possessed – but had forgotten to tell Ken about it. The teasing did not stop that day.

Our first holiday together was spent in Gibraltar. We wanted to go abroad but as my son was participating in the Falklands War and we knew that he was ill, we thought that if we were in Gibraltar we were more likely to get news and possibly see him on his way home to a hospital in England. We stayed at *The Rock Hotel* halfway up the rock, overlooking the naval yard.

I had hoped that this would be a romantic interlude and that once away from the pressure of business Frank would relax and not need to drink as much. However, he was just as dependent on alcohol and arranged that at four o'clock each day, whisky for him and orange juice for me would be taken to our room for our return from the pool.

I had brought a 'trousseau' even though this was not our honeymoon and I had every intention of 'seducing' him. I don't think he even noticed what I was wearing for every evening he would sit on the balcony overlooking the dockyard with his whisky in his hand, drinking – the big habit of his adult life. He really believed that he would not sleep without this nightcap and he seemed to be obsessed with his desire to sleep.

I think this was the first time I felt that I had competition for his favours. It was either me or his bottle – and in anticipated intimate moments, I was losing.

I am certain that this was mainly because he was no longer sure that he was able to make love when his head was telling him that his desire to do so was there. Somehow his body would not respond. He then felt that he had to apologise and that he was inadequate as a man. He could not understand that if he stopped drinking as much he would regain his libido. I had been without sex and love for too long and longed for him to satisfy me; but I had also been without close male companionship and he more than satisfied that. Frank was great company and he made me feel special when I was with him. He was attentive to my needs and thought that nothing was too good for me. I was totally spoiled by him and I was cautiously happy.

He had a special knack of getting the service he wanted. His approach was to quietly give a tip on arrival, then say, 'The other half of this will be given to you when I go.' It wasn't that he bought people off, rather that he could make it a pleasure for them to please him. Somehow he made them feel special too.

'Maître d', it is too hot in here. Can the air conditioning be turned up?' he asked, on one occasion.

'Certainly Sir,' said the maître d' as we ate dinner, having been given

the same, and probably the best, table every evening. A few minutes later
there was a complaint from another table that it was too cold.

'I'm sorry Sir, the air conditioning is not functioning properly and I am
unable to adjust it,' said the maître d'.

Frank had no feeling of pity for the freezing couple. 'If he bothered to
wear the correct clothes at dinner he would not be cold.' He felt he had
justified himself for the man did not wear a jacket and looked incongruous
in this famous hotel.

Frank may not have noticed my seductive underwear but he did notice
how I looked when we were in public. I often felt like a million dollars
because of his approval.

'You can always tell a woman by her accessories,' he would say, as he
knowledgeably glanced at my shoes and bag. 'And you look good.'

The hotel lived up to its reputation and provided us with comfort and
care which was second to none. We found Gibralter more British than
Britain and as two patriots, we appreciated this.

We ate cucumber sandwiches at afternoon tea as we drank Earl Grey
in the cool and peaceful conservatory overlooking the sea; we listened to
the news which was broadcast daily from home and relayed in the foyer
about the Falklands progress. We counted more Union Jacks flying from
private buildings than we had ever seen before and we saw dolphins diving
in and out of the sea as we spent an afternoon on a boat sailing around
the Rock. We made friends with a bank manager and his wife whom we
met at the swimming pool whilst reading and sunbathing. We found a
pornographic (or near enough so) book covered in plain brown paper and
on returning it to them, we became good friends. I learned what bank
managers sometimes do on holiday! We also became companions of a
recuperating soldier who had been blown up when defusing a bomb in
Ireland. His external injuries were horrific but his unseen damage was
far worse for his best friend had been killed at the time of the explosion.
We enjoyed ourselves.

The apes were still on the Rock. We laughed as they jumped up and
down on the bonnet of a car actually making a dent as the owner, a
woman, wringing her hands in horror, screamed 'That's my car,' as she
shooed them away.

The apes were not to be fed for once they'd realised they could successfully beg food they had started to go into the town to steal food from
residents. Our taxi driver encouraged them to take nuts from his pockets
and thinking that we had food too, they sat on my shoulders and were
quite frightening although very cute.

We shopped for bargains as everyone simply has to do. We rested and
we made friends.

Frank was frightened of flying, so on both the incoming and outgoing flights, he had to get Dutch courage and sank himself into his whisky. On reflection, he was totally dependent on his drink. I must had been blind to this.

I did not understand how he could drink so much without getting drunk, but he never seemed to reach that state. He was always in control of himself and the situation, I was proud to be with him and he was proud that I was his 'other half'. He was now as dependent on me as he was on his drink. I was beginning to become his crutch.

3. Tough Times

Frank had a contract with his company which was renewed yearly. He was proud of his work and believed that he was good at it. I was led to believe this too by the comments of his associates. However, this was the year that his contract was not to be renewed. He was shattered by this news. It had a devastating effect on him. His beloved Stock Exchange had turned its back on him. He had never had respect for his senior partner. There was no empathy between them. Frank believed that this was because the man's father had been an alcoholic and the son had reacted against this by becoming a teetotaller. Frank felt that he had always been penalised and that his forthright manner of saying what he thought and damn the consequences had not helped the situation. Now Frank, as a sick man in his fifties, would be made redundant. He needed every encouragement and support from me well as from his numerous friends. I would not judge him.

The City loves success but will turn its back on failure. So it did to Frank. Only one of his friends gave him any support at all. Whereas once they had all gathered in *The Stirling Castle* for a laugh and drink with him before going home, now they were either drinking somewhere else or had gone straight home. It was noticeable that they were all worried that their own contracts would not be renewed. Insecurity was beginning to show. It was a little like the kettle calling the pot black for most of them were drowning their sorrows in drink daily and would follow in Frank's footsteps. It is true to say that Frank had been getting slower. He had had odd bouts of absenteeism caused mainly by his bronchitis and heavy smoking but he was loyal and conscientious with a good track record of 25 years' membership of the Stock Exchange. He could still teach the younger ones a thing or two. Now he was being asked to relinquish this pride. He was devastated but put up a fight. I am sure that now he had someone to believe in him and back him, he would have been able to gain some ground but he had been dismissed at a crucial moment. He had a meagre bronze handout which was not enough to live on for the rest of his life but was just enough, with his savings, to make it impossible for him to get any state benefits. He nearly had to litigate for his money, which was certainly due to him.

He had been out of work for only three weeks before he was offered a directorship with a new company in the West End. Frank was told to find himself a City office for he did not wish to leave the City and he was still to deal with finance but now USM (the unlisted securities market) instead of the stocks and shares of those companies trading on the Stock Exchange with which he was so familiar. Relinquishing his share in the London Stock Exchange broke his heart and destroyed his *raison d'être*. He soon found a new address. Frank had always taken his acceptance and place in the City for granted and he was shattered to find that his 'Book' could function without him. Too many changes were being made and Frank did not like change. This made him even more dependent on me for he needed to have someone solid to cling to.

We no longer went to the pub together before coming home after work. I liked to be home first so that I could keep the house clean and prepare our evening meal. Frank did not prop up the bar after work for he now had a happy home to return to and was guaranteed a loving welcome. He could relax in his slippers with his pipe or cigarettes and his tumbler of whisky by his side.

I had continued to experience considerable pain in my abdomen which worried him to such an extent that I tried not to tell him about it. One night I was in great pain and could not lie down in bed. I spent the night doubled up in the bathroom and in the early hours of the morning I climbed into the bed in the dressing room so that I would not disturb Frank. He found me propped on pillows when he woke and I knew that he could not cope with my sickness. He also seemed abnormally concerned that I was in the dressing room and when I eventually opened the bedside cabinet I found out why, for there were empty bottles of whisky and a sticky, smelly glass half filled with whisky and water.

I knew that Frank could not sleep well and would often get up in the middle of the night and sit on the bed in the dressing room before returning quietly to our bed. This had become a habit.

My new doctor referred me to a consultant immediately who in turn insisted that I have a hysterectomy within two weeks. Frank was beside himself with worry and I was more concerned about him than with myself. He was in a terrible state and could not take me to the hospital, so I arrived alone. I was told that I would be receiving intensive care after the operation in order to prevent possible further trouble, and I dreaded Frank being aware of this.

Frank had promised that he would visit me in the evening before surgery but I received an embarrassing telephone call from him instead. I received the call while one of the two anaesthetists was at my side and I could not say all that I wanted to put his mind at ease. I was dreadfully unhappy and felt apprehensive and isolated from the world. Frank was consoling himself with his drink and I could not do anything about it. He promised to visit me during the morning before my operation but he made no contact with me. The morning seemed endless and was made worse by the trauma of a sick child in the next room. I sat by the window of my private room overlooking leafy Bryanston Square trying to take my mind off things by working on my tapestry.

My operation went well and at last my problem had been discovered and cured. I vomited through the night. I was not really aware of what was happening but I know that I was worried about Frank as I regained consciousness. I could not get him or his inability to cope with my absence out of my mind. I was already losing my true identity to him through his alcoholism but would never have considered leaving him to cope alone. I believe that would have killed him. I had to recover quickly to return home to him.

My son and his girlfriend stayed with Frank for the weekend and were with him when the surgeon telephoned Frank with the news after the operation on Friday evening. He talked to Frank for 15 minutes and Alan and Janet calmed him as much as they were able both during the operation and afterwards.

By now Claire was a more experienced nurse. Knowing that Frank should not be allowed to visit me alone in case he collapsed, she brought him to me after telling him what to expect. She held onto his arm as he stood unsteadily at my bedside. The tears rolled down his cheeks.

'I couldn't bear it if I lost you,' he said.

He bent to kiss me and he smelt strongly of drink. I knew that his whole being depended on my stability and it was weighing heavily on me. I received no flowers from him during my ten days in hospital, for he was overcome with worry and wasn't behaving with his normal generosity. He had no idea what to do for he was stunned and when I asked him to bring me clean nightdresses, he went out to buy them instead of bringing them from home, and they were the worst passion-stranglers I had ever seen. I needed to feel feminine at that particular time for it is an emotional strain to realise that your child-producing days have come to an abrupt halt. I wanted to see him but I dreaded his coming for I wondered what state he would be in when he arrived. I felt that no one would understand and didn't want people to find out that Frank was a heavy drinker for I felt shame for him.

During the week after I had returned home, Frank went into my business to deal with some urgent matters for me. Whilst in the office his nose started to bleed and poured blood as if a tap had been turned on. He was taken to hospital. The doctors wanted to admit him. He refused to stay as he wanted to look after me. However, on the following day his nose poured blood again and he had to be admitted to hospital for further treatment. I was alone at home. He was in hospital having blood transfusions.

I was determined to see him to put his mind at ease, so that he would not worry about me and I got a friend to drive me into the City. As I finally sat down at the side of his bed I realised the effort I had made to get there, and a nurse who had been walking behind me ready to hold my elbow smiled at me.

'Well done. I think you've earned a nice cuppa.' She went to make the tea.

Frank was delighted to see me. His estranged wife had been to see him and he was distressed by this.

'I have to tell you that she came to see me on the day of your operation,' he said, through his stuffed nose. 'She wanted lunch so I took her to the Gun, a riverside pub on the Isle of Dogs. She took £10,000 from me as her business is in trouble.' He had led me to believe that he had made adequate and generous arrangements for her before they had separated on condition that there was no more to come. Could it be that the family knew that Frank had received a handshake from his previous employer and would not really know what he was doing on that day?

'I want to be seen to be whiter than white,' were his previous comments. 'I'll come out of this smelling of violets.' He expressed himself this way when telling others how he had tried to do right by his wife.

Frank stressed that he had told the hospital that I was his next of kin and that he did not wish to see his estranged wife from whom he was awaiting a divorce.

The Sister of the ward asked me to stop his relatives visiting him on that day for his blood pressure needed to be kept down. She also said that she was receiving many telephone calls regarding him and that perhaps I could get the family to ring me instead.

I phoned Julia, his elder daughter, the only member of Frank's family whom I had met, and told her what the sister had said to me. Julia was perturbed.

'I was going to take Mum to see him,' she said. 'She won't like it.'

'Take her another day when he is a lot better,' I replied, for I did not want to make it sound as if I was trying to stop her going to see Frank at all.

I was angry to find out from Sister that Julia and her mother had gone to see Frank in spite of my request. As far as I was concerned, this proved what Frank had always said – they always put themselves first and didn't really care about his well-being.

'Don't worry too much, dear,' Sister said. 'I kept my eye on them the whole time that they were here and I only let them stay for ten minutes. Frank is OK.'

Frank was feeling withdrawal symptoms and the hospital started him on a drug which helped him to miss his drink a little less. I decided to telephone his sister to let her know that she could phone me for updates on Frank's progress and was met with the worst reception I have ever had in my life.

'You are not his next of kin and never will be,' she ranted on, in a bitter tone of voice. Her religion, she said, would not let her believe in a civil marriage or in divorce. She had dictated to and judged Frank all his life and he had always said that he wanted nothing to do with her. I was shaken as she screamed abuse at me on the telephone. Her husband was living with another woman. I remained outwardly calm and polite.

'I had been going to give you my telephone number so that you could keep up with Frank's progress but I will not give it to you now.'

It was obvious that the family were not interested in helping Frank but only in prejudging him. No wonder he was an unhappy family man who needed someone to believe in and care for him.

I was suffering tiredness and still felt weak myself when Frank came home. Frank's nose was subject to these massive bleeds and I learned to let the blood drip into a bowl on our way to hospital so that they could see the amount of blood loss. I used to stuff the nostrils and use ice on the bridge of the nose to try to help him.

Frank was not happy in his new employment and did not wish to be associated with the ethics of the company. When he went to the West End to train new dealers and control the dealing he realised that he could not work with the young whiz-kids and could not agree with the methods of work. He resigned. Frank's feelings about the company were correct and he resigned at the right moment, before the company was investigated and the news plastered all over the newspapers and television. We now had only his savings and my income to live off for as long as we could.

It became very difficult for Frank to adjust to this new life for he was used to the hustle and bustle and activity of the City. He appeared to accept that he would not get employment and did not put up a fight. He was drinking more and was trying to hide the fact from me.

I was out of my depth when trying to deal with the matter and made many mistakes by challenging him. This always made him retaliate with 'Don't you trust me?' as he looked at me with hurt eyes. I then felt guilty.

He started to sit in the lounge until the middle of the night with his glass, which no one was allowed to touch, on the nest of tables beside him. He always took a full glass of whisky into the dressing room when he finally went to bed, and now he would frequently sleep in the dressing room.

I couldn't sleep for I was waiting for him to come to bed, and when he

did come to bed I couldn't sleep properly, for he snored in his alcoholic
state. Often he would wake in the night when he needed to go to the toilet
or have another drink. Nevertheless he still got up early in the morning
and made me a cup of tea before I arose for the day.

I started to dilute his whisky in the bottle so that he was pouring a
weaker strength than he realised. I hid a bottle from him in the washing
machine but that only caused more aggravation for I was then becoming
as deceitful as him and it gave him ammunition to use against me.

He would hide a glass of whisky in the toilet roll dispenser in the
cloakroom and I did not realise this until I searched for the cause of
the stale smell and discovered a filthy glass which was thick with a sticky
mess on the inside. I learned to leave this where it was for if I had moved
it he would have found some other way of hiding his drink. Later he hid
a bottle in the cistern (and I became suspicious for he went to the toilet
so often) or in the integral garage where there were plenty of hiding places
including the wall cupboards and the dustbin.

He slept in the dressing room more often for he could hide bottles under
the bed or in the wardrobes and be able to get to them without being seen.
He stored the bottles in the boot of the car, both empty and full, only
removing the empty ones just before the dustmen arrived to empty the
bin. This way I would not find the bottles myself.

I was able to help him by having faith in him as he tried so often to cut
down his consumption. He would not accept that he was an alcoholic and
needed to stop drinking alcohol completely to be able to stop his craving.
'I'm just a heavy drinker with a drink problem,' he said. 'Leave it to me
to cut it down.'

He then started to drink lager which not only caused as much trouble
– for he did not give up his whisky – but made him increase his weight
dramatically. It was not long before he started to drink vodka instead of
whisky for now his breath and glass would not give him away as quickly.
He bought large containers of orange squash and emptied this into bottles
which would fit into the fridge. Now he could dilute this squash and
appear to pour orange into a glass when in fact it was extremely strong
vodka. He had a separate bottle for me but there was one occasion when
I poured a drink from the wrong bottle for my grandson who promptly
spat it out.

'Nanna, this orange tastes horrible!' I tried it, compared the colour with
the large container and threatened to return the bottle with a complaint
to the supplier for it certainly looked and tasted strange. Frank immediately said that he would take it back to the store, but of course he did not
do so.

Frank's distress was increased and made unbearable by the building of a new pumping station close to the house. The noise of pile-driving was horrendous and the house vibrated with the shock. This work went on all day for years with a break only on Sundays. I do not know how he managed to cope with the stress and strain of being in the house all the time during the period in which the area was being developed by the London Docklands Development Corporation. The constant noise was redoubled as it resounded off nearby buildings, and sound barriers of straw bales were demanded for health and safety reasons. The vibrations of the pile-driver could be experienced in the home to the extent that the bed would shake and an ornament splintered into pieces. Imagine living with that all day and every day, knowing that your future was bleak. It was a miracle that anyone remained sane and that we did not all turn to drink as an escape. We lost our river view, the river now being hidden by a pumping station resembling a Grecian temple or garish fairground monstrosity, depending on your opinion of modern buildings. The building achieved fame by winning architectural awards and sufficient praise from Prince Charles for him to include it in his book *A Vision of Britain*, and for tourists to include it in their itinerary. The locals could only look on in disbelief.

Periodically Frank would empty every bottle of alcohol away by pouring the liquid down the sink but he was fortunate in being able to replace the drink when he wanted more. I learned that I must not pour the drink away myself for that would only give him an excuse to blame me for everything and to purchase more immediately.

Frank was always affectionate towards me and was at all times kind and very much in love and dependent on me. I always loved him and did not consider leaving him alone to get out of this trouble for I am certain that he would not have wished to live without me by his side. I do not believe that you walk away from someone when they are weak and in trouble.

I was worried that the neighbours, my family and friends would think that Frank was an alcoholic and felt the stigma and shame that it brought. I withdrew from local people and covered for him.

We were for ever cancelling functions at the eleventh hour and not attending dinners and dances when expected. I was getting used to my disappointments. I dared not get enthusiastic about going out for I knew that there was a strong chance that I would not be able to attend. I was beginning to worry about leaving Frank in the house alone and was always in a hurry to get home. This did affect my business life.

I had always been close to my father and loved him dearly. When he was taken ill in Dorset and admitted to hospital I rushed to his side, leaving Frank to fend for himself. Frank agreed that I should go to the hospital. Terminal cancer was diagnosed and, understanding my father better than anyone, I knew that he should be told the sad news. The doctors were of the opinion that I was the best person to tell my father the facts but they would tell me the right moment to do it. I hated living this half truth as I sat by his bed chatting about everything other than what we both wished to discuss. I knew the facts. My father had guessed them.

When I had been called into the office to speak to the doctors they had said, 'This is the time to tell him, but do not raise his hopes for there is nothing we can do to save him.'

I walked to my father like a bat out of hell for if I didn't get it over now, I knew that I would not be able to speak to him myself. With my mother, brother and myself at his bedside I drew the curtains around us and held my father's hand. I tried to be gentle but inside I was tearing myself apart.

'Daddy, we have never lied to each other. I know that you know that I know what is wrong with you, and I know that you have guessed too.'

He held my hand tightly and smiled at me as I broke the news.

'So tell me what is different?' he said. 'Yesterday I had cancer just the same as today but today I know about it. It hasn't altered the facts. Never doubt that you did the right thing by telling me. Never blame yourself.' I laid my head into the sheets over his stomach and wept with his hand stroking my hair. I felt that I was about to lose the two men I loved at the same time for Frank was obviously very ill too. My father had his other arm around my crying mother.

'You'll never be alone,' he said to my brother and me, 'for you had the sign of the cross on your forehead when you were baptised as a baby. Always look at what you have and not at what you haven't got.' I was to remember those words in the future and get comfort from them.

I returned to my parents' home and lost myself in my father's vegetable garden. It is always comforting to be amongst growing plants at moments of the passing or anticipated passing of a loved one for it helps you to accept that everything must and will carry on as before. My brother hugged me and said that he would never have been able to tell our father of his sickness as I had done.

On the following morning the telephone rang very early. Dreading the worst, I rushed to answer it for my mother.

4. Happy Days

'**D**arling, have you got the radio on?' asked a wide-awake Frank. 'It's playing our song.' Stevie Wonder was singing *I just called to say I love you*. Frank was concerned for me and missing me very much. He was also losing track of the time of day. I wanted to be, and knew that I ought to be, in two places at once.

My father was to live for three more years and did not die as early as the doctors had predicted.

'I'll go when the good Lord calls me and not before,' he said. He had been a master baker and was brilliant at decorating cakes. He was making two important wedding cakes at the time he had been taken to the hospital for my son was to marry in August and my younger daughter in October. He stubbornly refused to give up and completed both cakes but was unable to ice one of them.

Although Frank and I were not married, Frank was treated as my husband at my son's wedding. He thoroughly enjoyed the hilarity before the event for Alan was stationed in Germany with the RAF, and many of his friends returned to England with him for the ceremony, staying with us.

Alan had climbed out of a toilet window in the pub at his stag night and had eventually escaped his friends by climbing a ladder into an upstairs window of his future bride's home.

The wedding was beautiful, relaxed and friendly. Frank had to save the day for me, for although I had bought two pairs of light grey tights to match my dress, I put my hand through both pairs as I got dressed. Frank jumped in the car and drove to the shops to buy me some more. He was always acutely aware of what would please me and there were many moments when I felt that I was thoroughly spoilt by him.

He had hired a chauffeur-driven Daimler to take the pair of us, and my parents who were staying with us, to the wedding so that my father could travel in comfort. We had an escort of cars bearing German number plates as Alan's friends were travelling to the same place at the same time. As we stopped at the red traffic lights a man asked who was in the Daimler. 'For security purposes, we can't tell you,' replied the airman, who started to laugh as he drove away.

Frank was proud as he walked with me to witness the happy couple sign the register and with Janet's mother afterwards. No one here was prejudging him and he was made to feel that he belonged.

Frank had given Claire a dinner on her 21st birthday on a boat in the docks. He had meticulously chosen the wine and ordered a special cake. She was delighted that he was treating her as his own daughter. He wanted to do something really special for her as he always felt that their own father had treated my offspring badly. Unfortunately he blotted his copybook a little later for when Claire and I had been out longer than we had anticipated as we prepared her wedding, he had become worried about us and he had started to drown his sorrows.

'I'm hungry and I'm fed up with waiting,' he shouted at me, and struck me across the face. It was the only time that he ever hit me for although he was a violent man, he never actually hit or even threatened to hit me. He was extremely upset immediately his hand had made contact but Claire was absolutely horrified and worried for she had had dealings with drunks in the hospital and was dreading the worst. Whenever he felt frustrated and wanted to relieve the frustration he would thump an object such as a cushion, a door or the wall. I hated these moments and it often meant that Frank would have to repair the damage later.

I had an enormous row with both the future bride and bridegroom over Frank's role in their wedding ceremony. They did not want him to take any part at all in the church, which would have meant that I would have been alone. I was very hurt and angry, for Frank was giving the reception in the best country club in Essex and paying a few thousand pounds for the meal. I was paying for everything else.

I did not tell Frank what the row was about but he knew that I was upset enough to say that I would not sit in the front pew in the church but would creep in and sit at the back.

Fate took a hand. Alan was unable to return to England for the wedding and Claire had to ask Frank to give her away after all. I took my rightful place.

The wedding was perfect and the bride looked radiant in her fabulous silk and lace gown. Frank had drowned his nerves before the ceremony and proudly supported Claire on his arm, but he'd forgotten his top hat, and had to borrow the page boy's for the photographs. It was a good thing that he did not have to balance the small size on his head. I was greatly concerned at the reception for there was no love lost between him and the bridegroom's mother, and he was well enough 'tanked up' to look as if he was falling asleep. I kept getting up from the table on the pretext of checking that the guests were alright, but it was really so that I could walk down to Frank and prod him awake. I breathed a sigh of relief that his speech was alright and not at all slurred.

'That wasn't only the wedding of the year, but the wedding of my lifetime,' said my weak and weary father who had made the ceremony to our joy and amazement.

Frank was godfather to my second grandson. He may not have felt that his own family wanted him. He knew that my family welcomed and accepted him. He was proud to belong.

It was difficult for me to belong in his world. His brother and sister wouldn't accept me at all, in spite of the fact that they had never met me and I was caring for their brother who was madly in love with me. It seemed that his younger daughter was making mischief but did eventually meet me after a long time. The elder daughter and I became friends. However, Frank's ex-wife did not want him but seemed to want to interfere in his life in a destructive way.

Frank was the Worshipful master of the Goodmayes' Masonic lodge and I was to be the President's Lady at the Ladies' Evening – an event that is a strain for any woman, even one who knows that she is among friends. I knew none of them.

It was so important to me that I would not let Frank down in any way. I bought a fabulous gold gown and thought of my speech. When the occasion arrived Frank had got more control of his drinking and was in fine form. He looked distinguished in his evening attire and proudly introduced his friends and guests to me.

We had chosen the menu carefully and our guests included both my family and Frank's daughters and their boyfriends. As we sat at the top table I could feel that we were being scrutinised by the Masons and even more by their wives. The time had come for me to make my speech and as I rose and commenced to talk the hotel relayed a Tannoy message.

'I knew something would upstage me,' I said, and everyone laughed. I think we all relaxed at that moment and I continued to speak from my heart. The speech was received well and the applause was loud and long from people who had warm smiles on their faces. I no longer felt like 'the other woman'. Frank had arranged that I would be presented with a hostess trolley and had spent many weeks finding out my favourite songs without my realising this. The toast and song to the President's Lady was followed with, *How to handle a woman* and many other beautiful lyrics sung by Alan Henshaw. I found it hard to control my emotions and at least one Mason approached me later with 'Did I notice a tear?'

My eyes were wet with happiness. Frank was a kind, generous and loving man. Unfortunately he was often misunderstood. I knew that I would back him through the rest of his life. *People who need people* was played, and we both knew that we needed each other.

Frank was a good dancer and was incredibly light on his feet for a heavy well-built man. We led the dancing and danced the night away. He was proud of me and I had learned that he was a good public speaker. We only went to two functions after that where we were not asked to make after-dinner speeches.

Frank and I had the sort of closeness that allowed us to go to a party and move amongst the guests without being together, and yet feel each other's closeness and presence all evening. It was great to be able to trust each other but I did worry about Frank and alcohol.

He had many months without alcohol for he tried very hard to give up drink, knowing that he had my support, but at social functions he was tempted to have just one drink – and that always became one too many and twelve too few. If I saw him with a drink in his hand, I knew that he was going to start a drinking spree which would last until he was so ill that he would need medical help. This addiction was a sickness that knew no boundaries. It struck anyone of any colour, race or creed. Age and sex were no protection, nor social standing and wealth. Intelligence appeared to have nothing to do with the craving either.

'Oh go on, one drink won't hurt,' was a cruel invitation to hear. So was the impression that a man is a 'sissy' if he drinks a soft drink. Frank started to say that he couldn't drink as he was on medication and that helped him, for no further explanations seemed necessary.

I was very proud of him when he managed to summon the courage and pretend that he didn't care what everyone thought of him in his fight against his demon. It helped him if I continued to have my glass of dry white wine for he felt that I must carry on as normal.

'I don't want to stop you drinking too. I can't bear the guilt if you stop as well.'

Frank was always the life and soul of a party. We arranged a luncheon party for my parents' golden wedding in my father's favourite pub, *The George* in Chideock, Dorset, where a painting had hung on the wall for sale for the last few years. I had wanted to purchase it but could not find the spare cash for the purchase.

My brother provided gold ribbon for the car and decked the car as if it was going to a wedding. My mother carried a bouquet and everyone went into the bar except for a friend and me. We went into the dining room to organise the place settings. I noticed that my beloved painting had a 'Sold' ticket stuck on the corner of the frame.

'Is that the painting which you like?' my friend asked. I nodded and continued to busy myself. Frank walked in to the room. He put his arm around my shoulders.

'I don't give a damn who has bought it, I'll make them an offer they can't refuse. You want it and I want to give it to you.'

'No, please don't bother,' I pleaded. 'Someone else obviously likes it as much as I do and I want them to have it. It doesn't really matter.' We forgot the painting.

We had a lovely family and friends' gathering in the informal surroundings. I sat between my father and Frank. My father had sat with me in the morning and written his funeral service, knowing that he would not be able to last much longer. I had the piece of paper in my handbag. He had also prepared a speech. There were a few things which I wanted to say as well. We all had a glass of champagne ready to drink the health of the couple and as I made a move to stand to propose their health, my father put his hand on my shoulder and pushed me down. He struggled to stand and spoke to us all. He took Frank and me totally by surprise as he came to the end:

'I could not have managed to live this long without the support of Ann and Frank. I have been blest with the best daughter in the world and I love them both dearly.' By this time I was moved to tears for I likewise believed that I had the best father in the world.

'I know that you had set your heart on something and I want to give you a little thank you for what you have done for Mum and me in the last few troubled months.'

The landlord removed the painting from the wall and gave it to my father who handed it to me. I was stunned and could not speak for I would have choked with emotion. I hugged the frail man, frightened that I would hurt him. Frank was completely taken aback too.

There were more celebrations to come. The luncheon had been on the Saturday before the actual anniversary so that the family could attend. The actual anniversary was on Monday and I had asked Ken Bruce to mention the occasion on his radio programme. He duly congratulated the pair as we prepared a party for the many friends of my father and mother. The party was a great success as many old age pensioners arrived to join in the fun. Frank was an excellent host and made sure that everyone was looked after well.

The elderly neighbour arrived wrapped in layers of warm clothing and said that she would not stop but did want to wish Harry and Dot well. When Frank offered her a glass of champagne she replied, 'I don't drink wine but I would like a small glass of sherry if you have one. I'll not take my coat off as I'm not stopping.'

Frank found her a glass of sherry and eventually, after a bottle of the same, still with her coat on and as the last guest to leave, he escorted her weavingly to her home next door.

In the meantime there was great hilarity when Frank had a puppet monkey on his arm and a cloth cap jauntily tipped to the side on his head as he entertained the old folk. A group of Brownies had been for a walk in the country and were returning past the front of the house. Suddenly we heard peals of laughter from outside and found that Frank was in the garden entertaining the troop with the monkey. It looked as if there was going to be a lot of food left over for I always overestimated the catering, so my mother and I took some food to the willing audience of youngsters. The small village won't ever forget that happy day.

We had decided that we would spend Christmas with my parents for it would probably be the last one that my father would have with us. We all became larger than life to cover our distress so we laughed too much and fooled around to try to cover our pain. We formed a kitchen orchestra by playing utensils as if they were musical instruments and I became Carmen Miranda with fruit on my head and bananas as ear rings.

My father was to be alive for another Christmas which we had hoped to spend with him again. I had delayed our travel to Dorset from London as Frank was too ill to travel the journey. He was drinking heavily and his stomach looked as if it had blown up. It was solid and hard to the touch. He was now spending nearly all day in bed in a form of stupor. I called the doctor and asked him for a home visit on Christmas Eve.

5. Renewed Concern

The doctor spoke to me in a state of great concern. He had just examined Frank who had been unaware even of his presence.

He told me that Frank was probably not going to live much longer for he was now in an advanced state of alcoholism. I was in a dilemma for I could not be with both my father in Dorset and Frank in London. The doctor said that it was not his place to tell me what to do but that if he was in my shoes, he would go to Dorset for if anything happened there, I would never forgive myself.

'Frank will not eat anything and he will not really be aware that you have gone.'

I was terribly worried for I knew that Frank could have set fire to the house when he was in a similar state recently and had forgotten that he was smoking. I had returned home to find that an armchair was ruined and the carpet had burn marks from such an episode. What would happen to him if left alone now? I had the Christmas fare with me for my parents so I drove to Dorset without Frank. I told no one in the family that the doctor had told me that if Frank continued in this manner he would die in a few weeks' or months' time.

I tried to function normally as I drove but missed the turning off the motorway. However, this turned out to be to my advantage for I then found a different route which I used thereafter.

Frank did not answer the telephone. I was dreadfully worried but did not wish to convey this to my parents.

Frank's brother called the police on Christmas day for he was concerned at Frank's conversation on the phone to him. The police hammered on the door and broke Frank out of his saturated sleep.

'Are you alright, mate?' the policeman shouted at Frank. 'We've had a call from your brother who is worried about you.'

Frank thanked them for their concern.

'Can't a man drink what he wants in his own house without any interference?' Frank belligerently asked. They could do no more that day. I was lying in bed on Boxing Day when I got a telephone call from a sober-sounding Frank.

'Don't be alarmed. The ambulance is here to take me to Bart's. I've been spewing up blood and I am in pain. I need you to be with me. If you don't make it in time, I love you. Don't ever forget it.'

I went cold. My father was incredible and put his arm around me.

'Don't worry, he is going to be alright. He couldn't live without you. I know he will make it.'

I got ready for the rush to London. I gulped a cup of tea and bit into a piece of toast for my breakfast. I couldn't swallow it. My mother was panicking.

'She is not to drive herself. She ought to have something stronger to drink. Roger, you drive her car and go with her. How has she kept this worry to herself over Christmas Day?'

I would not have a strong drink. I would never become dependent on anything other than my own will-power. My father understood and told my mother to leave me alone.

'She will be alright. She knows what she is doing.' However, I was grateful that my brother drove me in my car to the London hospital.

Our doctor had left a message for the doctor on duty in our area, saying that if there was a call from Frank he would need to be admitted to Bart's. This is what had been put into action. I arrived at the hospital before Frank was moved from casualty where the team were working on him.

To avoid confusion, I told the male receptionist that I was his wife. He looked puzzled. He went into the area where the seriously ill admittances were taken and returned to me.

'What is your name?' he asked. I told him and he breathed a sigh of relief.

'Thank goodness. I've instructions to admit only you, and that his family are not to be admitted or told anything.' He then took me into the cubicle where a very sick Frank was being prepared for theatre. I walked with him on the trolley beside the doctors and porter.

The hospital was quiet and there were the remnants of streamers and garlands of the day before. Many wards were closed but the few that remained open were caring for very seriously ill people. There was only a skeleton staff working so that as many nurses as possible could celebrate the Christian festival.

Frank was taken to the theatre. The staff nurse told me that I could use her kitchen to make myself a warm drink and also have one of her biscuits. Roger remained with me and we did as we were told.

When Frank arrived in the ward from the theatre I was allowed to sit with him. He regained consciousness and in his drowsy condition I knew that he was pleased that I was with him. I held his hand until he had been asleep for some time. The surgeon spoke to me. He had repaired as much internal damage as possible but Frank would have to return frequently for the remaining repairs to be made. I asked him how long he thought Frank had got to live.

'If Frank continues to drink he will only live for two to three years. He has cirrhosis of the liver which can repair itself if allowed to do so. If he is able to stop drinking there is no reason why he shouldn't live for a near-normal lifespan. He has lost a large amount of blood. He is suffering from malnutrition through his drinking problem (even though he had the same food as myself) and we need to keep him here for some time for tests.'

I went home to an empty house except for my elderly black cat. The toilet was covered in blood. There were stains of blood on the floor.

'Don't come in here,' I shouted to Roger. I didn't want him to be upset. I started to clean the small room at midnight on Boxing Day. The bathroom was in a worse state but it was apparent that Frank had tried to clean it for me. I cleaned the bathroom too. The dressing room stank of stale alcohol and tobacco. There were many empty litre bottles of whisky and vodka under the bed. I opened the window to let the stench out.

There was a jewellery box on the table with a note written by a shaky hand.

'Happy Christmas, Darling. I need you more than words can say. All my love, Frank.'

Inside was a string of exactly matched pearls. Frank had not forgotten these when he had to call the doctor for help in getting the ambulance to take him to the hospital.

Frank was to stay in hospital for a biopsy of the liver and many other tests as well as more repairs to his damaged insides. He was left in no doubt about the harm he was inflicting on himself. He was given advice and counselling but unfortunately, in spite of his desire to succeed, he was unable to refrain from drinking for longer periods of time than ten months. Now he went into hospital as a day patient, first weekly for theatre treatment and later once a fortnight. He worked out that if he refrained from drinking for a week before he went to hospital the doctors would not realise that he was in actual fact able to drink and be repaired. The doctors were well aware of what he was doing. I could not understand how they had patience and time for people who were basically killing themselves, and yet I was showing the same forbearance.

Frank started to see a counsellor in the house. His attitude was that he would give it a try but he was sure that it would not help. He would not go to group meetings and frowned on Alcoholics Anonymous. He would not be categorised, thinking that he was an individual; he was in no way humble, believing that he had a higher intelligence than the next man. He would not discuss himself or his problem with others with similar problems.

Frank did not appear to be interested in anything outside himself and really lived a life through me. If I had achieved something he would immediately think that we had done it. He did not read books but spent all day reading a newspaper. It took him this long to plough through it. He would never do any gardening or repair anything in the house. He would not paint or decorate. I learned later that he was not well enough to tackle the problems.

He seemed to have no interests. But there was no way that he would see anyone come to any harm. He had a warm personality and joked with everyone. He was popular with the local people, particularly the shopkeepers, as he used to amuse them with tales of his activities both current or in the past. His friends could have helped the situation more if they had kept in touch and been there when they were needed. Frank would have looked after them if the tables had been turned and they were in trouble.

He put me on a pedestal. He never allowed me to fall off. It was important to us that we were married before my father died. When Frank was finally a divorced man he got down on his knees in front of me and proposed in the old fashioned way. He had spent many months hunting for my engagement ring and produced the ring and placed it on my finger with pride and joy. He then took me to *The Grapes,* my favourite restaurant over the original Dickensian riverside pub in Narrow Street, and in candle-light I thought (like a far younger woman) that the world was looking at the third finger of my left hand.

I knew that in these moments of gladness our lives together would not be long and could be traumatic. Happiness was always tinged with sadness. Frank was a human being who needed my love and in his sickness I needed to stand by him as well as in his health. Of course, I was disappointed in the way that life seemed to kick me in my face. I really had needed to be looked after and wanted to be supported by my man. Instead I was the breadwinner and in the supporting role as I seemed to have been most of my adult life. Perhaps this is what fate had in store for me, but we all seem to have our cross to bear.

Doctor Boomla had told me that alcoholism was an illness, like a broken leg, except that a person with a broken leg will let you help.

When my father saw the ring on my finger he was absolutely thrilled. We told him that we were going to get married in Dorset so that he could be with us for he was far too ill to travel anywhere now.

'Do you mean it, do you really mean it?' he asked, with tears of joy in his eyes. Frank had done the gentlemanly thing by asking him for my hand. Frank gained new confidence and put up a tremendous fight in stopping drinking. He now had something to organise and occupy his mind. He also had me to believe in him and I had now committed myself to him, which helped him regain his self-respect.

6. For Better – For Worse

We got married in Bridport registry office on the Tuesday after the August bank holiday. The ceremony was immediately followed by a quiet church blessing at St Mary Magdalene, the parish church of Loders, a small Dorset village where my father worshipped and where Frank and I had hoped to retire. We had visions of him eventually relaxing in the local pub with a pipe and a pint after taking his dog for a walk in idyllic surroundings. Our families were present at the ceremony.

The weather was terrible with a 'hurricane' and floods. The family had trouble in getting to the wedding through the storm. It was so dark that I thought the photographs would not come out. We waited for a death to be registered before being admitted to the office for a ceremony conducted by a woman. I felt tense and unreal. I could do nothing with my hair which behaved like straw. My wedding ring needed to be pushed hard on to my finger and for one moment I thought that it was too small. I was cold in my electric blue pure silk designer dress in the thirties style. How was I to know that it would be like a winter's day in August? I expected to feel different when I came out of the registry office but I did not feel that I was married. My grandson Peter, on being told that he could throw confetti and that he could throw it all, threw the lot including the box at me after giving us a small traditional horseshoe.

However, after the brief ceremony in the church I felt happier and realised that I really was a wife again. Frank guessed that my son would want to hang 'Just married' signs and cans on the back of the hired car so in anticipation he had offered a handsome tip to the driver to say that the hire company would not allow it. We had also spread a rumour that we were staying in a different hotel for the night.

We had a family lunch in Dorchester, taking a whole room in the Wessex Hotel. We then left by train to stay one night in the best hotel in Southampton before sailing in the QE2 on the next day.

Imagine our horror as bedraggled and sickly passengers joined us in the bar when they had disembarked from the ship, which was a day late in docking, saying how rough it had been during the last two days. We heard these tales of woe but were not consciously listening to them.

Our suite was supposed to be the best in the hotel. There was a draught blowing like a gale through the sash window (which would have been rattling had there not been pegs inserted in the window frame to stop the noise). I found the creak in the floorboards amusing for it would let anyone know of activity in the room.

We embarked during the next morning and started our cruise into our married life. There was a wonderful flower arrangement from my daughters and son in the cabin and a saucy poster of penguins from the *Titanic* on an iceberg to hang as a dare on the wall.

We stood on deck and listened to the band playing *We are sailing* and enjoyed the send-off with streamers as the tugs moved us from the dock. Most of the passengers went below for it was windy and cold but we stayed on deck as we left England, waving to the smaller fishing vessels and motor boats.

Frank was disgusted with the seating in the dining room for children were clambering over the table close beside us and were throwing their food everywhere; hardly the romantic dinner of a honeymoon. He could not understand why they did not eat earlier at the special children's meals supervised by a brown-uniformed and highly trained Norland nanny relieving the parents to enjoy a romantic meal alone, nor could he understand why the parents ordered so many courses for them when they did not even eat one course.

Frank soon organised that we sat alone. A gateau was carried to our table with sparklers burning on the top as the waiters sang to us and we received a congratulatory message from the captain and another from the crew when we returned to our cabin.

Frank was disappointed that the ship appeared to be more American than British, using the US dollar for currency and having a predominantly American menu when the QE2 is the flagship of the Cunard fleet.

He drank no alcohol on our honeymoon and never left my side to go to a bar by himself.

During the talent competition we were entertained by an 80-year-old former trouper of music hall with bawdy and provocative songs oft associated with the suggestiveness of saucy Marie Lloyd. Frank roared with laughter and gave her a standing ovation soon to be joined by mesmerised Americans who had an even saucier meaning for many of the words. She became the celebrity of the voyage rather than the famous stars travelling with us.

We spent a week in the Waldorf Astoria in New York and behaved like 18-year-olds. If Frank had doubts about his virility he certainly need not have worried. As he was drinking no alcohol he seemed to be a new man. His former lack of sexual prowess was mentally as well as alcohol-induced.

It was disconcerting to find that there were armed security men in the corridors outside our suite for our safety. Whilst we were travelling in the lift someone accidentally pressed the wrong button and activated the alert. Immediately a voice boomed into the lift to find out if we were alright in case there had been an 'incident'.

We accidentally met British stockbrokers after visiting Wall Street. We were sitting in a fish restaurant in the area of the river and Stock Exchange and had eaten clam chowder followed by lobster served with fruit, including luscious Californian strawberries which tickled my taste buds. I passed a remark that I would have expected the brokers to be eating here when Frank recognised two men entering the restaurant. Frank called the waiter to our table.

'You see those two people who have just come in?'

'Yes sir.'

'Well, be careful about giving them a table. They are known to leave without paying and will take any cutlery or removable item with them when they go.'

The waiter hesitated. He did not know what to do about the predicament. At that moment Frank's friends recognised him and came over to our table.

'Well, fancy seeing you this side of the pond. What are you doing here?' they greeted each other warmly, shaking hands and patting each other on the back.

The waiter stood with his mouth open, wondering what to do about these crazy Englishmen. I didn't know them either at this point.

Frank introduced me to the brokers. He nodded to the waiter to bring them a drink at our table which would be added to our bill. The waiter did not take his eyes off us as he obliged. Frank laughed and told him that they were really alright and that he was only joking; however, I do not think the waiter really believed him by the look on his face.

'You sod, you . . .' they laughed. 'I see you've not been able to change the old devil,' they said to me.

We were invited to join them later in the evening but declined for on our honeymoon we had better things to do!

There are no superlatives too great to describe supersonic travel by Concorde. It was the most exhilarating experience of our lives together. Frank was not nervous and did not drink alcohol before or during the flight, in spite of the superb wines and liqueurs on offer.

I am sure every passenger was made to feel special by the mature and experienced stewards and stewardesses, but one of our fellow passengers from the QE2, who was on the same flight, had guessed that Frank and I were on our honeymoon and had let the crew know this. Pampered and deliriously happy, we watched as we reached 'Mach 2'. The side of the narrow but very comfortable plane felt warm as I touched it out of curiosity. We could see the white clouding effect around the wings as we parted the air which would join together again behind us with an enormous 'bang'.

On our return from the flight deck we found presents waiting for us on our seats from British Airways.

7. Down to Earth

As we touched down at Heathrow airport with the exciting pull against our seat belts caused by the rapid and steep decline, all the passengers applauded spontaneously. What a wonderful finale to a happy honeymoon. As we left the aircraft wearing our corsage and clutching our Concorde package and gifts we both hoped that we would be in a position to fly Concorde again. We had crossed the Atlantic from Kennedy airport in New York in three hours twenty minutes.

It wasn't long before we were back in the old routine at home. I had to spend considerable time in Dorset with my ailing father. He had remained as active as possible but had foolishly climbed a ladder in spite of being told not to do it. He had fractured his hip and was bleeding internally. After a spell in hospital I managed to convince the hospital that he would be better spending the rest of his life at home, pottering around. I had to put up convincing arguments for the specialists but had the backing of my father's general practitioner who promised me as much help as possible, including a Macmillan nurse. Sometimes the treatment is more painful than the disease itself. So often it is kinder to leave the patients alone to live a normal lifespan doing what they want than to remove them from their homes and loved ones. Better a short happy life than a long miserable one.

'They might as well put me in my box now,' my father had said to me. 'Staying in this place will kill me.' He was referring to the hospital.

My father loved to sit and watch the wildlife from his window and would painfully and now very slowly tend his garden. He hardly ever missed going to church on Sundays and amazed us all with his strength of character and faith.

Frank phoned me at five o'clock in the morning. 'I've taken the food out of the deep freeze and I thought we would have peas?'

He was now losing any sense of time. He was obviously drinking again after his ten months of abstaining. The guilt was mine for I had left him alone for a short but critical time. He had not lived up to my expectations. My hurt was acute but this was no time for self pity. I had to get home to help him.

'What time do you think it is?' I asked, as calmly as possible.

'Tea time. I thought you said that you were coming home today?'

'Darling, it is five o'clock in the morning.' I could hear the silence of the pause. He was stunned and slowly came to terms with the fact that indeed this was true.

Frank was continually admitted to hospital. The staff were fantastic. There seemed to be a good rapport between Frank and the medical team, including the nurses. In spite of the strain that his sickness was putting on me, he was supportive over my father's imminent death. He loved the man dearly and had spent many moments in quiet talk with him regarding what would happen to my mother and me when the inevitable happened. The telephone rang when we were watching television in the evening. My father had telephoned us and was upset.

'Ann, I love you. Never have any doubts that you did the right thing. (He was referring to the time that I told him that he had cancer. I had torn myself apart during the week before he was told, and he had found this out.)

'No man has ever had a better daughter and I want you to always remember this. Now I don't want you to rush here, for there is no need. God will always be with you and give you strength. Frank will be alright but he cannot do it without you. The garden is in fine shape and there is nothing to be done in the bungalow. I've made my peace with Roger. (He had not been too impressed with my brother of late.) Now I would like to speak to Frank. God bless you. Don't worry about me.'

In tears, I handed the telephone to Frank.

'Look after them for me, Frank,' he said, meaning my mother and me. My father died at six o'clock the following morning as he sat on the side of his bed at home. He had been given only weeks to live three years previously. I dreaded Frank would immediately console himself in his drink. I asked him if he would help by contacting the undertakers and he said that he would not drink even though he desperately wanted to drown his sorrows.

I had the treasured piece of paper on which my father had written his funeral service. I could not settle until I had visited the chapel of rest and seen my father's corpse but I had to wait a couple of days until after the post-mortem.

I could not understand how the rest of the house in Dorset slept that night. At five o'clock in the morning, I went into the kitchen and sat on a chair in front of the window exactly as my father had done at that time when he was alive. I had a premonition that he was trying to tell me something.

I watched the cattle come to the edge of the road on the other side of the hedge. I watched the dawn. I saw a mother bird fussing over her new offspring as she looked after them. I felt that I could hear my father saying, 'It's up to you to bring the young members of the family up in a

Christian manner now. Look to the youngsters just as the maternal bird is tending the young. Do the job for me.'

I felt that he had communicated with me. I knew that he was at peace. I returned to bed and appreciated the warmth of sleeping Frank's body and I slept too. *There was no nest in the hedge when I went for a closer look later.*

Frank said that the peace which my mother and I felt showed on our faces after we left the chapel of rest on seeing my father.

'You walked in looking drained. You came out smiling.'

My father was cremated after a funeral service in Loders. I turned to look at my family, his grandchildren, as we followed his coffin into church. I was so proud of them all. Frank supported me as my brother walked ahead of us with my mother, our feet churning the gravel on the path which we so recently trod in happiness on our wedding day. Alan wore his 'number one' RAF uniform in honour of his grandfather who had been more like a father to him.

In church, with my hand on his coffin and his prayer book in my hand, I spoke for my father as I had promised him that I would do. 'Laugh as we used to laugh' and more of the comforting words of Scott Holland which only brought tears at the time. Everyone remembered him as a sincere man with a sense of fun. It was only three years previously that he had busked wearing a lit-up nose, twirling his walking stick like Charlie Chaplin outside the annual amateur dramatics production.

My mother did not cry. She was too brave and we were worried over her. I contacted CRUSE, a charity for the bereaved, and they were very helpful and kind to us all.

Frank started to drink when we arrived home. He was shopping for me on the pretext of helping me, but I'm sure that it was so that he could smuggle the litre bottles into the house without my realising that he had the drink. I believe he'd got so bad that he was convincing himself that his glass of vodka was 'water', as he had told me. I did not challenge him very often but on one occasion I accused him of drinking alcohol when the glass looked as if it contained orange.

'If you think that, then try it yourself,' he said, as he held out the glass to me. I called his bluff and took it. I drank the strong brandy-tasting mixture and felt dreadful. I went to the bathroom and remember nothing until I awoke on the bathroom floor many hours later.

Frank was asleep in his armchair in the lounge although it was the middle of the night. He was beginning to realise, although he would not always admit it, that he was an alcoholic.

Counselling was not really working for he was not giving it a chance. He blamed the counsellors, although I had started to talk to Gail Priddey from InformAl instead of him, and he was grateful – as indeed I was – for the help which she gave to me over his problem.

I had spoken to Alcoholics Anonymous and listened to them, but when I was about to leave the house to attend one of their meetings for families of alcoholics, Frank was upset and I never attended. However, I did receive literature about private 'drying out' clinics and started to interest Frank in them.

He was now very fat and heavy. His ankles were always swollen and he slightly dragged one foot when walking. The palms of his hands were red and his face was puffy. He seemed to have bowel trouble and was always full of wind which he would discreetly allow to escape, making a squeaky sound against the leather of the chair if a visitor was present, but a loud fart if I was the only one in the room.

Frank decided that he would go to an expensive clinic for treatment as it was in the country where it would be quiet and he could get away from the building noise of the pumping station. He thought he would be able to rest and stroll in the massive grounds of the clinic. He wanted to have a room to himself and private guidance. He also wanted to be treated with some respect and as an older human being. He was assessed and the director telephoned me to tell me how seriously ill Frank was.

He admitted Frank that weekend. Frank stayed at the clinic for one week and then discharged himself.

The clinic was run on disciplinarian lines. Latecomers for meals were fined. There were two or three people in each room. During the day the inmates had to write essays. There were no manners like helping each other to coffee, opening doors or courtesy to the opposite sex. The language was filthy and swearing at each other was the norm.

Frank was too sick to move quickly and he had to have a bedroom on the ground floor for he was unable to arrive in the dining room without a fine. He could not write his essays for his concentration had gone and he was not able to express himself on paper at the best of times. He was belittled and made to feel foolish. He was much older than the other people. He could not relate to them. He was shouted at and sworn at and not allowed to go into the grounds of the old house. He was not allowed to communicate with the outside but he telephoned me at the end of the week.

'I smuggled the fare in here but I don't feel up to travelling home by train; can you get Freddy to fetch me? The nurse is with me and she wants to speak to you.'

Frank came home. It had cost £900 for the few days' treatment when I could have sworn at him at home, for nothing! I had said that I thought Frank was lazy for he would not even hang the kitchen curtains.

The nurse had replied, 'Have you not thought that he might be too sick to be able to do even that?'

It was obvious that the clinic believed that Frank was now too ill to be able to live much longer.

'I did try,' Frank told me; 'honestly, I did try. They could not understand that I won't swear at a woman. It was the wrong place and the wrong sort of treatment for me,' he explained.

Quality of life is variable, different people's ideas of it being dependent on the way each has lived. Frank needed to be mentally active for communication with the City was essential for him to be happy. Being isolated and basically immobile in the home would provide many with a reason to want to live. Frank found his life a living hell. His quality of life was depreciating rapidly. He spent all his waking time sitting in his armchair. He was depressed but always acted as if he was cheerful and positive when he had visitors. He slept for most of the day which did not help him to sleep at night. He developed sores on his legs. Doctor Boomla tried to get him interested in 'keep fit'. Frank would have none of it. Very occasionally he would pedal on the exercise bike at home for a few minutes. Doctor Boomla told him that he must try to go for a walk every day. He did go to the local shops in Castalia Square and had a laugh with his friends, particularly the shopkeepers in the butcher's, baker's, chemist's, greengrocer's and newsagent's where he teased the women at the counters 'pulling their legs'. When he was obviously weary he would be given a cup of tea and made to sit down in the shop or on the low wall outside before they allowed him to struggle home. He was very lonely and would chat to everyone on the days he was able to wander around Asda leaning on the shopping trolley for support and feeling crotchety as he waited at the check-out. One could help Frank more by giving him things that he could do than by telling him what he could not do.

We had arranged to take my mother on a cruise for we all needed a change of scenery after the death of my father. Frank did not want to go away. He persuaded me to take my mother without him, but I was terrified of leaving him behind. I could only think of the events of the recent Boxing Day with him having emergency surgery.

'I won't be silly,' he said. 'Go and enjoy yourself and don't worry about me.'

He waved farewell to us as we left to join the cruise liner in Portsmouth. I had left him a more than ample number of prepared meals in the freezer. He should not starve.

It was difficult to relax and forget him. I was always worried when he was not with me. I made friends with a couple of people, Frank and Audrey

Wright, and we had many laughs as we huddled under blankets in a determined effort to get a tan or wind-blown weathered look, for the weather was dreadful. I had mal de mer.

Returning to the cabin after a splendid dinner, I was searching for a shawl with my head down, when I realised that I felt queasy. I had never been seasick before but felt dreadful. I knew that I could have an injection to help alleviate the problem, so I rang for the nurse.

'There will be a delay, Madam. The doctor and one of the nurses are sick so there is only one nurse on duty. Half the crew are suffering too.'

My elderly mother was fine. She was worried about me for apparently I had gone a greyish-green colour.

The nurse asked me if I had actually been sick. 'I don't really like to give this injection unless you have been sick,' she said.

I shook my head and replied, 'If you stay here much longer I will oblige.'

She gave me the injection and I then enjoyed – although I was always worried – the rest of my holiday. Unfortunately I was unable to keep in touch with Audrey and our friendship, which I treasure to this day, has lapsed. Circumstances prevented our meeting again.

It was dreadfully rough and people dancing on the floor could end up on the far side of the ship in a bunch as the ship listed. Drinks on the tables ended in our laps, but the previous cruise had been far worse. During that cruise gambling machines had crashed on the far side of the ship, trapping the purser in his office. A window had been broken and a little Downs' Syndrome boy was temporarily lost. He was eventually found under a table without a care in the world, licking an ice cream, oblivious of the 'child overboard' scare.

Every time we docked a few passengers left the ship with their luggage to fly home. They had endured enough. I enjoyed the company of the entertainment staff who were very professional. Every evening the comedian sat and had a drink with my mother and myself, trying new jokes out on me. I missed Frank and wished he was with us. I was seated next to the captain on his table after his cocktail party and it did seem strange to be unescorted.

I telephoned home by satellite. Frank was delighted to hear me and he had so much to say. When I told him that the call was costing a fortune he replied 'I don't give a ... It's wonderful to hear you. I adore the ground you walk on. I don't want us to be parted again. I'll meet you at the coach station in London and hug you to bits when you come home. I'll not let you out of my sight again.'

It was one of those conversations when neither person wanted to be the one to say 'Goodbye'. I turned to the radio operator in embarrassment for he had heard every word.

When I arrived in London I had to wait for Frank to turn up. I was to introduce him to my new friends. Before all the luggage had been removed from the coaches, I saw him arrive in a minicab. He looked ill and as he smiled, I noticed a gap in his mouth where a front tooth had been knocked out. I was ashamed of him as I introduced him to my friends for in addition to his appearance, he also smelt of stale whisky. I thought it was a dreadful homecoming. At the same time I felt sorrow and love for him. What a dreadful addiction this alcoholism is when it takes over such a strong character with a high degree of intelligence.

I did not reprimand him for it would have served no purpose. He had frightened himself whilst I was away for he had haemorrhaged badly again. He had knocked his tooth out when his head hit the basin. He was admitted to hospital immediately I arrived home. The food left for him was untouched in the freezer.

Frank seemed to deteriorate mentally and was noticeably slower in his reactions and speech. After he had been discharged from the hospital he seemed to be thoughtful and rather negative. He began to think that as he was dying, he might as well go in his own way with a bottle beside him. He took the attitude that it was no one else's business what he did with his own life.

This was to the exclusion of me. He would hug me and say, 'What am I doing to you? You deserve better than this. No man has had a better wife.' I knew that he meant what he was saying. I also knew that I had to build his confidence and support him.

'We've been through so much together, we will have to fight this together too. You can only give up the drink if you really want to do so. You must give it up for yourself and not for me, but you must know that I will always be here when you need me. I love you too. I have no regrets.'

'But you should be out enjoying life instead of caring for me. I'm really buggering it up for you. I have no regrets except that I can't make love to you as I want to do.'

One Saturday morning Frank took action to let me live the life he felt I should have. He left me suddenly. He had been drinking heavily and had decided that he would go away and drink himself to death. He grabbed his passport, packed a minimum of articles, jumped into my car and sped off. At first I was too stunned to realise what had happened. I thought he would be home before the afternoon was out and then I worried as he was too drunk to drive. I wasn't angry. I was sad, for I started to blame myself, wondering what I had done to make him behave like this. I heard no more from him until Sunday morning.

'I've left the car at the airport and I managed to get a flight to Portugal.

I'm staying in a pleasant but frugal hotel and there isn't a phone for you to be able to contact me.'

I said, 'I'll collect the car from the airport.'

'No don't do that. You haven't got the ticket.' The telephone went dead. I made myself a coffee and pondered my next action. I was too ashamed to tell any of the family or friends for it would look as if I had another failed marriage. I did not believe that I should involve anyone in our problems, thinking that what happens between husband and wife is to be kept privately between the two people.

I did not believe that Frank had left the country and guessed he had gone to his younger daughter. I dared not telephone her to find out if Frank was there as I would only make her worried if he was not at her home. I went to the office on Monday and kept an appointment with the doctor in the early evening. I told him what had happened. Frank had phoned me during the day and chattered on about Portugal for over an hour. I was more convinced that he was in Essex.

I was nervous and unhappy. I was at my wits' end and as happens so often in moments of stress, I was careless and accident-prone. I cut my hand badly on an old rusty cat food tin. It should have been stitched but I did not have the car to drive to the hospital. I had to return to the doctor next day for a tetanus injection. He was kind and understanding towards me. I was beginning to think that if Frank wanted to die, it would be a blessing if God was merciful and took him without prolonging this agony for us both.

I received two long telephone calls from Frank on Tuesday.

'I can't get a flight home. I'm on a standby. I should be home by the weekend.' I realised that in fact he had not left me permanently at all – unless he was to kill himself.

This state of affairs continued until Thursday. Julia had been on holiday until Wednesday and on her return she had been contacted by her younger sister.

'Dad is drinking bottles and bottles of whisky. He can hardly get out of bed. I don't know what to do with him. I can't cope with this.' I was led to believe that she was also supplying the drink for him. Julia and I agreed that if he had not come home by Thursday, we were going to confront him and bring him home ourselves.

Terry, Linda's live-in boyfriend, drove Frank in my car back to London on Thursday. I arrived home from the office to find a sad husband sitting in his chair staring at our wedding photograph in his hands. The tears streamed down his face.

'Ann, Ann. What have I done? How can you love a person like me? I adore the ground that you walk on. I'm such a fool. I'm so frightened of the future, what little I have got. I'm not going to waste a minute of it by leaving you again, that is if you will have me back.'

Freddie, a good friend, was sitting in the lounge. He got up and said, 'This is the moment that I leave you alone.' I think he was embarrassed and very moved by our obvious love for each other.

Frank and I went to bed together and I cradled him in my arms just like a baby. This wasn't a moment to make love even if he had been able. This was a moment to feel close and reassure each other that whatever the future held we would be together. I had hated the idea that Frank could have died alone somewhere where he was unknown. No person should die alone, even though the journey ahead for us all must be made alone. There were no recriminations and he continued to try to lie about his whereabouts as he lay in my arms.

Gently I said, 'Frank, I want you always to be honest to me even though it could be something that you know I might not like to hear. I know you were with Linda — I guessed.'

He cried like a baby in my arms. 'I'll never leave you again.' He smelt of alcohol, stale sweat and cigarettes but somehow that was not important. He had looked so unkempt and I could see how easy it would be for him to become a 'down-and-out' if he lost a reason for living. He could not make it alone. Frank then told me where he had been. He had terrified himself with his drunken driving and had realised when he had pulled up by the roadside that he had been driving in excess of a hundred miles an hour. I do not know how I would have lived with myself if he had killed someone. I had debated with myself as to whether I should inform the police about him when he had taken the wheel. It was a difficult decision to make. I could not tell them.

Frank could not get in or out of the bath for he was unsteady and too heavy. I blanket-bathed him. I combed his hair. At least he now looked and smelt better. He said, 'I won't say that I'll never drink again but I will try to give it up. I'm going to have dreadful shakes and withdrawal symptoms. Please try to understand.'

He kept his word. He shook so much that it was frightening. I had to help him hold a cup as he put both trembling hands around it. It was hard for him to get it to his mouth. I boiled eggs and mashed them with tiny cubes of buttered bread in a cup so that he could try to eat with a dessert spoon. He was given drugs to help him in his craving for alcohol but it was essential that he did not drink alcohol at any time with them. He needed much more drastic internal repairs and went back to the hospital a little later as an in-patient.

I tried to get him interested in life. I managed to get two tickets for *Phantom of the Opera* which were as rare as gold dust at the time. He pretended to enjoy it for I was enthralled. Whenever I planned to entertain or go out, we had to cancel at the eleventh hour for one reason or other. We were beginning to live like hermits.

8. Away From It All

Some time later I took Frank to St Lucia to show him my favourite holiday isle. He fell in love with the island and appeared to be much happier. We stayed for three weeks and totally unwound. Frank, as usual, was popular with the staff who had greeted me with hugs when we had arrived for they looked on me as a friend. The beach boys were fascinated by Frank's half-frame glasses.

'See here,' he had said to them, 'I'm really a poor man. I can only afford to buy half a pair.' They laughed and patted him on the back. 'When I'm rich I'll buy the other half.'

'I like it, man.' He was accepted as a great character and we were never left without beach towels when others went without.

We had breakfast on our patio which overlooked the beautiful garden and the Caribbean. The hummingbirds busied themselves in the climbing plants on our wall. One pretty bird of a species unknown to us, would sit on the milk jug helping itself to a drink of milk. It even sat on our knives as we buttered our toast, seeming to enjoy marmalade too. Frank called this bird 'Joey'.

He loved watching the coconuts being picked by the boys, who with monkey-like movements walked up the trunk of the tree. He was given coconuts after they had been opened with a hatchet, and drank the clear liquid. He did not like swimming but watched as I thrashed around in the warm, clear and very blue water.

We ate well, mainly in the hotel, as we listened to steel bands and watched fire-eaters and limbo dancers.

We went to Capones night club. We had to knock three times and ask for Luigi, saying that Al had sent us. Inside was an atmosphere that said it all.

We felt like American gangsters in the black and white decor as the white piano was 'tinkled' by a black and white pianist. At the end of our meal, the waiter arrived with a suspicious-looking violin case. As it was opened we expected a rifle to be removed, but inside were mints and the bill. We were having fun. Frank, still believing that he was not an alcoholic but just a heavy drinker who had control of the situation, drank the odd rum punch.

I felt as if I had a film part as we were eating lobster in an outside restaurant when I realised that we were sitting among drug dealers at work.

A car had been left with the boot unlocked in the car park only yards from us. The occupants, a man and a woman from Puerto Rico, were at one table with two bouncer-like minders sitting nearby. Cars came one by one and flashed their lights at the couple. At a nod, the boot was opened by the newcomer and something removed. They then drove off. The minders had a heavy-looking holdall under their table. I tried to draw Frank's attention to the dealing.

'Don't look round,' I said, as he did precisely that, looking to see what was interesting me. I leant a little closer to him. 'Ssh, I can't talk to you about it now. I'll tell you later.'

'For Christ sake, woman, what the hell are you going on about?' he loudly asked me.' I wanted the floor to swallow me as I tried to behave normally. It suddenly dawned on Frank what was happening.

'Let's get out of here now,' he said. There was to be no after-dinner chat or small talk with his cigarette.

'Whilst we can,' I thought.

He did seem to be able to control his drinking during the holiday.

As we were returning to our room through the hotel grounds at night I saw the ugliest animal walking towards the hotel from the beach. I pointed it out to Frank.

'What on earth is that?'

'I don't fancy waiting to find out,' replied Frank. The woman in the next room threw a fit, but as she was German I could not understand what she was screaming. Frank noticed the electrician.

'Hey, mate,' he shouted at the man, 'what is that goddamn animal?' The electrician came over to us and glared towards the beach. Once his eyes had focused on the long-legged, long-snouted bedraggled creature, he threw his arms in the air.

'Man, him bad,' he said to Frank in fear, as he made to move away from us. 'Him a manacou,' I thought I heard him say. 'He bite bad.' The electrician departed and we went to our bedroom. I got a fit of the giggles. I peered through the window pane as the creature pressed its nose against the glass from the outside. We glared at each other.

'I don't know who is the uglier of the two of us,' I said to it, 'but if you don't disappear quickly, I know who will be the deadest.' The mangy boar-like creature was hungry. It was pregnant. It went into the kitchen where it chased a hatchet-wielding chef around the large table, having a nip at his leg. The hatchet came down on the creature's back and divided it into two. The chef went to hospital.

Next day, the staff were telling the tale to everyone but it seemed to get more and more far-fetched with each narration.

Frank spent some time in the beautiful church in Castries. He lit a candle and prayed silently and privately. Outside the building was poverty and destitution. The inside was glorious and opulent.

Frank went to the bar without me every night before going to bed. He said that it was to get the ice for our ice bucket and as he did not appear to have been drinking when he returned, I was inclined to give him the benefit of the doubt.

It was in this bar that he made friends with other guests. Apparently there was a friendly argument between an arrogant American and a German when Frank got involved. He could not resist joining in. 'Lead the world! What rubbish. I don't care what you say. America will always be five hours behind us.'

The guests loved it and encouraged him to continue joking. He went to bed as a happy man who had found his old self that night. It was time to return to reality from my dream world. I was given the largest bouquet of sprays of tiny mauve orchids by my 'friends' as I arrived at the airport.

'We'll give you a party next time you come.' I did not believe that Frank and I would be able to return together.

Frank realised that his manly chest was changing. He was developing breasts as a side effect of his drugs. He accepted that this was the lesser evil but was embarrassed by it. He needed the diuretics to help remove fluid from his body, so for the first few hours of every day he did not like to move far from a toilet. At times this did cause problems. Once he took the drugs accidentally when I was driving to Dorset. It was in the area of the Palace of Westminster that he got the first strong urge to pass water. I learned where every toilet was between London SW1 and the motorway, not that there were many anyway! Appointments had to be organised for later in the day.

Frank never sent me flowers or a card on Valentine's Day. 'Every day is Valentine's day as far as you are concerned for I always love you,' he said. However, he sent me flowers on Mothering Sundays.

'I have not got a mother to send them to and I wish that you had been the mother of my children.'

His own mother had been dead for a few days when she was found by the police in her armchair at home. Frank had found this hard to accept and it had a tremendous impact on the rest of his life. April 14th was his mother's day and he always went to her grave by himself with a bucket, scrubbing brush, trowel and flowers to tend to her needs.

I had developed a lump in my breast. Frank started to drink for he could not cope with the idea that I would be ill again. I then felt a guilt complex over the whole matter. On reflection, it was also a fact that he was looking for an excuse to drink. The lump was removed the day after

I had seen the consultant and was benign. Frank did not stop drinking though.

9. Slippery Slope

Now he was on the slippery slope again. Things got rapidly worse. He would telephone me in the office at the most difficult time when I had important clients with me. If I indicated that I could not talk he would sound very hurt and say 'goodbye' in a way that worried me.

I had started to leave the door to the house unlocked again so that there was easy access. I set the burglar alarm so that any intruder would activate the alarm, however. I would leave Frank in bed in the morning with his food and soft drink for the day and would return progressively earlier each afternoon to find that nothing had been touched. There was always another empty litre spirit bottle under the bed and the smell of stale drink and cigarettes in the air. I would attempt to blanket-bath him and keep him looking loved and cared for.

Christmas had come around again. It was going to be bleak. I do not think Frank was really aware of the proximity of the festival season. He was now living on a disability pension but spending money as if he were still earning a big salary as a stockbroker.

It was so sad to see a man deteriorate as he had done. Life is so precious but he was finding it a burden. When I prayed for him, I did not know whether to pray for him to live or die. Instead I prayed for guidance to do the right thing and that I would have the strength to accept that it was right.

I went to St Mary-le-Bow to join in the Parish Carol Service on the Thursday before the holiday. It was the most beautiful service I had ever attended and the words of the sermon touched a raw nerve. The church was so full that even though chairs had been placed in the aisle, some of the congregation had to sit on the floor. I left the church feeling better. I was determined to get out of bed earlier the next day to go to the Eucharist in the crypt.

I realised that I was missing my religion and that I had to give up the time for worship. The quiet contemplation was helping me to cope with the destruction being wrought in me by my illogical love of a man. I had help later from Father Victor Stock who told me to make a note daily of just one thing that had given me pleasure in the day and to be thankful for it. I found this an excellent exercise for it was mainly small things of inconsequence that had given me joy. I realised that life was still good and worth living. After all I was giving up a day of my life for each day that I wasted.

I don't think Frank took any notice either of the tree with its candlelights or the food prepared. He couldn't eat his lunch on Christmas Day and left the table in the middle of the meal, not to return.

I would not be hurt by his sickness, for it was totally alien for him to upset me. I was still on a pedestal. I was all that he could depend on. In January he thought that he would die in the night. In the evening he asked to see his daughters. They would not come on the first asking. He was dreadfully upset and he threatened to cut them out of his will, not that he had much to leave to anybody. They came on my second asking and found him oblivious of their presence. As he regained consciousness, he spoke to the girls individually but I know that he asked them to respect my feelings and to be helpful and not oppose me. He told them that he loved them both.

My son-in-law, Phil, had been a great help to me during the day for he had called in to see me and had instantly rung his office to say that he couldn't leave me alone.

Frank was incontinent and the bed was in a mess. I had to bath him but could not do this alone. Frank could not stand and I really do not know how we managed to get him to the bath, let alone in and out of it. I know that Phil bore the bruises on his arms for some time after the event. He had supported him while I dried him with a bath towel. Frank was aware of this help and told Phil that he had misjudged him in the past.

I was totally exhausted but my stepdaughters did not think to look after me. Phil made me a cup of tea.

When he went, he was near to tears. He put his arms around me. 'It's a shame that it takes a tragedy to make people close and really know each other.' We had so much respect and love for each other after that day.

Freddie was a great help as well. He was the only person who could tell Frank that he was a fool or even challenge him. He was a hunk of a man and his strength was useful at difficult moments.

Frank was delirious at times and would ramble on about me having protection from the boys.

'If you see a large Merc outside, don't worry. It's the boys protecting you.' He would thump his fist into his other hand. 'No one will touch my woman!'

He picked the telephone up once and gave a person a ticking off. 'I'll stand no nonsense. If Crad says do it, do it!' He slammed the phone on to the cradle. 'There, that will put paid to their nonsense. You will be OK now.' As he had dialled out someone somewhere must have received a troublesome call.

He did not want to live. He took sleeping tablets and alcohol but never managed to take enough to kill himself. I sat through one night holding his hand and talking to him although he was unable to respond.

'Rest quietly, I will have to live without you if God is ready for you. I love you dearly,' I said.

He came to with a start in the early hours of the morning and vomited smelly yellow-green bile.

His life had changed so radically from his exciting City of London days and although he had me to back and love him, it was apparently not enough. He felt a failure and as a proud man, he could not cope with this 'shame'. He believed that I was a 'survivor' and would get over his loss and carry on successfully. I don't think 'happily' or 'loneliness' were in his vocabulary, but certainly they are in mine now.

I felt that I was in danger of changing my views on euthanasia. I did not support Frank in his idea that his life was his own and that he could do what he wanted with it. He was continually asking me not to allow him to be taken to hospital. He made me promise that I would not allow him to be kept alive on a life support machine. I agreed to this and felt that I would not want to be kept alive artificially if I would not be well afterwards.

'If I were an animal I would be given an injection and that would be that,' he frequently said to me after our cat had been so badly hurt by a greyhound that it had to be 'put down'. He had been in depression over the cat for a few weeks and I was upset – for the owner of the greyhound, trying hard to say sorry, had given flowers to me and some whisky to Frank. That's it, I thought, you have killed the cat, now you will kill my husband.

Frank recovered sufficiently to be able to walk about and take his daily shopping expedition. He was drinking still but said that he would not give himself an overdose of drugs while on alcohol again. The help that our excellent GP gave us both was over and above his call to duty. We could speak to him at any time without an inquisition from the receptionist. Julia was to marry David and this was used to bribe him to stop drinking.

'It will break her heart if you do not take her down the aisle and give her away.'

He continued to drink, but as he was trying to hide the fact it was obviously cut down drastically. He was shaky and tried to make me go to bed earlier than normal so that he could go into the garage and bring his drink into the lounge. He convinced me that he could have a can of lager each evening as it helped stop the craving and he would not touch any other drink. He touched no other drink in my presence but made up for it in my absence. He was now deceitful in the extreme. He was desperately worried over the wedding and the fact that his two wives were to meet.

Frank started to drink very heavily during the fortnight before the wedding although he had cut his drinking down for a couple of months prior to that. It was difficult to make him understand the futility of the situation as no one could reason with him and he really did not appear to know what he was doing.

His internal organs were struggling to cope with the abuse and his legs were constantly swollen. The sores were being treated daily with hydrocortisone cream and his skin irritated to the point of distraction. He needed piriton tablets (antihistamines) to calm the irritation. He bruised easily and bled under the surface of the skin. He found it hard to move about as he was heavy and his breathing was laboured. He had a smoker's cough. He did attend the wedding rehearsal during the week but I had a difficult task to get him ready to go and he could not drive himself the few miles to the church. He needed a drink to give him courage to meet his family again.

The wedding was to be at lunchtime so I knew that it would take all morning to get him ready. He could no longer put his socks or shoes on and could not lace them up for he could not reach them over his extended stomach. He said that it had been weeks since he had been able to even see them. It took him ages to wash or do normal tasks which once would have been completed in a mere moment. I helped him to get ready but nevertheless we were an hour late leaving home, sufficiently so that the bride phoned to find if we were on our way. There was an uncle on standby in case he did not get there at all.

I wanted to look my best and was nervous of meeting the family for the first time knowing that they disliked me even though they had not met me and did not know me at all. I had no time to spend on myself and felt flustered. Julia sensed that I was having trouble and had begun to suspect that her father might not be able to give her away.

We did not arrive at the bride's home until the bridesmaids had left for the church and the bride's mother was about to follow. I did not wish to arrive at the church after her, so asked the chauffeur to drive as fast as he could and get me there before her.

I nearly ran as I was walking so fast down the path to the church door where my son and daughter-in-law were waiting as support for me. My picture hat blew off and I plonked it back on my head. Now I knew that I definitely was not looking my best. It was me at my most flustered and worried who entered the church, feeling like a lamb being thrown to the lions. I wanted to be calm and composed.

I sat in front of my brother- and sister-in-law thinking how destructive their attitude towards us had been. Whenever Frank disagreed with them they accused him of being drunk. It would have been just if it had always been the case, but they managed to pick on him when he was abstaining and had been fighting his desire to imbibe. I often wondered what part they would have played in helping Frank if I had not been around.

Trumpet Voluntary was played by the organist and Julia supported Frank down the aisle, or they supported each other. The drink had been flowing for hours before the service for the family and friends. Frank did well and was justly proud of his daughter who looked radiant in her gorgeous gown. Frank joined me as soon as he was able and travelled with me to the reception. His speech was reasonably humorous but he did say that he would return to this earth as a pigeon and shit on the lot of them!

Julia gave me a look as she left for her honeymoon which said that she did not believe that she would ever see her father alive again. I thought she might be correct for Frank was really drinking now because he felt so ill and could see no future for himself.

For many months I used to arrive home from the city in mid-afternoon for I dared not leave him alone longer. I never knew if he would still be alive and would look at the window for a hint of change since I had left him in the morning. More often than not now, the curtains would not have been moved and Frank would be lying in bed just as I had left him. He managed to lean on the wall and drag himself to the bathroom in my absence, marking the paintwork with his signet ring. The food was rarely touched and remained by the bed. He had now missed two hospital appointments, giving them excuses as to why he had not kept them.

The doctor and I were greatly concerned over his behaviour and health.

'There is no point in calling me if he is just drunk for he won't know what I am saying. Don't however hesitate to call me if you think I can help,' the doctor had said. I was extremely worried and felt as if I was playing God by working out when he should be called. I felt as if I were carrying a burden. I had guilt complexes over Frank and blamed myself for things that were totally out of my control. I think that this was because Frank made me feel that everything depended on my support and belief in him. I was trying to be superhuman and in that context, I was playing God.

I had left the house as normal, during the week following Julia's wedding, feeling that all was far from well.

I had an important business meeting during the early part of the morning when I was interrupted by one of my staff.

'I know that you do not want to be disturbed but Mr Craddock is on the line and he says that it is urgent.'

I excused myself and took the call.

'I'm missing you very much,' Frank said. What could I do?

'Are you listening?' He sounded very strange.

'Frank, can I telephone you back so that I can talk to you at length? I'm in a meeting at the moment.'

'Don't bother,' he shouted, 'I won't be around. I've phoned to say goodbye. I do love you but the time has come.' He replaced his receiver and the telephone went dead.

10. Au Revoir

I did not know what to do for he had said farewell to me on a few occasions before. What would happen if this was not a case of crying wolf? In my heart I think I prayed that there would now be an end to his torment, perhaps this was going to be the day when I arrived home to find that he had passed away. I could not play God. I phoned the doctor and told him what had happened. I told him that I was on my way home when the minicab, which had been ordered for me, arrived.

The doctor told me that he would come to the house when I got home. 'Phone me as soon as you get there if you think you need me. It could be that he doesn't really know what he has said. I will join you immediately.'

Although I was finishing the meeting as quickly as possible, I was then interrupted again by my staff.

'It's the police on the line from your house.'

I apologised to my business visitor.

'I'm sorry, I must take this call. Please do excuse me.' I dreaded the worst.

A policewoman spoke to me.

'Your back door was unlocked so we were able to enter your house. We received a call from a person in your stepdaughter's office and have found your husband unconscious on the floor at the bottom of the stairs. We are not sure whether he has fallen down the stairs or not. He has been drinking and there is an empty pill bottle in the kitchen. The ambulance is on the way.'

'Thank you. Please try to get the ambulance to take him to Bart's as he is receiving treatment from them and is often an in-patient. There is a briefcase on the table. Please open it for inside you will find a list of the drugs prescribed for Frank and the names of the specialists who are repairing his insides. I am coming home to him now.' I felt guilty that I was not at home. Illogically I began to blame myself.

'I've got the letter from the briefcase. I will give it to the ambulance men with the pill bottles. Have you any idea how much he could have drunk? We have found a quarter of a bottle of whisky left.'

I could not answer the question because I did not know and because I felt a loyalty towards Frank who could die without me with him. I thought 'How deep is the ocean?' I just had to get to him in time.

'I will let you know where your husband is taken,' I was told by a kind voice on the telephone.

I put my coat on.

I saw my visitor out of the door. The phone rang again for me. 'Your husband has been taken to Newham. The driver wouldn't go to Bart's as the traffic is too thick to get through quickly. I gave him all the details. I will lock the house with the keys I have found in the briefcase and put them through your letterbox. Good luck.' She did precisely what she said she would.

I left the building and was driven to the hospital. I was told that Frank was in casualty and then asked to sit and wait. I rang Claire and told her what had happened. She then informed the rest of the family.

I sat for an eternity of a few minutes and felt like a spare part. I had to get to Frank. I saw that some doctors had gathered and I could hear some of the conversation which I was sure related to Frank. I got up and walked to one of them and said who I was. I told him what I could about Frank's medical position.

'We have his wife here,' he said. 'I'm grateful for the information, it will be a great help.'

I was taken to Frank who was lying naked on the trolley, his best pyjamas thrown in a heap on the floor. He was in a coma. I removed his watch and put it in my bag. I sat in the large cubicle alone with him wondering what was happening.

The doctor needed to take a sample of blood from an artery and there was no nurse to help him. I offered to hold my thumb over the artery to stop the flow of blood and was accepted. I seemed to be standing beside him for some time as I pressed down on the cotton wool on the arm.

Suddenly all hell was let loose. I was taken to radiology for they needed me out of the way and that seemed to be the nearest place to put me. Frank had died. The doctors got him to breathe again. I had heard him choke as I left the cubicle. A doctor was breathing for him with the steady rhythm of a balloon being pumped. He was wheeled away to intensive care with white-coated staff bending over him. I could see this from where I was sitting but it did not register in my brain.

'Your husband has been removed to the ward,' I was told.

I sat still for a little while and then thought I might as well go home for it was unlikely that I would be allowed to visit him until visiting hours that night. The pyjamas assumed importance in my mind. I wasn't going to leave them on the floor for any Tom, Dick or Harry to pinch. I approached a nurse who was behind a desk.

'I think I will go home. I'll take his pyjamas with me.' I made a move towards the cubicle and bent to pick the striped garments up off the floor.

'I'll get you a bag for them,' the nurse said to me. 'How about a cup of tea first?'

A door was unlocked and I was led into a small room. The nurse left and my tea was brought to me by a pink-uniformed angel. She obviously had a high rank and deserved it. She handed me the tea.

'Your husband technically died for a few moments. The doctors made him breathe again and they are fighting for his life. It is touch and go at the moment. He is a very sick man.' She was gentle and kind.

'I know he has not long to live,' I replied. 'He has been sick a long time. He does not want to be kept alive on a life support machine and I want you to respect his wishes. Please let him go,' I pleaded.

The doctor came to speak to me.

'We are doing everything possible to save your husband. Things look very grim.' The doctors were working so hard against Frank.

'Please let him go,' I said. 'Please do not keep him alive artificially. He wants to die.'

'We can't do that,' he said to me.

'We had a pact that I would speak for him and stop you doing this. It is his life,' I calmly said.

'We can't do what you ask.' He was being kind to me none the less. 'We have to keep him alive artificially for 24 hours. He is very sick and we are fighting hard.'

I knew that they could not do more to save him at this time. I pleaded over and over again all afternoon.

On reflection, I felt they had every right to tell me to stop asking them to stop doing their job, but they remained kind and considerate. There was havoc in Outpatients that afternoon for no one else was being given treatment on time.

'They have to keep him alive for the first 24 hours by law,' my angel told me. 'What happens after that is a different matter.'

At five o'clock the door opened and I was told by another doctor,

'We think we might have saved him this time but we haven't really saved him for he will be back again soon. These cases always do try it again (meaning suicide and alcoholism). We don't have a spare ventilator and have been ringing around to find one. There is one available at St Andrew's so we are moving him there.'

'Please let me go with him,' I pleaded.

'Sorry, that is not allowed,' the doctor replied.

Quietly and undramatically my angel spoke for me.

'She should be allowed to travel in the ambulance. I know that she will be alright and it will be better for her.'

'Only if you realise that we will be working on your husband, and as there are a few of us there won't be much room and you must stay out of the way. It could be hairy if anything goes wrong,' the doctor replied, turning to me.

'I will stay in the corner,' was my reply. The angel had not left me all afternoon and escorted me to the ambulance which had been reversed up to the hospital. I had been told by the doctor who had saved Frank that there was brain damage due to a lack of oxygen reaching the brain during his period of 'death'.

Frank was still unaware of anything. He was still in a coma with the team beside him working hard. I was in a predicament for it seemed wrong yet merciful to pray that they would not succeed.

I sat in the rear corner of the ambulance as we sped through the rush-hour traffic, going against the traffic lights on the wrong side of the road. We weaved in and out of trouble. In out, in out, went the black balloon in the tiring hands of the female doctor. In out, in out, it went as it breathed for him.

On arrival at the friendly smaller hospital, no time was lost. The medical team ran with him, the balloonist bent double at the same time, to the intensive care unit. No entry unless authorised. I did not know whether I was expected to enter and on noticing a payphone I decided to use this to contact Claire before I tried to follow. I could not get through to her for she was trying to find a means of getting to me. She could not leave her baby alone and her husband was away on a business course with the car. One of the nurses who had been in the ambulance came out of the unit.

'You can come in now.' She smiled at me. 'He is being kept alive on the ventilator.'

I walked into the intensive care unit where Frank was lying on a high bed in the middle of the large ward. There were two other patients in the ward. One was behind a curtain and the other was in an iron-lung-type machine.

Frank was now connected to 'blinking' and 'bleeping' machines as well as the ventilator. He had drips attached and was attended by a doctor and nurse at all times.

I sat in the office with a second doctor who told me to make myself at home. I was to use the telephone when I wanted and was given coffee. He asked me many questions as the Tannoy was relating the results of tests being carried out on Frank.

'No paracetamol,' it said. 'No valium.'

I sat in the unit until the early hours of the morning; then I was called to his side. I held his right hand in mine and bent over him slightly, not knowing if he would hear me.

'Frank,' I said quietly.

He seemed to jump and turned his head rapidly towards me.

'He knows you,' whispered the nurse.

'You are in hospital. Just have a nice sleep, dear,' I said to him as he looked as if he was still in a coma. 'I love you. Sleep tight. God bless. No regrets.'

His hand moved slightly in mine as he tried to grip it. I knew that I could accept his death if he did not make it through the night for I would always know that he loved me.

I looked at the nurse. She had tears on her cheeks. I sat with his hand in mine for an hour. The doctor tapped me on the shoulder.

'I think you should go home for a couple of hours and try to get some sleep. I'll call you if there is any change but he does not know you now.'

I agreed to this but expressed my worry over Frank's attitude if he came out of the coma for he had wanted to die. I felt that I should be there.

'Don't worry. We can handle that,' he said, before he ordered a taxi to make sure that I got home safely before the world started another working day.

The taxi driver had reassured me by telling me that I would be given priority treatment should I be needed urgently in the hospital. He did not drive away from my house until I had unlocked the door and gone inside, making sure that I was safely at home.

Someone dialled my number and my telephone rang immediately after I had got into my bed. The person did not speak but replaced their receiver. I had to be certain that it was not the intensive care unit trying to get in touch with me so I checked with them.

'There has been no change. Try to rest a little. We will definitely let you know if there is a change in his condition.'

I slept fitfully. It was comforting to be snug in a warm bed and I cuddled the duvet to myself with the softness of the fabric and filling giving me a feeling of security, rather like a child with a teddy bear. I had found Frank's keys to the house on the mat inside the front door, just where the police had said they would be. The house bore no sign of the drama of the previous day.

I spent the next day in the intensive care unit. Frank was kept on the ventilator but had regained consciousness. I had phoned Linda, his younger daughter, and offered to take her to see her father. She went to see him with me and was obviously very shocked to see him in this state. I held her hand as we sat by the sedated man. I needed to provide comfort to them both. Frank managed to ask Linda if she was the one who had 'split on him'. As she nodded I had to grip her hand more tightly so as to stop her getting upset.

'Now, now Frank. Don't have a go at her. Save your energy for getting home,' I said, gently. He tried to nod agreement.

He started to fight to get fit and was determined to get home before the end of the week. I could only wonder whether this was because he wanted to come home or whether he wanted to get access to alcohol.

Meanwhile I took Linda home with me at lunchtime and cooked a substantial lunch. I treated her as if she were my own daughter. I spent some time in explaining what was happening to her father and how the support and unity of the family would help him. I told her why her father wanted to shorten his life, believing that he felt like a trapped animal with no other way out. I explained that he was addicted to alcohol and nicotine and that although he had put up a great fight to kick the habit, he knew he was unable to sustain any periods of abstention. He also knew that he only had a short time to live. She listened and appeared to agree with me. Unfortunately, she went into near hysterics when she returned home, rushing to her mother, and the family telephones became redhot with tittle tattle and, as it appeared to me and Frank later, malicious mischief. It was hard enough to deal with Frank alone without the family pulling against me and upsetting him at every opportunity.

Frank was moved out of intensive care and spent two further days in hospital where he was given counselling and excellent attention. I had a feeling that he had discharged himself when I collected him, for he could hardly walk and virtually collapsed in the long corridor as we struggled to the exit. He was stubborn and would not use a wheelchair, trying to convince everyone that he was fit and a fighter, and aiming to get a few 'Brownie points' and clear his conscience of the fact that his own behaviour had put him there in the first place.

I thought of the doctor's words to me: 'We think we have saved him this time but he will be back very soon.'

What could I do to stop Frank trying to take his own life? We talked about this and Frank had obviously been thinking very deeply over the matter. He told me that he would not take his life in any way that would be construed as suicide for he was concerned that I would then not benefit from his life assurance. He could not promise that he would not drink again, and seemed to respond well to my suggestion that as he thought he had only a little while left, he should try to make the most of that time and we should enjoy it together. Unfortunately, enjoyment meant drinking to him, and this would then mean that he had a good excuse to drink as much and as often as he wanted.

I was concerned that he would use the Samurai sword to kill himself. He thought this was funny and assured me that it would be too messy and that he treasured the sword too much to sully it with his own blood.

The Samurai sword had been a gift from me and it stood in glory in pride of place in our lounge.

Frank now promised me that he would not drink 'behind my back' as long as I tolerated his drinking in my presence. I thought this might be better as I could keep an eye on him. I had been terrified that he was driving, for although he did not get drunk (for his blood was used to being saturated with alcohol), he really believed that he was safe to take the wheel. I told him that I would tolerate but not condone his drinking if he promised not to drive the car. He promised, but accused me of not trusting or believing in him when I tried to get the keys. I knew that he was less likely to drive if he kept the keys to the car but then I had to try to remove the vehicle from the garage when I went out without needing the car.

Every drink he poured knotted my stomach muscles. I was constantly tense and did not relax for a moment. Everywhere smelt like a pub when the glasses have not been washed from the night before. I was embarrassed but knew that I must not criticise him but reason good sense with him.

I felt annoyed when Frank told the doctor that I did not mind him drinking any more. It would have been better to have no alcohol in the house so that drinking could only be in the sociable atmosphere of the local pub had it not been as dangerous to drink as much as possible in a short time for the liver has no time to recover.

I was terribly worried when I left him alone each day as I tried to carry on normally. I was relieved that we now had a Homelink box which could be activated by Frank if he needed help; the control panel would telephone me in the office as they alerted the emergency services to his needs. Frank had a new kitchen designed and built to make my life easier. He changed the garage door from a manual up-and-over to a remote control system so that I did not aggravate my spinal problem. He said that he was 'closing his doors' so that when he left me alone in this world, I would have as easy a life as possible. He showed me great love and devotion.

Frank sat on the bedroom balcony during the summer months. He looked dreadfully ill and other than leaning on the wall to get to the bathroom, he could not move about. Daily, he sat outside without shaving or combing his hair. He no longer washed himself or knew what time of day or night it was. He sat with the daily newspaper on his knees but could not read it. He looked like a very old tramp. Frank did not come down the stairs to the lounge for he would not have been able to manage the stairs. His only friends were the blackbirds. He talked to them.

'Look Ann,' he said, excitedly, 'the birds know me.' He called to one of them, 'Hey Joey, get off that roof and come and keep me company.' Few of his friends were around now that they were really needed. How they

could have helped me get Frank interested in normality again or sat with
him to give me a break from constant caring.

I do not know how he got the drink but he was obviously being supplied
with at least two litres of spirit a day. I bought him one bottle of vodka
once for he was in such dreadful withdrawal pain that I was frightened
for him and for myself. I felt as if the whole world watched me as I
paid for the bottle of drink and I was very upset. The guilt complex was
enormous and not worth bearing.

'I'll come to you immediately he asks for help,' the doctor had said, 'but
it is no use unless he asks for me, not you.' There was nothing the doctor
could do for Frank without his co-operation.

I was now trying to run my business and behave normally. I went to
the office at ten o'clock every day except Friday (that was my housework
day). I did not open my business at weekends. I would return as early as
possible, but normally at three o'clock for I dared not leave Frank longer.

My heart would be in my mouth every time I drove into the square for
I never knew what would greet me. I would then try to blanket-bath and
shave my husband. It was usual for the food and soft drink that I had left
for Frank to have in my absence to be untouched. He slept a lot.

I tried to spend as much time with him as possible, talking about my
day and joking about inconsequential matters. I refused to believe that I
could not get Frank to behave in a sensible and positive manner. I was
sure that he was just very sick and troubled and 'there but for the grace
of God go I.' We talked about religion and politics. We talked about travel.
Frank was reliving his past. He likened me to his mother on one occasion
and wished that she had met me for he was sure that she would have
liked me. He wished that I had given birth to his children and that we
had met each other earlier.

'I've not given you a fair chance of happiness,' he would say to me so
very often. 'You deserve better than this.' He was sad. He no longer had
money and was living on a disability pension. He had used all his savings
for our old age. I had invested all my savings in the business and now
had nothing for my rainy day or old age myself.

I would not give up in my battle to get him interested in life again even
though it now seemed that I was wasting my time. I was not going to give
in or shirk my responsibility.

Things got worse. Frank was becoming incontinent and sometimes dirty.
I heard him drag himself along the wall to the bathroom in the middle of
the night. There was a loud crash and I jumped out of bed. (Frank had
been sleeping in the dressing room for some months.) He had fallen over
and couldn't get up. I struggled with his 19 stone body. It was a dead
weight but somehow I managed to get him to stand again with his arms

stretched out in front and the palms of his hands flat on the wall. I then used my own body as a support and, picking each of his feet up in turn placed it in front of him, telling him to transfer his weight to that foot.

I manoeuvred him into his bedroom and manipulated a turn of his body so that he had his back to the bed. Now he had only to sit down on the bed. He promptly fell on the floor. Eventually he was settled in his bed. I returned to mine in the hope of getting more sleep before a busy day. Just as I was about to enter the land of Nod, there was another disturbance from the bathroom. Frank had used the wall as a support and guidance to the toilet. He could not return to bed without my help. He had vomited some blood and bile. I managed to get him to the bed.

There was a third problem during that night. Frank had again got out of bed for the bathroom. He had looked hilarious as he tried to return to bed without help for he had his feet flat on the ground, but his body was straight and solid at an impossible angle of 25 degrees so that his feet were walking 18 inches ahead of his shoulders! He had to take small mincing steps as fast as he could to get back without falling.

He was terrified of returning to hospital and never stopped asking me to keep him at home 'come what may' and not to call for an ambulance if he was unconscious again. He longed to die at home and end his long and dreary days which were making his life drag on unbearably.

On arrival in my office I rang the doctor and told him of my concern. I felt that the responsibility for his life was too heavy and subconsciously I thought that it would be a merciful release for Frank to be able to end it all.

The doctor talked to me for a few minutes and said that he would call to see Frank either 'today or tomorrow' and would then speak to me again. Incidentally, Frank was now a diabetic as well as having trouble with all his internal organs. His external organ, the skin, was problematical with dark red blotches, irritation and open ulcers on his legs. His mouth was black and ulcerated. The skin on his feet was thick and rough and his toenails were long and jagged. I tried to deal with them but was not very successful for they were so strong that the scissors couldn't cope.

I was beginning to feel that it was cruel to continue to prolong the life of a person who would never be well and wanted to die. I felt so sorry for him. I had been told by the doctors that I would wonder why I had ever got involved in the situation and that I should think of the man I had originally met and not the man he had now become. I always knew why I had become involved with the man and did not have recriminations. He had needed me at a moment when I needed to be needed. He had always loved me and in his own way had cared for me as best he could.

11. Crisis

I received a phone call from the doctor at the end of the morning. He had gone to see Frank and had let himself into the unlocked house. He found Frank trapped in an empty bath in a filthy state for he had emptied his bowels whilst in the bath because he could no longer control the bowel movement.

It appeared that Frank had gone to the bathroom and fallen over backwards, hitting his head on the taps and bruising his back as he landed in the empty bath. His flailing arms had hit the soap dish, knocking it from the wall tiles in which it had been built. The broken soap dish had landed in the basin in small pieces. Frank had been lying in the cold bath for four hours.

The doctor was shocked to see the extent of his deterioration and was having Frank admitted to hospital immediately. He had summoned an ambulance and had hosed Frank down with water from the shower after removing the stinking pyjamas, dumping them at the end of the bath for me to deal with on my eventual return.

The doctor asked a male neighbour to help him to get Frank out of the bath but try as they might, they could not manage to lift him out. This was left for the ambulancemen.

'Don't bother to come home, Ann,' the doctor advised me; 'make your way to Bart's hospital instead. I've already spoken to the consultant and they are waiting for Frank and you. Frank really is in a poor way and unless he changes radically, I think it may only be a matter of days or weeks at the most before he dies. You know where I am when you need me.'

Frank asked the ambulancemen to pass him his half-emptied glass of whisky as he was gasping for a drink before they left the house.

'Not likely, mate,' he was told. Frank protested that he needed drink and he was passed a cup of water instead.

I arrived at the famous City teaching hospital at about the same time as Frank, entering by a different door. He was immediately attended by the liver specialist team who were on duty for accident and emergency admittances. I was taken to Frank who seemed totally confused and at times did not know where he was. He rambled on, talking a lot of nonsense. Frank interrupted and argued with me when I was asked questions and answered them truthfully. I again helped the doctors with the odd blood test from the artery as I had done in the other hospital and I was allowed to look after Frank who was to remain in the admissions section for the rest of the day. Frank would not admit that he had been drinking, saying that his last drink had been on the previous evening, and I believe that he really thought this to be correct.

He would not accept that he had not been able to stand because he had been drinking and made himself believe that he was only in hospital because he had hurt himself in the fall. I had a long and helpful chat with the doctor when Frank went for his X-rays. It was the one time when I was able to speak to them without Frank arguing with me. His future was very grim.

I had to keep fetching the urine bottle for Frank who was unable to use it. He could not pass any water, but he was dreadfully thirsty and I was for ever filling a paper cup with water, which he gulped down.

There had been an accident which had claimed two lives and very badly burned five other workmen during the afternoon. One more died in the department before the four remaining patients were rushed to the Billericay burns unit. As one nurse went with each patient it meant that the department was short-staffed and outpatients were getting irate. One man who had been waiting for attention since eight o'clock in the morning burst into the treatment area and tore a strip off the sister. She calmly and quietly replied to him but I did not hear what she said.

'Sister, I'm sorry. I feel very ashamed,' the crestfallen man said in return.

Frank was removed to a ward which I can only refer to as providing semi-intensive care. It was beautifully decorated in quiet yet cheerful colours. The nurse was absolutely charming and kind. Frank was now too ill to lift his head. He was so weak that he could not support his own limbs for tests. He was obviously not drunk but very seriously ill. I left him there in the capable hands of the nurses and doctors whose skill is second to none in the world. He had so much internal damage to so many organs that he was anaemic, diabetic, dehydrated, malnourished and mentally beaten. Everything was stacked against him except God, medicine and myself.

We had been having problems with his family and I received a telephone call of abuse at midnight because Frank had not been in touch with his daughter on her birthday. There had been no thought that there could have been a good reason for the neglect and no concern over Frank's health or well-being. I continued to get telephone calls from someone who would not speak to me, replacing the receiver if I answered the phone. Eventually the culprit admitted the fact to Frank and we had our number changed to get peace from the unwanted calls at home.

I was never accepted by his family as his wife, even though I had not been instrumental in the break-up of his first marriage and I loved and cared for him in his desperate moments. I had no support from them, only criticism and hindrance. This created additional stress for Frank who took it all very seriously.

I was told that Frank had a maximum of ten months to live. He was moved from the cheerfully decorated ward to the liver and kidney ward, – the Rehere ward upstairs which was to become familiar to us both over the last few years. We were both tired with the struggle of day-to-day living and had accepted that the end was getting nearer. We were able to talk to each other in an open manner about death and our parting. In future we never parted company without finishing our conversation to our satisfaction for there was a danger that we would not speak to each other again. Frank had informed me of his arrangements that I must carry out for him when the time came. He had filed documents in order. We needed to be together alone as much as possible and it seemed to us that people intruded into our privacy.

I felt that most of the doctors, both here and elsewhere, were treating Frank as a liver and not as a person. My feelings did not seem to count at all and I was not asked questions which I would have thought were relevant and extremely important in view of the events which were going to overtake us both. I appreciate that Frank was the patient and not me, but certain matters regarding one of the partners does affect the other and the whole family at home.

Religion meant much to us both. Frank had received instruction from Father Victor Stock from St Mary-le-Bow on Wednesday afternoons at home, with the priest travelling from the City for the weekly chats. I was delighted that at a midday service in Easter week the congregation, of which I was one, were told that on the next day the church would be welcoming back a man into its fold. Little did I know that this man was my beloved Frank.

The service was a special one for Maundy Thursday when the priest washed the feet of some of the congregation. Frank was anointed on his hands and forehead with holy oil during this service, having confessed his sins on the day before. We had been married for two years by that time and had never taken the Eucharist together. It had been a very wonderful and inspiring moment as we knelt on the altar steps together. We had spent many hours discussing the differences between the Anglican and Roman Catholic churches. I was of the first and Frank had been of the second; now we were united in our worship. We believed that families who pray together, stay together. How long had we got together on this earth?

Frank was adamant that his family were not to be told that he was in hospital. He did not wish them to visit him or cause a nuisance to the staff. I felt that his eldest daughter should know of the deterioration in his health so that the end, when it came, would not be too much of a shock to her. I persuaded him to see her and her husband on the understanding that they kept his whereabouts secret.

Frank had been in hospital for a fortnight without smoking a cigarette and he thought that he would not smoke again, for if he could go without nicotine for that amount of time, he could abstain forever. Likewise, he had not drunk any alcohol and could now manage for an indefinite period without his prop. He made me promise that when the time came for him to die, irrespective of where he was, – at home or in hospital – I would put a glass of whisky to his lips. His attitude had recently been that, as he was dying anyway, it did not matter whether or not he speeded the process by doing what he wanted with his life, for it was his life anyway and he was going to die. There was nothing anyone could do about that.

I visited him daily, spending as much time as I could with him. He was always pleased to see me and watched his wristwatch tick away the seconds if I was the slightest bit later than anticipated. His face would light up as I came into his view. He made friends with a kidney transplant patient. The patient's sister was donating one of her organs to her sick brother. Another father who had received a transplanted kidney would not allow the nurses to transfer him to bed 13 for his young daughter was terrified that it would bring him bad luck. Frank smiled and offered to have his bed moved into the space. The rest of the ward breathed again with relief, for all were apprehensive.

My telephone rang at around ten o'clock at night. A nurse told me that she had an upset Frank on the line to speak to me. Frank sounded extremely agitated. He was so upset that he could hardly speak to me. It appeared that a telephone call had been received in the ward from a person who said that she was the elder daughter of Frank. She desperately needed to talk to her father. Noticing that Frank was awake, the nurse went to ask him if he wished to take the call. He had said that he would speak to his daughter and was helped into a wheelchair for he was too ill to stand by himself. He was wheeled to the desk on which the telephone was lying, off the cradle.

'Hello!' was all that he was able to say before the caller interrupted.

'What the hell do you think you are playing at?' she said.

'Who's that?' an ashen-faced Frank asked. 'You are not my daughter. How dare you trick the nurse like this . . . off, you bitch.' There was laughter on the other end of the line as it was disconnected. Frank had managed to tell the staff that it had been his ex-wife before he collapsed.

The consultant had been called and there had been considerable concern over the damage this stupid action had caused. Security was alerted and no one other than myself or a person with me was to be admitted to see Frank in future. I had a code to use if I phoned the hospital so that they would know that it was me, his legal wife, and not another hoaxer on the line.

Frank chain-smoked three cigarettes. He was shattered and as always when he was in trouble, would not settle until he had leant on me.

I hope I comforted him. He was drugged to sleep. The elder daughter rang me at midnight in hysterics. She had been told the story by her sister.

'Ann, I'll never speak to them again. How dare they use my name. How dare they do such a stupid selfish thing.'

I was cool towards her for I was beginning to wonder how they knew where Frank was. When challenged over this point, she satisfied me with her explanation.

'My sister's boss has a friend in the ward and she noticed Dad was there.' I tried to assure Julia that I believed her, but by this time she was in such distress that her husband had to take over.

I spent a wakeful night worrying over Frank. I am told that elsewhere two women, his ex-wife and younger daughter, thought that it was screamingly funny and laughed themselves into an unladylike state matching their previous disgraceful behaviour.

Frank was handed a card by the visitor who had informed the family where he was. The card was from his daughter. He tore it into small pieces and he would not accept anything from her again. As far as he was concerned, neither his ex-wife nor his younger daughter existed. He was never to see them again. He wrote specific instructions to them not to attend his funeral and had a copy of this communication sent to his solicitor for safe keeping. It was unlikely to, and indeed did not, have any effect.

The doctors and consultant were upset that Frank had had this setback and spent a time with me when they apologised that it had happened but I could attach no blame to them or the nurses and felt that no apology was necessary.

Frank was particularly fond of one of the senior doctors. He had a heart-to-heart with him, expressing the thought that he did not wish to be kept alive artificially any more. Frank asked that he should be allowed to stay at home as much as possible and live a normal life without interference. He said that he considered that we needed every moment together for our time together had been so short. Frank had been a patient with this doctor when we had got married and he had noticed the tremendous improvement in him at the time and the months which followed. Frank had not drunk for ten months after our marriage. It had been overconfidence that had started him drinking again when he had been sure that he could drink a bride's health: the one-too-many drink, the twelve too few.

He could not stop drinking once the alcohol was in his blood. I heard this conversation and the doctor asked me if I agreed with what had been said. I said that I did agree and I felt that the doctor agreed too. There was a sense of peace and relief in us at the time.

The doctor left us and went to speak to the consultant who later toured the ward. He walked past Frank, saying 'I'll be back to see you after I've seen everyone else.' He obviously wished to speak to Frank and when he returned he told me to stay where I was sitting as he sat on the bed. We were shattered by his next remark for there was a sense of peace in us at the time.

12.   A Lifeline for a Drowning Man

'Have you considered a liver transplant?' It seemed like a cruel joke and I was stunned into complete silence. This could not be happening to us. This only happened to a few other people on television or in the newspapers. I was dazed. Of course, I wanted Frank to live but not at any price. Liver transplant patients were rare and did not have a long lifespan even after the operation.

Frank was flabbergasted. His first question related to drink.

'Would I be able to drink again? I would not be considered for a transplant, would I? I'm 59 years old, have a drink problem and have buggered up the rest of my body.'

He didn't add that he had also tried to commit suicide more than once and had just asked to be left alone by the hospitals, but the doctor knew that.

'We are not equipped for liver transplants so it would be done in Addenbrooke's Hospital in Cambridge or at King's College Hospital in London if they accept you as a patient.

'You must convince them that you have not had a drink for six months before I refer you for transplant. You would be able to live a normal life again and have the odd drink for you would not have cirrhosis with a new and strong liver.'

I found this an incredible answer for I did not understand how a man could drink alcohol when his life would be dependent on drugs, but I am no expert on such matters. I believed that Frank was being misled and that his future was being made glossier and better than real life. I stumbled over my words as I asked if it were possible to place a new organ into a body with kidney, heart and vascular problems. He nodded to me.

I could not understand how an alcoholic could be given a new organ for surely the organ alone would not cure alcoholism. I was holding Frank's shaking hand and felt as if I were trembling too. We could not say any more at that time but on reflection I believe that consultant was irresponsible and devoid of compassion and understanding.

We could not say much to each other either. I asked Frank to pinch me so that I knew that I was not dreaming. 'I don't want an answer now. Think about it.' He told me he was concerned that Frank had become negative. 'He used to be such a live wire.'

The doctors were arguing in the corridor. The argument was very heated and very long. It was about Frank.

I knew that this was not a unanimous decision. I continued to sit by
Frank's bed. We could not really talk to each other for we were pensive
and in shock. I was going home to think alone and leaving Frank to do
the same.

'Darling, whatever you decide to do, you will have my backing and
support.'

'Don't tell anyone about this yet, please,' Frank said. 'Let us keep it to
ourselves for a little while. I cannot believe that I am worthy of being
given this chance.'

I drove into the square and my car was surrounded by my neighbours
wanting to learn how Frank was getting on in the hospital. I could not
speak. I was still so stunned. I felt like a robot which had been pro-
grammed to move without being able to think what it was I was doing.

'I can't really talk to you at the moment. Things are about the same,
thank you.'

I went into the sanctuary of my own home. I paced up and down my
lounge thinking hard – so hard that it hurt. 'I've experienced everything
now,' I thought. 'Surely it is humanly not possible to experience any more.
How can I face the world if he has a transplant and then tries to commit
suicide again? How can I live with the shame if he starts to drink with
the new liver? This is only going to prolong his death for he is a sick man
with serious problems with other parts of his body. We cannot take any
more suffering. Surely he will be rejected as not being suitable for a
transplant. It won't ever really happen. How can he possibly be accepted?
And if he goes forward and then is rejected, what will that do to him
psychologically?

'God please guide us to do the right thing and help us to accept what
we have in front of us as being right. Help me to understand that it is
ethically and religiously correct to use the organ of another to prolong a
life. If they decide to give Frank a liver, it can only be experimental. I'm
tired and not sure what this move will do to my own life. I am already
allowing his sickness to begin to ruin my career.

'I know that I can cope with Frank's death. I love him enough to let him
go. Can I now cope with his renewed life? I don't think I believe in this
transplant and I hope that Frank will say no. Whatever I think is not
going to make any difference but, come what may, Frank will have my
support. God help me now. I can only accept the transplant if that is what
Frank wants but in my heart of hearts I believe that his living or dying
should be controlled by God rather than man.'

Frank was lying in his bed deep in thought, too. He thrashed about.

'If I agree to have a transplant the medics will learn from my death and
I will be repaying them for the way I have been treated and I'll make

amends for the trouble I've caused them. It can only be experimental. I won't live through the operation but my life won't have been useless and wasted then.

'If I live, I will be giving Ann a fair chance of happiness for our time together has been far too short. I only want to live if I can live normally and have a better quality of life. I have had assurance over that. I will be able to drink again with no worries. Life to me is only worth living if I can drink and I have had assurance over that as well.

'I will be able to counsel others with my problems. I want to help others see the foolishness of this addiction. I want to stay and make Ann happy. How can I say no to this chance. I'll do it for her.'

I returned to the hospital next day.

'I feel like a drowning man who has been thrown a lifeline,' said Frank. 'I have to clutch it.' The tears streamed down his face and I wiped them away with my fingers. We were so close. He was under my skin and I felt his sorrow and pain as if it were my own.

He had a 50% chance of living for ten months. He had to abstain from alcohol for six of those months before he could be sent for assessment regarding the life-saving operation of a liver transplant. It seemed strange that at a time of massive cutbacks in the NHS, amid claims that there was never enough money to provide the service for routine cases, a costly liver transplant was being considered for a man who had, only a few hours ago, expressed his wish to be allowed to die peacefully at home, and who was an alcoholic.

Our way of life was being taken out of our hands. It was extremely hard to adjust to the fact that Frank might not die in a short time when we had bravely come to terms with death. How could we come to terms with life if indeed it were to be granted?

I thought of a reading:

One night a man dreamt he was walking along a beach with the Lord. Across the sky flashed scenes from his life in which there were two sets of footprints in the sand; one belonging to him, and the other to the Lord. But he saw that at the saddest points of his life there was only one set of footprints.

'Lord, you said that once I decided to follow you, you would never leave me. So why during my most troublesome times is there only one set of footprints?' The Lord replied, 'My son, my precious child, I love you and would never leave you. During the times of trial and suffering, when you see only one set of footprints, it was then that I carried you.'

Frank and I climbed on to the Lord's shoulders for a long nail-biting wait. There were many moments when Frank doubted that he was doing the right thing, never more so than when he picked up his *Daily Mail* which carried a letter from a medical lady stating that, even as a medical person, nothing could have prepared her for the last six months of her father's life with the trauma of a liver transplant. He worried that it might be too much for me to take.

'I'm made of sterner stuff,' I confidently replied. He was unsuccessful in trying to trace the sender of the letter but thankfully he did not think of contacting the newspaper itself.

Part Two

Borrowed Time
November 1989-March 1991

13. Unkept Promise

There had been frequent news reports (with a news update on most evenings) of a young mother who shortly after the birth of her baby was fighting for her life, due to her reaction to drugs. A plea had been made for a donor liver and at the eleventh hour, a generous family had allowed their son's organ, now of no use to him, to be used.

At first all seemed to be well, but now things were looking very grim.

The morale in the liver ward was so low and even appeared to be sinking fast. I could not get it out of my head that this would be one of the worst places in which to die. It was becoming more and more obvious that Frank was losing the very little confidence he had ever had in this hospital.

The atmosphere was filled with a militancy against the government and Maggie Thatcher in particular, she being the scapegoat for any inadequacies on their part. This, combined with the frustration of ongoing battles frequently unsuccessful to save lives, the aggravation of unwanted media – at one point newsmen prohibited from a sterile area placed ladders outside the windows, and attempted unsuccessfully to climb them for a scoop photograph – and the natural fear of the unknown stifled the air.

Patient after patient seemed to get worse. The nurses had no time even to smile at Frank as they scuttled about. There was no continuity of staff, most of them being agency nurses who had a 'here today, gone tomorrow' attitude which was so easily interpreted as a don't care one. One thing was sure, they certainly were not enjoying their work. Where was the dedication of yesteryear?

I sat quietly beside Frank's bed hoping to build his confidence and play down any aggravations and worries. It had been a struggle to live long enough to get this far and I did not want him to fall at this nearly final hurdle. How I would have loved to tell the busy staff what I thought.

Frank's life would be in the balance and the result of the tests to be completed in the next few days could give him the chance of a future. Without it he would certainly die in the next few months. He had squandered so many opportunities in his 59 years for a healthier and more fulfilling existence. I prayed that it was not too late to make amends. I always had doubts that he would find it possible to stop drinking alcohol but would not let him know this fact.

Frank desperately wanted the transplant for two reasons. He felt that he would be repaying the medical staff for their time and attention if they were to learn from his death this way and he really believed that he would not drink again anyway, this opportunity being a sign that the doctors believed in him. Frank had always needed people to believe in him and their trust was very important to him. I will always remember the day I hid the whisky in the washing machine. It wasn't the fact that I had hidden it, but the knowledge that I had not trusted him that hurt him so much. Of course, with an alcoholic, trust is a rare commodity, the deceit being a large part of the sickness.

Frank was inwardly praying, 'Please God, give me the strength and make them see that I will not drink my time away. At this moment when my life is slipping away, I really want to live, even though on some other occasions I have been eager to die, not believing in myself and my ability to give up the booze. Will they understand that I feel that if I am given this chance I will be able to help others?

'There really is so much that I want to do. I can help others avoid the mistakes I have made. No one was around to understand me when I needed them, please God spare me so that I can be the one to help and understand people like me in the future.'

I had spent many a wakeful early morning hour wondering if the brilliant surgeons would consider the massive and expensive life-or-death transplant on an older man who had abused his own body by his way of life. I suppose that if I were really honest, I would write that I did not believe that it could ever happen. Common sense itself dictated that it was not right to prolong the daily struggles of a person with Frank's problems when there were other needy people to help. I did not believe that there was any chance of his living when the other organs in the body were having to cope with this abuse too.

It would have been different if Frank had been in a sudden accident and the rest of the body was in fine shape. Yet here he was in a famous liver unit, second to none, all 19 stone of him. How I loved this man, unreasonable or not. I suppose my view of the ethics of the situation was constantly changing, but it can be finally summed up in the thought that it would be inhumane to refuse a man who was dying of cancer through smoking a life-saving operation, even if it was perceived that he might start to smoke again. It would be equally cruel to deny a reformed alcoholic a chance of life – but heaven forbid the anguish and shame we would feel if this should happen and Frank should start to drink again. This problem was beginning to haunt me, but believing that we should 'not trouble trouble until trouble troubles you,' I pushed it to the back of my mind.

Frank began to wander around the small two-bed ward. The menu was brought in and he was offered liver for lunch. At least the kitchen staff had a sense of humour, but I felt that it wouldn't exactly have tempted me to eat!

'I expect you get a lot of that here?' Frank said, with his tongue in cheek and his eyes sparkling with mischief, 'but I'd prefer bacon and onions with mine.'

We wandered into the passage. The struggling young mother was meeting her Maker in intensive care. Her husband grabbed a cup of coffee from the kitchen at the side of the passage where we stood. He was unaware of anything or anyone as he walked somewhere, anywhere to do something, anything. He was lost and at his wits' end. Exhausted from the days and nights of worry, never leaving the hospital where his wife's mother and sisters were also keeping vigil, he could find no privacy, no counselling and certainly no comfort. The weeks of torment, fight and many moments of grasping at straws were coming to an end. This time should have been a celebration of new life with a baby daughter.

Frank looked at the weary man and put out his arm to touch his shoulder, their eyes locking in that moment, and comfort passed from one to the other, their suffering souls united. They drank the understanding and comfort as a parched person in a desert.

I decided that this was the time to leave the hospital. They needed to communicate without me.

Frank was to be assessed as a possible recipient of a liver transplant and, if this was positive, tests made for a match. These tests normally take a few days and there are very few local people as patients. It does mean that whereas most of the patients have to stay in the ward at weekends, a local person is allowed home on Saturday and Sunday, so after a few days of exhaustive tests Frank was to be allowed home each weekend; but his tests took four weeks instead of the anticipated four days.

I returned to the hospital in the latter part of the afternoon a few weeks later when everything depended on the results of that week. One of the doctors was doing his rounds. He was an ordinary fellow who if met in the street, would bear no resemblance to the sort of man one might expect to carry so much responsibility. He stopped at Frank's bed and said that it was pointless to keep the patient there any longer.

'I promise to phone you with the results and our decision tomorrow,' he stated. The decision would mean either that Frank would now be left alone medically for the short remainder of his lifespan or that there would be an attempt to save him and his details would be added to the liver transplant waiting list of 11 people, not necessarily in order of first come first served for it would depend on organ compatibility. The transplant could take place at any time but would have be within three months, for that was Frank's projected lifespan.

My beloved Frank was coming home for Christmas; the knowledge filled me with the mixed emotions of gladness, apprehension and fear that this would be the last festival that we would spend together.

Frank left the ward to change into his day clothes from his pyjamas, his uniform of late, in the filthiest bathroom he had ever entered. He was too preoccupied to take much notice of this. I gathered his belongings together from his locker with tiredness sweeping over me as I waited for him to return. I could not allow myself the luxury of admitting that the daily journeys to visit my husband, the constant worry, the numerous telephone calls just as I was about to eat and the running of my business were beginning to wear me down.

The matronly figure of a nurse who had been born in the Caribbean approached me with kindness written all over her face.

'My, you are not your normal bright self today. You look tired. You must look after yourself you know and keep your chin up.'

I realised that this was the first friendly gesture shown in the month that I had been going to this hospital. I found it hard to understand the aloofness of the staff but expect that they dared not get too friendly with patients who are not likely to live long. They must feel the frustration and helplessness daily, but I am glad that this is not apparent in hospices which on the whole are happy places. Frank had been joking and trying to be bright and cheerful in the ward, but the response had been sour. We all joke or talk too much when we are nervous. This was his way of trying to camouflage his true feelings.

'Yes', I thought, 'I am tired, but it isn't just through our own troubles.' I had spent a few hours last night consoling my young neighbour when she learned of the drowning of her boyfriend.

The nurse snapped me out of my melancholy thoughts. She gave me the best cup of tea I had drunk for weeks, even though it was in a plastic cup.

'Ssh, I'm not supposed to give you this but I think you have earned it. Don't let the others see it; they'll all want one.' She busied herself in her cleaning up and found a pair of new-looking slippers, telling me not to forget to take them home. They were not Frank's. 'Course not, silly me, but the owner won't be needing them where he has gone.' She took them away. 'He was very friendly with your husband.'

'As if a patient isn't suffering enough pain and problems without losing friends as quickly as they are made,' I thought as a very young and apprehensive priest put his head around the curtain, asking me if I knew someone of whom I had never heard. I got into conversation with the man and asked him which church he was from. He was a Roman Catholic but felt that it didn't really matter which faith one had at a time of crisis. Any faith is better than none.

He seemed so young to be faced with the constant trauma – the drips, drains and anguish that were for ever present. He was only human and at this stage the strain was showing. I wished him well in his new post. It was a strange feeling that both Frank and I experienced as Frank bade farewell to the patients and staff. We both wondered what the future held for us and whether he would ever return to this hospital. We had a love for each other that would see us both into the future and beyond. Together we could face the world. Together we would not be alone. Frank took my hand in the minicab and held it all the way home, occasionally raising it to his lips. He seemed weak and I had to wait until we were home to hold him to me.

That night was spent peacefully in our own bed with us luxuriating in the warmth of each other's body. 'I have him for a little while longer,' I thought, 'and for that I must be thankful.'

This was to be the last night of complete relaxation for quite some time. We both knew that we would not receive a telephone call from the doctor at the hospital with the critical results as he had promised to inform us *on the following day*, so neither of us was listening for the ring of the telephone.

Frank had in a way already become hospitalised for his conversation and his life revolved around the events within the ward. He told me of the complete dedication of the Sister tending the mother who had died. She had appeared first thing in the morning from the intensive care area, which was behind closed doors (leaving the mind to conjure up thoughts of what lay behind that blue door) in an old and very thick grey cardigan to keep her warm against her exhaustion. She had been on duty for over twenty-four hours, not wishing to leave the patient nor the family in their sorrowful state. When she finally and dejectedly went home she was too tired to cook for herself but, knowing that she needed a warm and nutritious meal as much as sleep, called in at the local fish and chip shop. Feeling stupid as she realised that she had left her purse behind, she had to explain that she could not pay. The 'chippy' unwrapped the cod and chips and returned them to his warm compartment. Sister Fran felt that the world was against her as she fell into her bed, too tired to feel her hunger pangs.

Then there was the other side of the story, the complete opposite of the dedication of a totally overworked leader with no time to supervise the laid-back nurses. The ward was divided into smaller wards of between two and six beds with a nurse on duty in each of these wards at all times. All the patients were extremely sick but only a minority were there for transplants. However, at night the agency nurses would sneak into the smoke-filled day room. I was fuming with anger as I heard this and vowed to report it to one of the three sisters on the ward when I returned to the hospital. I was beginning to feel worried about the care that Frank would receive but assumed that as a transplant patient, he would not experience this lackadaisical and careless nursing.

Frank was a very strong character, someone you either loved or hated, and he certainly could be extremely trying at times. He was a creature of habit and didn't see why his daily routine should be altered if he was away from home. He demanded that I take eggs and tomatoes in to him daily for his breakfast as he was of the firm belief that this was the most important meal of the day. He also wanted his salt and spent some time explaining to sceptical doctors that this was not proper salt but only a substitute. He was on a low-salt diet.

He teased the dietician on being informed that he was not to eat anything salty by asking whether he was allowed caviar. The dietician went away to find out if this was on the prohibited list, only to return to find Frank trying hard not to laugh as he was informed that this luxury was not to be allowed. I told him off for time wasting but secretly I was delighted that he was still his old self.

No one other than the staff was allowed in the kitchen but somehow Frank had charmed or cajoled permission to enter and look after himself. This pleased him and probably kept him out of the way and quiet. The only problem which was sure to occur was that some of the other patients, watching Frank, decided to try to copy; they were told off. I think this helped to make him feel special and helped in the building of his confidence. Like most of us, he needed to be liked. His family had smashed his confidence and always managed to belittle him.

I loved him just as he was, including his weaknesses and faults. We tended to agree over most things but I knew that in any disagreement, he would get his way, probably partly because this was how I wanted it to be. He was the one who wore the trousers in our house. He used to say that he was his 'own man.'

Frank had always been a heavy smoker, smoking cigarettes which, he said, had 'no spats'. This was his term for non-tipped cigarettes or ones without filters. He had been told in no uncertain terms by the director of the unit that he would not consider a transplant for Frank if he continued to smoke. He demanded that Frank immediately stop smoking. Frank told him that he could not give up smoking that way. He had given up drinking and thought that his body would go into a state of shock if denied nicotine as well. He promised the director that he would give up smoking if he was allowed to do it in his own way. His way was to halve the number of cigarettes he smoked every few days until he got the number down to five. 'Then I will give up smoking completely and, what is more, I'll never smoke again,' he said. The compromise was made and accepted.

It was to prove a very hard bargain to keep as anyone who has ever smoked will know, but true to his word Frank started one battle he was determined to win.

I think we both woke early but pretended to be asleep so as not to disturb the other, every now and again dropping off. Dawn seemed extra noisy, particular for a city, with the birds returning to the docks in their flocks. Eventually we discovered, with great relief, that it seemed a reasonable time to get up. Frank as always was the first to rise and he brought me a cup of tea in bed. This was a daily routine which had previously been taken for granted but with the disruption of late it was a welcome return to normality. It was essential to Frank that he had his *gathering his thoughts* time every morning and evening, being the first up and the last to retire. Those quiet half hours were important to his equilibrium. We would have made a good Darby and Joan in our old age as we were old-fashioned in our attitude to marriage. The woman was created to love her husband, raise a family and tend the home as the main part of her life. Careers were important for a woman but the man ideally should be the main breadwinner. In turn he would love, care for, provide for and protect his woman. It had been a great problem for us both to accept that in Frank's sick state of the last few years, the breadwinning role had been taken over by me as well as the usual housewifely duties.

Frank did not clean the house nor tend the garden. At first I thought this was laziness but, when moaning to an attendant at a drying out centre sometime earlier, I was asked whether I had not realised that he was not fit enough to do this. It is hard to accept that a person has drunk himself into a state where he's become physically incapable of doing odd jobs. It would have been all too easy to condemn him to death then instead of giving him the support he needed to face life with a loved one, creating a future which need not be alone. Frank could not have lived without someone caring about him and believing in him.

Frank had an enormous 'pot belly'. People would laugh at him about this, asking him how much or how long it had taken him to get it. Although he laughed with them, it used to hurt him very much. He wanted to look smart as he was a proud man, conscious of his good dressing.

It was becoming increasingly difficult for Frank to find clothes to fit him and his shirts were now pulling at the buttons with gaps of flesh showing in between. This often depressed him and he would occasionally fly into fits of rage and frustration when the depression became too much to bear. It had been months since he had been able to see his feet or his shrivelled dick, he said, not in self pity but in anger. He was angry with himself that, although mentally he wanted to make love, his organ would not obey his brain. His mind was sexually active but his flesh was unwilling. He could never accept that it was his companionship more than his sex at this worrying time that was so important to me.

Frank had gone through bouts of wondering if I was 'getting it' elsewhere when he was drinking but had never accused me of this and obviously knew that it was only in his imagination. All I needed from him was his undying love, trust, dependability and most of all his terrific sense of humour which I had missed in my 12 years of living alone after the break-up of my first marriage.

I could not leave the house on this pre-Christmas Thursday as I needed to be with Frank when the anticipated and promised telephone call came. We felt that sometime around lunch the call would come and we would then know whether Frank was to be given the lifesaving transplant or at least be placed on the waiting list. We knew that without it he only had a 50% chance of living three months. Come what might, I had to be with Frank when the telephone call came as he should not be alone when he learned the result, whether good news or bad.

My worry over his attitude would not subside. If the answer was negative I wondered if he would try to commit suicide by drinking himself to death. I imagined that bottle after bottle of vodka and his favourite whisky would be poured down his throat. He had always said that he didn't want to cause me more heartache and in his confused state would not realise that this action would cause me more pain and anguish than caring for him to his natural end.

The telephone did not ring that day. Midday came and went; five o'clock and more than a few cups of tea came and went. Shall we or shan't we telephone them? It's nearly Christmas and they don't want to give us bad news, we thought.

Frank convinced himself that he had failed one of the tests. In his anxiety to get as fit as possible he had started going for walks and when he had been home during the last weekend he had walked too far. On returning to the hospital for continuance of the heart tests, he had had to walk on a treadmill. Every muscle in his body and, in particular, his calves, ached. He got cramp and was not able to complete the test by walking for the full time.

Now he started to wish he had not been out for that walk. If only the doctor had experienced this side of his business he would not be so callous as to not keep his promise. Surely he could have phoned to let us know there was to be a delay, we felt. No news isn't always good news. We became nervous and very edgy.

We slept badly, tossing and turning and whenever we looked at each other we were both awake. I made a warm drink of Ovaltine in the middle of the night in the hope that it would encourage sleep. It did not work. The night seemed very long.

The next day was a carbon copy of the day before with one exception. Under great stress and unable to wait any longer, Frank took matters into his own hands and rang the hospital. He had the doctor concerned bleeped. Eventually he received an apology but no reason why the promise had been broken. He was further assured that we would receive a call with the long-awaited and crucial information on Monday.

There is a lot in favour of being cool and calm in a crisis but sometimes this coolness and calmness causes stress in itself. 'Don't they understand?' was followed with 'Don't they care?' by an apprehensive and increasingly depressed couple over the weekend.

The promised call on Monday did not come. It did not come during the whole of the week, nor over the Christmas period. It all seemed remote and unreal. We felt as if life was going on without us and that we were not part of the real world, possibly being in a nightmare of our own.

That doctor never phoned Frank.

No plans had been made for our celebration of Christmas apart from the purchase of food. We had stopped looking too far ahead and had begun to take each day as it came. The family had made their own arrangements and we were pleased that they were not allowing our problem to spoil their own lives; consequently they did not visit us. I longed to be with my grandchildren but kept that misery to myself. It would have been unbearable for Frank to suffer the excitement of three small boys clambering over him, shouting with the festive joy. How I missed people around me. It is possible for two people to be together and yet feel lonely. I do not know what thoughts Frank was keeping to himself.

The programmes on the television were typical of the usual bank holiday selection-circuses, pantomimes and ancient films which had been shown a multitude of times before. We ate traditional Christmas fare but had to be careful with the diet as Frank's weight was always a problem. I had not used salt in cooking for some time as this only serves to exaggerate fluid retention and raise an already high blood pressure. Actually, after a few days the lack of salt is not noticeable, and placing a salt-cellar on the table when guests come usually alleviates any problem.

Frank would never have been considered thus far if he had not given up drinking alcohol for at least six months, so the spirit of Christmas was accepted as being a non-liquid one. It helped Frank to see that his problem did not stop me having the odd glass of wine although at times I felt as if it would choke me. He felt less guilty if I partook.

The dusty old Christmas tree had been found at the bottom of the cupboard under the stairs and brought into the light of day. Somehow the candle lights sparkled more and looked prettier than before, or perhaps it just felt this way this year. We both made it a very special time.

Frank still managed to consider others with troubles and went to Mass, which was being said for the drowned boyfriend of our neighbour a month after his death. She would otherwise have been alone in the church.

He went to give her comfort in her suffering at her sad loss on this magical day in the year. He had never been to a local church service before or since, preferring to attend a City service.

We were so close to each other physically and mentally but doubts about the transplant were uppermost in our minds and began to haunt us both. Any respect for the hospital and the unsympathetic doctor was by now non-existent. It was all I could do to keep Frank from backing out of the situation. We had lost faith in the hospital through the experience of the last month. The nursing was of a very low standard. There was no continuity of staff and they took no trouble to find details of the patients. Agency staff came and went, even more so now that the patients who were able to move around had taken to waking the sleeping nurses in the night by entering the day room and turning on the lights and television at full volume to get them to go back to work! The doctors were remote. Sisters talked politics in the National Health Service and berated Maggie Thatcher who I am sure was not responsible for the filthy state of the toilets and washrooms. They did not appear to notice the tardiness of the nursing staff as part of their duties. And now the doctor had not kept his promise.

Despite all this, I was confident that things had to be different for patients with a transplanted organ. There had to be sterile areas, as yet not seen by us, and very specialised nursing. As Frank was a dying man with a short time to live, I was determined to help him in his choice of going ahead with this unexpected chance of a lifetime if indeed it would still be offered. Now seemed the wrong time to change his mind. But we were both very frightened.

Sill no news. After a week and a half of listening to the clock tick louder and louder, every hour feeling like a day, our nerves were frayed.

It was now December 27th. Frank had gone into the integral garage to cut his finger nails, something he always did as the nails were so strong that, when cut, the could be seen competing with Concorde in their flight across the room to climes unknown.

14. One of Eleven

The telephone rang, sending fear shivering down my spine. I rushed to pick up the receiver before it had a chance to ring four times (when our answerphone would cut in).

'Hello, I'm Kirsty, the transplant co-ordinator. Frank's tests show that there is a chance that his heart will stand up to the long operation and he is now on the international liver transplant list.' Perhaps I should have called Frank to talk to her but I was frightened that at this stage he would have told her where to put the liver and that would not have been in his body!

I was trembling. I asked what would now happen and was told that when the compatible liver was found, Frank would have to be in the hospital within two to three hours. The hospital was about 35 minutes away if the traffic was light. She also said that we would be told more when we next visited the hospital.

Could this really be happening to me? This was a drama one reads about but in which one is never a player. This only happens to other people, I thought. Another organ needed to be found in the next three months to be in time to save Frank's life and it was now that I felt that somewhere a person had to die to save him. This was the first of many times that I thought of this sudden death, so tragic and so sad. 'It is better to give than to receive' could not be true to the family left behind. Frank had to be told the good news. Being a man who called a spade a shovel his comments were, 'Now it's a case of shit or get off the pot.'

Once he had made the decision to accept and go ahead he would not turn back. When the next call comes from the liver unit it is likely to be a case of the two to three-hour dash to the theatre.

Relief, fear and love swept through us as, with our arms around each other, we cried buckets of tears.

Each and every day was another of waiting and yet each day was one spent of our lives. No day should be wasted as it will never return.

It was very hard to keep going and to live a near-normal life. As a businesswoman, I knew that the months ahead would be doubly hard. I needed respite from the pressurised business and knew that I had to make arrangements for the period of time ahead when I would be needed in the hospital.

I went to talk to the bank manager to explain what was happening, to ask him for his advice and to tell him what arrangement I proposed to make regarding the business in my anticipated prolonged absence. The strain of the last few years of Frank's sickness was taking its toll and this was not helped by the ever worsening financial state of the country. Interest rates were high and looked set to rise again. I knew that I needed to find an experienced manager to take over from me – someone who was also an administrator. He agreed with my idea and I started to look for a person with the necessary experience whom I could trust. By this time the account was in debit and the overheads would rise with an increase in salaries.

It was a gamble that I could ill afford to take but I knew that I was not able to give my best attention to the business when my heart was elsewhere. I found that I experienced guilt and extreme worry when I was in the office for I really wanted to be at home with Frank. I used to arrive home daily and look at the window to see if the curtains were open or closed against the day, always preparing myself in case he was dead. When I did stay at home, I always felt guilt about not being in the office. It became a Catch 22 situation. The doctors had advised me to carry on as normal but I needed to be superhuman to do that.

The bank manager and I went carefully through the costings and cash-flow in an amicable and understanding way. I've always found that in a crisis one's best friends are the bank manager, the accountant, the solicitor and the GP. If these people are good, you will not go far wrong.

It was unlikely that Frank would ever work again; he was proving over and over again that his great gift was in the help he wanted to give to others with drink problems. He was commencing to make this his purpose in life. It had crossed my mind that if Frank lost his battle for life his assurance money would get me out of any financial problems, but I would face the ongoing battle that most of us have in making ends meet if he lived.

Neither Frank nor I truthfully believed that he would live and we were gradually accepting death as inevitable and imminent. I tried so hard to keep financial worries out of his way. Material and worldly things were assuming less importance in our lives.

I suppose I was coming to terms with his expected death and also that life had to go on. If I started to talk of death I felt it would be construed as being negative and that I had no confidence in or gratitude for the work being undertaken to save Frank.

The forthcoming transplant had stopped the comforting, deep and rather moving conversations between us – intimate ones in which death was spoken about in unemotional ways. We could no longer talk freely in these terms for now there was uncertainty in the near death and neither of us was able to handle the fact that this might not now happen. This was so much harder to handle. I knew that I loved and needed him with every inch of my being. We certainly needed each other.

However, the bank manager found that I had carefully thought about everything. I was always referred to as a survivor and had never learned how to lose. The manager seemed to understand how difficult it was for me to cope with running the business and looking after Frank. He agreed that I would not be able to put in the required time for a few months and that work would take second place in my life during that time. He stunned me by telling me that when this episode was over I should have at least two months out of the business before returning. He was actually concerned at how tired and pale I had become. Then I heard words from his lips which I never thought a banker would utter, even under his breath: 'Money isn't everything'.

His comfort, understanding and totally human approach helped me at that moment but will be remembered with gratitude for the rest of my life. There were many business problems and the staff were not strong enough to cope.

One of the saving factors was that I was chairman of a charity in the City of London and we were preparing for a massive three-day festival. The work involved helped me to keep my sanity. We hoped to raise thousands of pounds to send children who had been treated for cancer on holiday with their siblings to Disneyland. The Kenton Trust recognised that the young relatives suffer greatly when a member of the family is seriously ill in hospital. The whole family's life is totally disrupted, as indeed Frank's illness was disrupting ours. I felt a complete empathy with the youngsters, believing that it must be devastating for the poor children if it was unbearable for me. How wonderful for them to be given the chance of laughing together as they commenced enjoyment of life before returning to pick up the pieces of normality.

The festival was also going to raise funds for a new coronary ambulance for St Bartholomew's hospital whose staff had been so good to us in the past. I hated to admit that every time I heard the klaxon of an ambulance I wondered if there had been an accident with a fatality in case there was a liver to transplant. The remaining money was to go to the East End homeless.

I had far too much work but Frank was eager to help with any of the charity jobs whilst he sat in his armchair, a soft drink in his own crystal glass (which no one else was allowed to use) by his hand even though he was often too tired to get too involved.

Frank always had his own cup and glass. Earlier in his life, the glass would have held a treble whisky at all times. Now he was only drinking what he was allowed. He had gone through an era of drinking Lucozade because it looked like the whisky. Now that was forbidden also.

He was struggling to cut down his smoking and now had an everlasting dummy cigarette to suck when the desire became overpowering. Quite soon the cigarette was thrown dramatically into the air with the wry comment that if he couldn't manage to stop smoking by sheer willpower he would not give it up at all. He did not need props!

Frank refused to substitute the 'non-spatted fags' with sweets or more 'nibbles'. He did not increase his eating at all and maintained that unless he remained cheerful, no one would want to have anything to do with him. The struggle continued. Sometimes he finished a whole cigarette but I noticed that not only were the numbers smoked daily dwindling, but the stubs in the ash trays were getting longer. Frank had always liked to believe that he lived by the motto of the London Stock Exchange: *dictum meum pactum*, my word is my bond. He had made his promise that he would try to stop smoking if he was on the transplant list. He found it incredible that his 'unproductive' life was considered worth saving and his morale was boosted.

Religion was of paramount importance to us both. Frank had been brought up as a Roman Catholic and was proud of the fact that he had been an altar boy in his youth. He had been taught by Jesuits at school.

He had found that church too demanding and unreasonable in certain aspects, mainly its unbending attitude to birth control and the more modern service now being in English and not Latin which he loved to use whenever possible. He was no longer allowed to take Eucharist at a Roman Catholic Mass but, being a welcome member of the Church of England, was delighted to have weekly visits from the Rector of St Mary-le-Bow.

I attended the midday service every Wednesday and without doubt felt uplifted after each attendance. It was so peaceful to sit in the church, which became my second home, and have the time to allow God to communicate with me, making me stronger to cope with the future. I would light a candle which would burn away the deep hurt that I felt tearing me apart. I would look up at the large wooden cross, above the heads of the tiny congregation, which had been given to the Wren church by our late foes, the Germans, and join in and appreciate the prayers being said for us both. Prayers which gave us strength and love. Whenever I felt desperate and unable to cope with it all, I would always go to church and shed many tears of sadness, pain and desperation, praying for help and guidance to do the right thing.

Frank always kept his prayer book beside the bed and never went to sleep unless he had read part of it. Whenever the struggle and pain seemed too much to bear he would quietly pray with this book, which was the only relic of his association with the Catholic church.

The director of the liver unit had said that he wanted the operation to be performed three months after the assessment, provided that Frank had stopped smoking and continued to abstain from booze. Frank was determined to be as fit as possible, knowing that his chances of a successful operation would be considerably greater if he had stamina. Occasionally he would walk to the local shops where he was greeted like a long-lost friend. Sometimes he needed to sit down in the shop before returning home, but the people were so kind and helpful. They appreciated his incurable sense of humour and the warmth of his personality. How this always boosted his confidence and willpower.

When the weather would not allow this walk, he would work out on the exercise bicycle in the spare bedroom which he always referred to as his dressing room. He was rapidly out of breath and exhausted, and would flop onto the single bed and fall into a troubled sleep. He was sleeping very badly anyway and night after night would roam around the house like an animal on the prowl. This meant that I could not sleep well either as the bed felt cold and empty without his cuddly fat body beside me to snuggle against. However, when he did settle into a sleep, he snored so loudly that I could not sleep properly anyway.

Winter set in; snow settled in London but only for a short moment before turning into dirty slush. We panicked, thinking it might be difficult to get out of the square to the hospital. Frank lost his temper with a cocky student neighbour who continually blocked our drive. It would just be his luck, he felt, for there to be some reason why he could not make the journey to the hospital in time.

We did not go out, so our social life became nonexistent. If we had to get to the hospital within two to three hours we did not really have the choice of visiting friends as they all lived too far away. We dared not leave the house together.

Every time the telephone rang we were in two minds about answering it. Would it summon us to heaven or to hell?

We were obviously hoping that the organ would be found in time if it were to save Frank's life, but if the operation were to fail, that call would be the beginning of the end of our lives together on this earth.

There had been a lack of communication from the hospital with no more contact from the co-ordinator. We were totally isolated and alone. No one helped us in our wait with any form of counselling. It would have been a relief to talk to someone with experience at this dramatic time.

But we were fortunate in our great love for each other and we became so very close in our emotions and thoughts that we were truly as one being. I did not want to leave Frank alone with every moment of the remaining time being so precious. I dreaded him receiving that telephone call when he was by himself. As previously stated, he had a communication box, now nicknamed *Big Brother* which was situated under the answerphone which was linked to the emergency service. It could be activated by him if he squeezed the disc which he wore round his neck. He would then be talked to until the ambulance arrived which would have been summoned by this marvellous service. I would have been alerted along with the hospital. This knowledge helped me to keep my sanity when I had to be away from home. I continued to leave the back door unlocked so that the emergency services had access to the house but I also activated the burglar alarm to stop giving the freedom of our home to unwelcome intruders.

January became February; time was running out. It was nearly three months since the director had said that this would be the best time for the transplant. *D* day was drawing nigh. I was in two confused minds, knowing that there was a strong chance that the operation could bring a rapid end to Frank's life and shorten the span even if only by a few weeks.

Alternatively, it could add a handful of years and hopefully improve his quality of life. Some would have said that his quality of life wasn't that bad in comparison to other disabled people's, but for an active man who had a brilliant brain and been the centre of hustle and bustle, sitting in the leather chair every day, unable to concentrate enough to read (it took him all day to read the newspaper) was like being in prison. He was unable to co-ordinate enough to wire an electric plug. He did not want to have his life prolonged if it meant that he would remain in this state. He was expecting some sort of miracle should he survive.

We dared not leave the house for longer than half an hour together in case the call came while we were absent. My working day became shorter and shorter. I left the house later in the day and returned earlier. I could not have lived with myself if I had not been with him when he needed me. A sort of aura was enveloping me through which normality and the humdrum could not penetrate.

I believe that my priority was correct. I also had a premonition that the transplant would take place on February 25th but I was wrong. The day came and went as normal with our tension heightening. Tempers were becoming more and more frayed. There had been no communication from the hospital and this somehow felt like an anticlimax from the previous activity, and somewhat like neglect. We were going through a form of hell.

Frank appeared to be less fit. He had been a physical training instructor in the army for a short time and knew how to make the most of his strength. Time didn't stand still and soon it was March. We were now sure that if the transplant did not take place in March, it was unlikely to take place at all. Frank had a moment when he believed that no one had truthfully ever meant to operate, having played him along to keep him positive until the end.

I was given instructions to carry out in case of his death and he had picked out a stick pin from his collection for each of the male members of our family. He put them to one side. He had made his will and now he sat with me and discussed his funeral arrangements. He showed me where his documents were to be found.

We were both organised people and decided to write a list of all personal articles that we would need in the hospital and work out the things that would need to be done when the organ was found. We felt that it would be easier to do this when we were calm and not under stress.

I actually part-packed the cases for I knew that we would be in a terrible hurry to get to the hospital in the allocated two to three hours. Frank would only need a few toilet articles, not even pyjamas for some time, in intensive care. However, I needed to take money for the telephone calls to our nearest and dearest, night attire, change of clothes, underclothes, tights, toiletries, make-up, my Bible to read for comfort, paperback for relaxation, knitting to keep me occupied, etc. I prepared a note for the milkman to stop milk until further notice but did not put it outside for him yet. I tried to keep the refrigerator as near empty as possible so there would not be the smell of rotting food later.

It was like preparing for a holiday without knowing when we would be going or for how long. I was continually making sure that I had my hair 'done' so that I could always look my best for Frank to stop him worrying about me, hiding the strain that I naturally felt. There came a day when I had to cancel one appointment owing to pressure of business, remaking the appointment for the following Monday. I never kept that appointment and, when the time came, I felt scruffy. We both had a feeling that the call would come on that Mothering Sunday, March 25th 1990, but, because there were no facts to substantiate our feelings, we both kept them to ourselves.

15. In Haste

I had always felt that the most likely time for any transplant was at weekends when there tend to be more car accidents.

We only had a snack lunch, preferring to eat in the early evening in front of the television. I prepared chicken in a strong garlic sauce so after partaking, we both smelt somewhat unpleasant. I remember wearing old laddered tights and not being dressed to go out of the house. We tried to have a normal relaxing Sunday. The phone rang three times that day. The first two calls were from the family for me with messages to add to those in the Mothering Sunday cards and flowers on display. When the third call came Frank picked up the receiver. It was exactly nine o'clock. I knew instantly that this was the moment we had waited for and went numb. I started to busy myself immediately, looking for the cases and the milkman's note, and setting the timed light switch so that lights would turn on and off in our absence while he listened and talked on the telephone.

He remained totally calm as I heard, 'Yes, I am a big man, I stand around five feet ten inches, weighing eighteen stone.' This was followed after a pause with, 'I last ate at six o'clock.'

He was told to keep the line open and not use the phone as he turned to me and said in a quiet way that the operation was on.

The telephone rang immediately again. This time Frank flew into anger and shouted down the receiver 'Stuff your liver', followed by 'I am not coming without my wife.'

I knew that we had a problem and I was worried that Frank was going to back away now. I spoke to the calm lady doctor at the other end of the line who told me that we only had one hour to get to the hospital, not the anticipated two to three hours, that the organ was being 'harvested' now and that a police car was on its way to collect Frank. The problem was that the police car wasn't insured to carry me. I told her that I would make sure that Frank got to her in time and that I would follow in another car. She told me to drive carefully, but the matter was taken out of my hands by Frank insisting that I did not drive myself. We tried to get a friend who was a minicab driver to help but he had gone to bed early so a neighbour immediately reversed his car off his drive in readiness to take me behind the police car.

Frank threw a cigarette packet into the air. He had not been smoking but always kept some cigarettes near to hand as he had said that helped him to stop. He shouted that these were the last cigarettes that he would ever touch. I am certain that he was longing to have just one last cigarette.

Everything then happened so quickly that I am not quite sure how. A brand new police car came quietly into the square. Frank was sitting in the back as it went equally quietly from the square until it was on the main road. Then I could hear the squealing siren, noisy at first, becoming quieter in the distance as it took Frank away from me.

I set the burglar alarm, put the note out for the milkman, locked up the house and got into the waiting car to follow him.

The police car drove through the heavy weekend traffic returning to London after a weekend out of the town. It rushed through the Rotherhithe tunnel, squashing vehicles into the curved outer wall; it went through traffic lights at red, with the co-driver issuing instructions as navigator: 'Go, go, go, right now, go, go, go.'

A silly woman, sitting bolt upright, clutched the steering wheel of her dilapidated 'clapped out' beetle, got in the way and froze.

'Get out of the way you stupid . . .' the driver muttered, almost under his breath.

'Cow' added Frank, finishing the sentence.

The police car sped past the turning, but one U-turn later was in front of the famous hospital, at the bottom of the steps so often seen on TV when bulletins on liver transplant progress were in the news. Recently there had been news of the wonder drug to help with anti-rejection of donor organs which would be used on Frank.

Frank was escorted to the unit by the police. I followed, less dramatically, around the Elephant and Castle and along the Old Kent Road. I would learn every bump and bend of this road in the months to come.

The police car was still parked in front of the entrance when I arrived. I hurried as fast as I could, weighed down by the weight of the cases, along the long empty corridors, up in the lift. I felt numb and as if I were dreaming. I was aware that I was alone. I walked past the two theatres which were not in use. They were not sufficiently equipped or large enough for the task in hand, I thought.

I met the body of the voice I had spoken to on the telephone. Dr Fagan was busy but not too busy to tell me to sit down beside her. She was in constant touch with the medical team who were 'harvesting' the liver – bringing it in from somewhere about 20 minutes away. She seemed pleased that it was a local organ. I learned that it was a rather large liver, bigger than the normal ones used, which would be marvellous for Frank.

I learned little else about the donor at that time.

Frank was to be anaesthetised and in the theatre by 11.30 p.m. and there was slight panic for there was hardly enough time to complete the tests and prepare him. Many people were involved and I tried not to be in the way. I was so relieved to be told that I could be with Frank and help to speed him up for he could not help being so slow in all he did for himself. Every task was an effort.

I found him sitting on the bottom of the bed in intensive care. I felt my love overcome me and I filled with pride at his courage and calmness. There was a staff nurse looking after him as she busily read his blood pressure and commenced a series of tests.

Frank was obviously relieved to see me and was exhilarated by his exciting car ride. It had reminded him of his advanced driving lessons and his earlier rally driving, he said – a part of his life that I had not shared with him. The nurse had been trained at Bart's and had nursed on the Rehere ward. This pleased Frank and gave him confidence as he had enormous respect for that hospital above all others.

'If I thought that my journey here was exciting,' he said, 'it was nothing in comparison to the lady in the next bed. She had been transported from home in a helicopter.'

She was obviously critically ill with liver failure but was not to be a transplant patient.

I had been given permission to use one telephone at the busy desk – where doctors were busy controlling the situation of the donor organ, the theatres and all aspects of the lifesaving operation. I rang the Revd Stock for it would have been perfect for Frank to be anointed before the operation. However, this was not to be, as he would not have had sufficient time to arrive at the hospital before Frank was in the theatre. Frank had already been anointed previously. In any case he smelt of garlic and this is said to keep the devil away. I think the devil would have to retire and pack his bags with the strength of the odour! Hopefully, it would not upset the surgeons.

A porter had been called to wheel Frank to radiography in a chair. He had been told that it was very urgent and to come as quickly as possible. In the meantime the ECG was taking place at the bed and the porter, arriving and being told to wait, took the 'hump'. I was told that I could go with Frank. The porter, feeling that he could make up the wasted time spent waiting for the ECG, decided to try to break the world walking speed record and I had trouble keeping up with him and the wheelchair, as I tripped along behind the pair with a frequent skip and jump, my heels clip-clopping along the spacious and empty corridor.

Radiography was empty when we arrived on this Sunday evening. Frank was wheeled behind the closed door with the usual signs to stop anyone entering at the time of actual X-raying. He was then wheeled back to sit with me and wait for the results.

It seemed an eternity but probably was not long at all; I was edgy as I knew that we had so little time before the 11.30 p.m. deadline for the theatre.

'Oh no!' The X-rays were not satisfactory and needed to be repeated. Frank returned to the camera as I sat and waited, twiddling my thumbs and trying hard not to allow panic to set in.

The porter disappeared. He returned with a casualty patient who was making the most of the occasion, moaning and shouting in a drunken state with his friends in a similar condition but without the injuries. They would just have thick heads in the morning. They all sat and waited. The porter returned and wheeled this man away but he did not return for Frank.

We sat and waited for an eternity. I was going to wheel Frank back to the ward myself but thought that it might provoke a strike in this militant establishment. I think the porter had gone for his coffee break and eventually after the radiographer had received a call from the doctor in the ward asking where we were, a different dawdling porter turned up to escort us back to activity. He moved like a snail. I kept trying to speed him by walking quickly myself but aborted the thought that he would keep up with me. 'Clippity-clop' my feet said in this eerie atmosphere, the lull before the storm of Monday.

We walked past the previously unused lift which always appeared out of bounds. It was fully lit and was obviously and unusually about to be active.

Frank had the X-ray plates on his lap. These were taken, hung up on the wall behind the desk with light pouring through them and pondered over by the medical team which appeared to be increasing. There was obviously a problem and I was certain that Frank could not have a clear chest after all the years of smoking, even though he had not smoked recently. One lung appeared to be covered on the lower half on the plate. Whatever the problem was, it was swept aside.

I was told that I should now bath or shower Frank as quickly as possible. The time was 11.20 p.m. Only ten minutes more of our life together? I was handed a fistful of razors in green sterile packs and a crisp white hospital gown. There were no more instructions other than to prepare him all over. I was so grateful for this privacy and will never forget the relief that I could have a few stolen moments with Frank in this unreal drama. Every moment was so precious.

I was not prepared for the appalling state of the cold derelict bathroom. I did not know where to hang the theatre gown as nowhere was clean enough. I could not use the shower and Frank always preferred a bath anyway so I did not persevere with the unyielding spray.

There wasn't a nurse in sight as I looked around, prepared to ask for help. The bath was filthy. Someone had urinated over the back of it and the whole bath was covered in grime along with the dull yellow streaks of the urine. I was horrified. I started to clean the bath before Frank could be allowed to get into it. I then realised that some of the dirt was blood and that there were blood and urine splashes on the floor.

There was no time to make a fuss but I will never understand how this bath could have been used before major surgery. I part-filled the bath for Frank and in a daze washed him all over like a baby in the shallow warm water. This was the only way left to show him the overwhelming love I felt for him. I no longer felt shut outside the trauma now that I was encouraged to be part of it.

Thankfully, as we were in a hurry, emotions were kept under control. I shaved him all over as instructed. We joked as I took particular care over certain areas of the body.

Frank was being brave. 'I think I'll ask for a dick transplant whilst they are at it,' he said. 'That'll make medical history and bring tears to your eyes.'

Blinking away tears to clear my blurring eyes and not let us down, I said 'I love you,' followed by 'No regrets.'

I tied his gown at the back.

Frank replied, 'No regrets. If I could live my life again I'd do the same with you. Your life must go on. Live it to the full. Live it, but not necessarily alone.'

It felt as if a knife had been twisted in me. I couldn't bear to think of being without him as I fought with tears about to flow, which thankfully I controlled.

'Ann,' he said, 'we've not had long enough together.' He oozed love and gratitude.

We returned to the bed where his few belongings were placed. The theatre trolley was waiting with a porter and nurse. They discreetly closed the curtains around us. We hugged each other. There might not be a tomorrow. We kissed.

The nurse and porter returned, the curtains opened and we started the walk to the theatre.

I walked beside the theatre trolley holding his hand all the way. The porter pushed it. The doors to the unit were already open for us to get out into the corridor to the mystery lift. Those doors were also open and waiting. The lights were on. Our entourage entered and the lift went down to within a few feet of the massive theatre.

There was the sound of great activity in an area hitherto always very quiet. I went to the theatre door, still holding Frank's hand.

The nurse told me that this was where I had to say 'Goodbye.'
At the sound of that word, I went cold. I will not say it, was my thought.
This might be the last moment that I saw my husband alive.
'I love you. God be with you,' I gently spoke.
'And also with you,' was the soft reply from a pale Frank. I realised, as
I looked at him, that he had given a fleeting glance of defeat.

As he entered the theatre I managed to smile and give him a thumbs-
up sign and a wink.

The look on his face changed. I knew at that moment that Frank was
going to fight to live. He knew that he might not make it but he was going
to give it a good try. He knew that I would be waiting for him.

16. Life or Death

The theatre door closed gently as the rubber sealed it quietly shut. I was in the wide corridor all alone. I felt the loneliness and was cold, tired and frightened. I did not have to pretend to be brave for him any more but tears did not come. It was only two and a half hours earlier that we had been watching television at home.

The nurse came out of the theatre to take me back to the ward. 'We now have to find you a bed for tonight,' she said, 'but I think we could do with a cup of tea first.'

The door to the mystery lift was now closed but the lights were left on. I was taken into Sister's office and sat on a chair surrounded with the staff's personal belongings. Lots of holdalls cluttered the floor with my case and Frank's few items, which were to remain in my care, joining them.

I was given a large mug of tea which I drank alone in a world set apart from the rest. In my stunned state I struck up a conversation with a young doctor, expressing my doubts about the rights and wrongs of transplant surgery. I must have rambled on and on in shock, believing that I was behaving normally.

The nurse returned to show me where Frank would be when I saw him next. No one said, 'if he makes it'. I was to see behind the blue door – the extremely special ward where doctors were engaged in a constant fight to save lives. At this time there were only facilities to care for two critically ill patients. This was the area where one had to scrub up on entering and leaving, wearing a gown whilst inside which was thrown away on each leaving. There was only going to be entry allowed for myself and one other person for the duration of Frank's stay inside. No one could enter without permission, which was obtained by pressing the buzzer on the door. There were specialised staff trained for this ward who were hardly ever seen outside the door.

It was quiet on this late Sunday night. The space was empty for Frank but it would be many hours before he was expected to arrive. His battle was taking place elsewhere.

At last a bed was found for me. It was only vacant for one night as it was really a private patient's room. I went to the room with the nurse who had been looking after me since the dramatic exit of Frank. It was at the end of a long passage.

I was assured that I would learn of any change and would be informed when Frank was out of the theatre, but that would not be before 7.30 a.m. on Monday March 26th 1990 at the earliest.

We had walked past the hospital chapel so I returned to sit at the back in the large dimly lit and empty place on the hard wooden pew. I wanted to light a candle but there were none there. I prayed that if Frank were to die, he would not regain consciousness for I did not want him to suffer any more. I felt that if he died it was God's will and that any amount of interference by the medical profession would not change that. However, if he were to live, that too would be God's will and that was the only way that I could make myself truthfully accept any transplant surgery. I prayed that the surgeon and staff working through the night would be given the strength and skill to save lives. I thanked God for the life which I had spent with Frank and asked for strength in the months ahead. I needed guidance to do the right things.

I also prayed for the soul of the donor and for strength to be given to his grieving family whoever they were, for I knew nothing about them. I was so alone in this longest night of my life. My father had said that I had the sign of the cross made on my head at my christening so that I would never really be alone, and although he had died some time earlier, I thought of him now.

I went to bed. It seemed strange to get out of my clothes and into my nightdress. Normal actions assumed a feeling of abnormality. I set the travelling alarm clock for 6 a.m. as I had to telephone the family. I had not contacted any of them yet for they would not have been able to get to the hospital in time to see Frank, although they would have been able to support me now, through the long worrying wait. At least they will be sleeping through a normal night, I thought.

The toilet was on the other side of the corridor. I must have nearly worn the carpet threadbare as I crossed from my room to it over and over again in the following few hours. My stomach was churning over with collywobbles and nerves. I would have been comforted if the nurse who was sitting at a desk at the far end of the corridor near the phone had shown any interest in me.

I felt as if I were in an oven. It was so hot. I got out of bed to open the window, which overlooked a railway line. I then felt too cold and it was too noisy with trains being shunted into the right places for Monday's commuting, so I closed the window again. This happened a few times. I did not sleep at all. I had the most terrible feeling of cold and a total void: at 2 a.m. I felt a great numbness. I was sure that at that time Frank could no longer live, as his liver had been removed. Perhaps I was anticipating some form of contact with him that was not there. No one came to see me.

I felt that as far as the hospital were concerned I did not exist. I wanted to cry but I could not find any tears.

I did not need my alarm to wake me at 6 o'clock for I was still wide awake. I went to the payphone at the end of the passage, creeping quietly with each step so as not to wake the sick patients. I dialled my stepdaughter's number but I had been cross-examined by the hospital staff before I had been allowed to use the telephone.

Everything around me was so strange and hostile. My stepdaughter was getting ready for work but thankfully her husband answered the phone. I heaved a sigh of relief at talking to him for I felt that the news would be better broken to Julia by him. He was a solicitor in a City practice.

David had said that Julia would come directly to the hospital. They had been anticipating this call and they both guessed what it would be that early in the morning. Frank had stopped seeing his other daughter, or rather she had stopped seeing him. He had expressed his opinion that he did not want certain people involved in his life or death and she was one of them.

When David tried to return my telephone call he had trouble in getting me.

There was a knock on my door about half an hour later after I had spoken to David.

'Who's there?' I asked.

'You're wanted on the phone,' I was told. 'It's your husband.' I shuddered. The careless mistake hurt.

'It can't be my husband. He's in theatre having a liver transplant,' I said, as I went to the waiting phone. In fact it was David, confirming that Julia would be with me as soon as possible.

Tea was taken to the few private patients kept in hospital over the weekend but I did not get the offer of a drink. I was too shaky to even ask for a cup. There was no mug over the handbasin so I scooped some water in my hands to swallow my normal daily dose of pills for my blood pressure.

It is at moments like this that little things mean a lot. Any kindness would have helped and been so welcome.

I was coping with the unusual and stressful things but wasn't coping as well with routine and less important matters.

As far as the liver ward were concerned I did not exist as no one had the courtesy to keep their promise to me and inform me that Frank was still alive and had come out of theatre after eight hours of surgery.

I was informed of this by Julia who had been sent by the private patients' wing to the liver unit, who in turn had returned her to the private patients' wing in her search for me. I heard her arrive for she argued with the nurse that I was definitely in a room for the night.

She had learned that Frank was out of the theatre as she had only narrowly missed seeing him being moved to the specialised liver intensive care. She said later that she was glad that I had warned her of the dreadful things she was likely to see on a normal visit to this area of the hospital. This was her first visit.

The corridors are kept clear when a transplant patient is moved out of the theatre as it can be a most distressing sight. There are so many doctors around the unconscious patient at that time with equipment keeping the body alive.

Now he would be on a ventilator with so much happening around him that some doctors would be sitting on a table over the bed in order to find the room to get to him and continue with their own specialised tasks. He was in such good hands with the finest team in the country working to keep him alive. Julia was embarrassed to learn that I had not been told that Frank was alive and out of theatre as she so casually let it slip. She also had instructions that we were to keep out of the way until late morning for we would only be upset and would not be allowed to see Frank. At least he was holding his own for the time being.

The case of where I would sleep later was causing a problem as there were a few relatives staying in the allocated rooms. I could well have done without this but I am certain that the ward sisters have enough to do with looking after sickness without looking after this sort of arrangement which should be an administration responsibility.

We collected both Frank's and my belongings and sat with them on the plastic-covered bench outside the room in which Frank's vital life signs were under constant scrutiny. I remember wondering how it is that life appears to be carried on normally by everyone else and that people do not stare at you as if you have two heads when your own life is in a turmoil? By now I had telephoned my youngest daughter Claire who in turn had informed the rest of the family about this medical crisis. I also rang my staff who had been speechless and stunned, finding it difficult to reply to me.

'Do a couple of things for me please,' I asked. 'Go into St Mary-le-Bow for me and light a candle. Also explain why I have not kept my hairdressing appointment to Debbie, the hair stylist.'

I was later told that sixteen candles were lit that day in the church. All of our friends were praying for us and our families then, and on many days to follow.

I had been steeling myself for the worst news. The fact that Frank was still alive was in itself unexpected. Eventually we were told that we could visit Frank and Julia and I were both terrified of being able to face the future. I thought that I would want to hold him in my arms and would find it hard in not being able to do this. This was furthest from my desires as I looked at this stone-cold body, so white and lifeless. It did not seem possible that this ghost could be the husband I knew and loved. He was as pale as the white blanket which left only his face uncovered as he lay flat in this gown as if in his coffin. In fact the only sign of life was in the activity around him.

There were tubes everywhere and drains leading to bottles and bags under the special bed. He was on a ventilator and not breathing for himself. To all intents and purposes he was dead. The machine was doing everything for him. A pipe was strapped to his face and went down his throat into his body. Another tube came from his nose and others went into his neck and other parts of his hidden body. There were bleeps from numerous computers with graphs and numbers displayed on the equipment which were constantly changing.

He was receiving expert attention from a professional team of specialised doctors and nurses. They were cool, calm and quietly reassuring. Warmth and understanding radiated from them. Frank's eyes were closed with tapes and he was thankfully oblivious of it all. However, he was being treated as if he were able to hear every word spoken. He was still a person and not a freezing cold body.

I was grateful that I had been into this area and had much of what I had just seen explained to me previously. Julia had never been into intensive care before and the shock of her father brought tears to her eyes and she nearly blacked out, stumbling as if to crash onto the floor. Sister Fran cradled her in her arms. It was alien to me not to want to touch Frank. I hardened myself to cope with the future and not to be a nuisance to anyone by truly showing my feelings. I wanted and needed kindness but I am sure that this would only have broken me down.

Neither of us stayed with Frank for long. I felt so useless. There was nothing I could do for him and I would have been in the way if I'd stood by his bed for too long. There were no chairs near the bed as there was too much activity and although there was plenty of space around the bed, it was needed by the medical team. There were at least three people with him at all times and they made me confident that he was receiving good care. We washed our hands again in the liquid soap and threw away the compulsory plastic aprons. I still had not spoken either to the surgeon (who must have been resting after the eight-hour night-long operation) or to a doctor, but when Sister told us to get a coffee, I realised that I had not drunk anything that day.

We could not find the staff canteen even though we had received instructions before setting out. We must have walked by it a number of times. Eventually we waited until we saw nurses on their coffee break and followed them. The coffee machine was very complicated to use but I had to master it because I would be using it frequently in the days to come, unpredictable as my stay in the hospital was. The coffee machine coughed, spluttered and spilt scalding liquid over my hand. I could not eat anything but found the hot coffee a help in steadying my nerves. Food would have choked me at that moment.

We returned to the busy ward and sat on the bench near the closed door on which was a sign making it clear that there was no admittance to staff, patients or visitors. It was in this room that the battle to give Frank life continued.

One of the many attending doctors approached me to give me news. Apprehensively I heard that Frank was on the danger list. He was doing well considering the seriousness of the operation. Rejection of the liver could happen at any time but at present the new liver was functioning. His kidneys were just standing up to the trauma but his heart was causing some concern through irregular rhythms. The main problem with Frank was that his whole body was showing signs of being worn out – the wear and tear of modern living. This doctor believed that the spleen had been removed to make room for the large liver but he had not actually been present during the long operation and this idea was later proved to be untrue.

It was emphasised to me, already feeling worried, that time was young and that I was not to get too optimistic as anything could happen.

'You will have to face months of uncertainty,' the doctor said. 'Don't get excited.' Sombre yet positive, I made my way to collect the key to my allocated bedroom.

It was handed to me by a middle-aged woman who was full of apologies regarding the room. She escorted me up the wide stairs past the luxurious boardroom where a splendid buffet lay on the polished table in readiness for a working luncheon for visiting consultants. A security pass number was given to me to punch into the lock on the first floor and enter the nurses' sleeping quarters. This opened onto a bleak, dimly lit corridor with waste bins lined along the wall like regimented soldiers against the numbered green doors. There were a few primitive toilets; only the outside ones received light (from their dirty, draughty windows) and the doors had broken unusable locks. Pink toilet rolls were unwinding on the floor through puddles, there were chipped baths in the middle of vast austere concrete-floored rooms and a couple of dilapidated showers.

Standing at the end of the corridor was a cleaner complete with a cigarette hanging from the side of her mouth. She appeared flustered that there were people moving about.

'Me no speak de Englishe,' she said to us, and in her slovenly, lazy state, she had no intention of understanding any English either. She was never known to do more than empty the regimented bins daily.

The key unlocked the door to room 731a but no one could have been more shocked or depressed at what I found on the other side. I felt, and still feel, that it is criminal to expect anyone to sleep in such appalling conditions and when I think that student nurses are given this room when they leave home for the first time to start a dedicated career, I fill with anger.

Apparently a new nurse can expect to live here for the first three months of her training. I am sure that this must be an important factor in the shortage of permanent staff at this particular hospital where their priorities are so wrong.

The damp musty smell hit Julia and me as the door creaked open. The walls were damp and stained. Paint and plaster were peeling away in great leaves. There was a massive hole where the heating pipes went through the wall into the next room. These pipes were cold in spite of the fact that the heating was on in the building. Dank brown sacking with massive holes hung on string for three-quarters of the way across the badly fitting and dirty window as a curtain. String was also tied over the washbasin and dirty cups with a mould growing in them on stale tea bags were on the floor.

There was a phone for incoming calls only on a filthy bookcase against the outside wall. The wardrobe on the far wall was tiny but smelt so awful that I was frightened to open it in case there were nasty creepy crawlies inside and I am petrified of spiders. The floor was covered with dusty felt. A lumpy old bed had been made and the sheets looked clean and did not feel damp. There were two naked light bulbs but no electric power point inside the room.

This room would have been condemned if it had not been in a hospital. I'd seen photographs of rooms with cockroaches and peeling walls in the newspaper and this room, I thought, would cause a sensation too if exposed to the media in its current state. I do not believe that squatters would have considered living in it.

This will teach me to appreciate what I have, I thought, and really know how lucky I am to share our comfortable home with Frank. I would have slept anywhere near Frank in his crisis. Anywhere to lay one's head is acceptable when your loved one is fighting for his life. I could only be grateful that a bed had been found. I would not have left the hospital for any reason at this time.

'Sleeping in the day room is not allowed,' Sister had said earlier. There are two well-furnished double rooms complete with fridge purely for the purposes of accommodating relatives, but both of these were already in use. Often a small lecture room is used to sleep a relative too, but this was already occupied.

Julia was not prepared to sleep in the hospital so I quite expected to occupy this room alone but in the meantime my family had been rushing around to make arrangements to give me support.

On returning to the ward I was pleasantly surprised to find my son Alan and his wife Janet waiting for me on the bench outside Frank's isolation ward. They had travelled to London from Wantage immediately they had learned the news of the transplant. Frank was still alive. As no one other than Julia and I were allowed to visit Frank, neither Alan nor Janet could see their stepfather, however. There is a great risk of infection after the transplant as the resistance has to be broken down in order for the body to accept the donor organ. This organ could only last for a period of six hours from the death of the donor unless it is temporarily preserved in fluid for up to sixteen hours – hence the haste and rush of the previous day. The donor and the recipient must also be under 65 years of age in this country but must be even younger in America.

Later that day, Lydia, my elder daughter, arrived from Banwell, a village in Avon, where she lived with her husband and two sons. She had organised the two boys and taken the first Inter-city train from Bristol on hearing the news. She was going to stay the night with me in the spooky room.

Alan Andersen, the minicab driver who had been very helpful to both Frank and me in the past, often driving Frank when he was too ill to drive himself – in the better early days he had driven him to and from the city Stock Exchange each day – once again came to our aid. He delivered a camp bed and blanket from home to Lydia and with horror and disbelief saw the state in which I was to live when he left them in my room.

Our family were cool but not really calm. We were all too frightened to be grateful or confident yet. We all prayed silent prayers that God would guide and guard us. We prayed for the courage to accept His will which will be done.

Frank and I were together every few hours but only one of us knew it. Frank was still unconscious, with machines and drugs doing the work of living for him. He was so white. He lay so flat and so still. He was deathly cold. Not a sound. Not a movement. Certainly not from him, as the computers continued to bleep, flash, click and show mysterious and fast changing numbers.

Drugs were constantly being injected by the finest staff, who never seemed to flap or panic. They cared for the dying just as lovingly as for the living and must have been part of so many dramas.

I was exhausted and knew that I must get something to eat soon or collapse. I did not want to eat and was unaware of the time. Alan and Janet had returned to Wantage knowing that there was really nothing more that they could do. Julia had returned home to her husband, David.

The canteen would not open for another two hours and I knew that I would not last that long for I would be asleep before I had eaten. Lydia persuaded me to leave the hospital to buy a meal outside. I was moving like a robot, not knowing how to lift my heavy swollen feet and place one in front of the other. Somehow we walked the distance to McDonald's, not the sort of restaurant that we would have used in other circumstances, and entered to eat. Today was totally unreal. It crossed my mind that Frank would never have eaten here for the seats were fixed to the ground and too close to the table for him to have got his stomach between the table and the chair.

I ate my cheeseburger and string chips not really knowing what they tasted like. It was food. I was disturbed by tramps who were on the bottle hanging and falling around the doors, and being chased away by the manager. I spent a little time in the chapel and visited Frank to say 'Goodnight, God bless, I love you,' as I did every night.

Then Lydia and I flopped wearily into bed, but not before attempting to go to the strange toilets in the dark. None of the lights worked. I stood guard at the door, keeping it open, in the hope that there would be a little light from somewhere to help us see. Lydia felt her way to the toilet, running her hands around the bowl to find the seat . . . along the wall feeling for the paper . . . and in the air to grab the chain . . . in a distant single beam of light casting shadows from the corridor.

Then we changed places with Lydia on guard for me. I think I peed in the pot for I heard the right sounds as it hit the water in the closet. We both hoped that our bladders would hold out for the duration of the night.

It was a tremendous relief to find that although the room was freezing cold and smelt musty and unhealthy, the water from the dripping tap was boiling hot.

Sleep descended on us quickly but I awoke totally refreshed and thought that it must be time to get up. The illuminated clock disagreed. It was only two o'clock in the morning. I wriggled around, changing my position in the lumpy bed and trying to get to sleep again, but to no avail.

I was not alone as a relative in the nurses' quarters. Bad news had been received by the family in the room next door. This Italian family were stricken with grief as they screamed in their effort to come to terms with their plight. The sound of their anger and sorrow tore through me. I did not know how I would react if there were a knock on my door to summon me to Frank. No one really knows how they will behave at a tragic time.

Our telephone did not ring, nor was there a knock on our door that night. Lydia seemed to be comfortable on the camp bed as she ground her teeth together in her sleep, something she had done since a child. It had the same effect on me as the sound of chalk slipping on a blackboard. In spite of the paper-thin walls, she slept through the sadness next door whilst I struggled with unforthcoming sleep.

I felt fortunate in having the love and support both physically and mentally of my family as I had certainly needed them more than ever in the last twenty-four hours.

We went to the staff canteen for a yoghurt, tea and toast. I felt that we were intruding into the time off for doctors and nurses we had met in the wards and tried to avoid eye contact with them in the pretence of not recognising them out of the ward. Their bleepers were continually calling them away from their breaks.

Lydia was required at home by her husband and the two boys later that day, so she left me alone around the middle of the day. Before Lydia left to travel home by the Inter-city train – her first journey alone like this since she had married some years previously – she and I met the brilliant transplant surgeon. We were both sitting on the padded plastic bench near the blue door when this oriental man approached.

A prominent medical genius is imagined as large in stature, loud and dominant and with his minions following to heel. Mr K. C. Tan (known and fondly referred to by everyone who really knew him as K.C.) was as well dressed as a City gentleman and distinguished in appearance, but he was small in stature and softly and kindly spoken. He had a kind, untroubled face and an understanding manner. He hid his stamina and was extremely humble considering his marvellous and famous achievements. His current success rate was incredible. (He told me, at a later date, that between January and June, he had performed twenty-eight successful liver transplants out of twenty-nine operations; the unsuccessful one had had massive heart problems of which he had been misinformed by the patient, who was a doctor himself.)

17. Cautious Optimism

K.C. was alone as he introduced himself to me. I was told not to be optimistic. Frank was showing signs of his hard life and good living with the food, smoking and drinking abuse. In this so-called 'good life' he had furred his arteries and caused a massive oedema under his heart.

'Did you know that he has an aortic aneurysm in his abdomen?'

I certainly had never been told of this and indeed did not know what an aneurysm was.

'No,' I answered. 'What is that?'

K. C. explained that in parts of the body the arteries and veins were clogged up, with narrowing of the tubes, but in other parts, including the aorta, the tubes were thin and blown up like balloons and could burst. It was obvious that the operation would not have been performed if this and other facts had been known about Frank. I had never believed that Frank was a good subject for this operation and already I was sadly learning that I had not necessarily been wrong in my unqualified lay-person's thoughts.

'Frank's old liver was in a bad way,' continued K. C., 'and would have given him only around five more days' life. The new one is from a 25-year-old man, is large and is functioning well at present. I will get a heart surgeon to see him in due course,' he added, 'but at most I have given him only a few more months to live than he would have had.'

I felt that it was inadequate to just say 'Thank you' to this genuine genius for saving my husband's life. Even though the facts were grim, I found it comforting to be told them, and I was now confident of being kept in the picture in the future. A complete trust had bonded between surgeon and patient's wife, and the fear of the unknown disappeared.

The team answered questions and explained everything fully because they had the finest leaders setting an example.

I immediately felt that the news would be too much for Frank to absorb when he regained consciousness so I proposed to ask that he should not be told all the news. How awful to go through all he had done only to learn that the battle is not over. I was still trying to protect him mentally and I was frightened that he would slip back if he felt that this had all been for nothing. He had said that he did not want to regain consciousness if he were to have complications within the next few weeks. We had seen too much of this during the previous November when he was being assessed for the transplant. There had been many cases of lung collapse and massive fluid retention and infection with the slow fights being painfully lost. He had said that he could not face this.

In spite of this disturbing news, I was determined to remain cheerful and positive even if it were only on the outside. Inside I was greatly disturbed and insecure. I was determined not to be a misery or to upset those people around me, but I desperately wanted someone to put their arms around me and let me weep until I could weep no more.

I have always had to be the strong one in the family and would have benefited from being weak now. I dared not let go for I might smash into little pieces and not be able to regain composure. I could not send Lydia away with worries over how I would cope.

Sister was not at all pleased to learn that my dreadful room was unheated so she complained to the workmen and the heating was turned on. She also reported the lack of lights but in the meantime gave me a torch to use. It was now the first Tuesday after the operation. Frank had not yet regained consciousness. That morning I wanted to see him alone so before his daughter arrived I rang the bell to the unit and was admitted. The soap was making my hands sore from the constant scrubbing up. The jet of the liquid soap squirted everywhere, never in the right direction and certainly not on my hands.

'I must be cleaning the whole area around here,' I thought, but would never have given voice to this. This had amused me, and also Julia, on the previous day in a moment of light relief. Apron on, I went to the life support machine and noticed that the covers were not up to Frank's chin any more. The 'tin foil' showed underneath but his arms were still hidden and were tightly by his side. I found his hand and touched it. It did not respond and I willed his fingers to move as they had done once before in intensive care during one previous fight for his life, but this did not happen. I was appalled by his ashen-white face. I needed to sit with him alone to gather my thoughts and feel that closeness which had become extra special to us. Even though he did not respond there was still the magic of our love between us. I was unaware of the marvellous staff who were personally caring for him alone.

His skin was clearing of the many blotches which had been part of him before. Even I could see that the liver was functioning.

I returned to talk to Lydia in the main ward and I noticed the most beautiful bouquet of white and soft blue flowers that I had ever seen, being delivered. I was surprised to learn that they were for me from the best friend that I could have been blest with – a near neighbour, Nancy. The perfume was sweet and full of the joys of spring. I am sure that it is rare for a visitor to receive flowers instead of the patient but this gesture was appreciated by me more than mere words can express.

Sister found me a big mottled blue ceramic vase and gave it to me to take the flowers to my 'dungeon'. I said farewell to Lydia and went to put the flowers in water. The musty smell was not as prominent as I expected when I unlocked the door to the room. There on the bookcase was a drinking glass filled with freesias. Beside the glass was a loving note from Lydia to me, her mother. How considerate she had been and how surprised she must have been when the bouquet arrived. All the stress and strain had not made me cry but the simple kindness of a wonderful daughter and a dear friend made the tears flow in pain, love and gratitude. The flowers looked beautiful in the vase which joined the glass on the bookcase.

The dreadful room was now more habitable and actually smelt wonderful. Spring had come to me. The torch was to become very useful!

Julia did not go to her office but came to see her father, keeping vigil with me. She persuaded me to have some lunch. It is always more pleasant to eat with someone else and I acknowledged that I was hungry. That afternoon we both visited Frank again. We were told that he was beginning to show signs of regaining consciousness. He wanted to live.

There was now another patient in the unit. He was a very good-looking young man who had tried to commit suicide. Doctors dialysed him and fought for a life he did not want. They had slit his arm open and joined a vein and artery with a filter between. (We had to wait for this to be completed and the blood cleaned from the floor before we were allowed to enter the unit.) They lost their fight. The young man won. But I could only think that if his life had been so unbearable, it might not be such a bad thing at all, just a total waste.

Frank was blissfully unaware of the drama. On our next visit to him, a few hours later, we found his head raised a little on pillows. He looked better this way than unnaturally flat. He was still on the ventilator and all the tubes, drips and drains were still attached. But his eyes were now open and the whitest that I had ever seen them, instead of the yellow tinge we had come to take as normal. He was conscious. He was awake but could not talk because of the tube in his mouth and throat. He indicated that he wanted a pen and paper, a familiar request and one anticipated by the nurse, who had both ready.

'What day is it?' he wrote. 'Can I have my spectacles?'

He had gone to 'sleep' on Sunday. It was now late Tuesday. He had given up two days of life to gain a few months but did not know that.

It seemed very cold in the unit and Frank felt cold to touch as we held hands. We didn't need to say much to each other for we knew what we

were thinking. A miracle had been performed, but this was not the end of
Frank's suffering and in so many ways it was the beginning for us both.

I went to the chapel and wrote my thanks in a book kept for prayer
requests. I sat for a long time in the quiet chapel, praying silently. Subconsciously I had accepted death and learned to accept our anticipated premature parting as inevitable. Now I had to accept life and help Frank to do
the same.

God, in his wisdom, had granted Frank bonus time. A new life, his
greatest gift of all.

I went to my dreary room, number 731A, which seemed less dank and
it now smelt like Covent Garden first thing in the morning when it was
full of fresh flowers. I was unable to concentrate enough to read or knit.
Julia was becoming worried that I would not eat and kindly brought
tempting dishes daily to me; I struggled to eat as much as possible, finding
it difficult to swallow much at all. I slept fitfully. Frank survived the night
too.

18. Bonus Days

A certain routine was beginning to develop. I would have a strip-wash first thing in the morning, trying to hide behind the torn sacking nearly stretched across the window overlooking the laboratories. The shower and bathrooms were too cold and bleak to face and I'm not certain that there would have been any privacy either. The hospital was beginning to wake at this time, with cars spewing out staff into the car park outside the window. Hustle and calm bustle was under way for the new day. I would then get breakfast in the canteen with the doctors, nurses and maintenance staff; apparently I was looking more and more like a member of staff – the cashier had stopped asking me, 'Staff or relative?' and was assuming the first. I'd then stroll to the W. H. Smith hospital shop and queue for my *Daily Mail* with staff who had no time to waste, and mobile patients with masses of time to kill. This was followed by a few quiet moments in the empty chapel.

Thus prepared for the day ahead, I arrived in the ward after the doctors' first round of the day.

I was granted permission to enter 'Frank's hide-away' after ringing the bell. I scrubbed up, put on my apron and found that he was fully conscious and no longer dependent on the ventilator. However, the various monitors were active, the drips were still dripping into him, the drains and catheter were still draining from him. The bile drain seemed to come out of his chest and culminated in a bag that required frequent emptying. This would remain for eleven more weeks.

The doctor informed me that Frank kept forgetting to breathe and that although he was doing well there was a long way to go yet.

Frank's skin colour was vastly improved and his eyes were white and clear, showing no signs of jaundice and proving that the new liver was continuing to work. His previously ulcerated legs had borne reddish, often weeping scars but these were now turning browner in colour and were obviously healing well.

Frank was unaware that in a chair beside him sat a young girl who was on dialysis. She was to be saved, but at this stage was struggling with the doctor and nurse in the hope that she could remove the tubes from her body. She had tried to commit suicide by taking drink and drugs after an argument with her boyfriend. She had been transferred from another hospital by air ambulance.

I realised that although the hospital seemed to lose so many lives, they were really dealing with those patients who could not be saved by other hospitals and had been rushed there as a last resort in the knowledge that many of the cases were likely to die anyway.

The staff are firm and believe in what they are doing and the few patients who come through the trauma and ordeal must give them great satisfaction and make it all worthwhile.

So many people find life too hard to bear and resort to drugs or alcohol or both together. The drugs which do the most harm are so easy to obtain, such as paracetamol, and if mixed with other drugs and not found quickly could possibly kill.

The overdoses are taken in a weak moment and later when the damage is irreversible the sad person may change his or her mind and struggle to live. Death may not come easily or quickly, often taking many painful and anguished weeks. I can't imagine the horror of knowing that you have killed yourself and are unable to stop the process of dying when clinging to life.

Alcohol can poison quickly but may kill slowly. It isn't necessary to drink spirits daily to damage a liver. An enormous binge where a large amount of alcohol is drunk in a short time can do the same damage to a liver. So many people who are not normally big drinkers need emergency help in hospital too.

I had found that so far the staff had been professional; their expertise was reassuring and my confidence in them was total. No one could fault their dedication in their care of Frank. However, some counselling for the family at this stage would have been very welcome. It should not be left to the relatives to ask for counselling at a time when they do not wish to create more work for the busy staff, distracting attention from their loved one and making them feel a burden.

It was at this stage that I began to feel emotional. I was becoming deeply aware that somewhere a family were grieving over the death of a loved one. Was the death a sudden loss of a husband, son, father, brother or best friend? Who was the donor, the person who had given Frank new life? How unselfish his family had been.

It would have disturbed me to learn that the donor organ had been given unwillingly. At present in Britain the family are asked if the organs can be used even when the donor is carrying a card giving consent. I can accept this, but if the law were to be changed to make organs free to be used unless a card is carried to say organs are not to be used in transplant, the gift of life would be automatic and not always in the best interest of the grieving family, and therefore not as easy to accept by the recipient and family.

I felt that the bereaved family would be wondering what had happened to the liver and I wished to let them know of my gratitude without causing them more pain. But no form of gratitude could ever be enough.

Perhaps if Frank continued to live, that would give them comfort, but if he died they would suffer their bereavement twice.

I asked to speak to the transplant co-ordinator; it was four long agonising days before she responded and then our emotional conversation was in a busy corridor of the hospital. We did not sit in a room in peace and privacy to discuss the mental anguish I was experiencing in this rare life-saving action.

Eventually I learned that the pregnant co-ordinator was on her last day at work and that the donor was a 25-year-old, six feet two inches tall and well built male. It was suggested that if we wished to say thank you, an anonymous letter could be sent for forwarding to the unknown family a few months after returning home. Some people leave matters alone but some families actually become friends eventually.

Both Frank's and my offspring visited the hospital in the first three days of his operation and although he was so seriously ill none of them was offered a cup of tea in their worried state. They had travelled to London from Avon, Colchester and Oxfordshire. Their stepfather was too ill for them to see and they could only imagine the battle going on behind the blue door in their own form of shock. Of course the staff were busy but I wonder how they would have felt if the roles had been reversed. What was routine to them was a tremendous ordeal to us. A little kindness and understanding at a time like this would have made the ordeal a little less harrowing. I do not feel that sufficient thought was given to the family at any time: how this drama would affect their future lives or the tremendous strain and stress they would have to overcome in the next few months. The patient could not be isolated from his way of life and family for ever, nor vice versa.

Leaving Frank in the isolation ward to learn to breathe for himself and gain strength, I joined Julia and my daughter Claire, where they were sitting in the main ward area. I wondered how I would have coped without the frequent visits of my family and friends over the next few weeks. Claire was as horrified as Julia and myself at the filthy state of the ward. It seemed incredible that on one side of the blue door all was as sterile as possible whereas only a few feet away was fluff, dust and dirt and an attitude of sheer militancy to disguise the slovenly laziness of the domestic and temporary nursing staff. They had obviously not heard of a fair day's work for a fair day's pay, not that they would have agreed with me that the pay of their tasks was to be considered fair.

Claire understood that she could not be admitted to the isolation unit

because of the risk of a two-way infection, but in a matter of hours Frank
was to leave this sanctuary and enter an area which by any standards was
totally unsatisfactory and unacceptable.

'My God, you should have seen the size of the liver in the bucket. I've
never seen one so large or with so many colours,' we heard one staff nurse
say to another. We wondered if she was referring to the liver which had
been removed from Frank or the one which was now functioning in him.
Probably it was neither and the patients could well be eating it for lunch
for we didn't learn whether the bucket in question had been in the theatre
or carrying an animal organ in the kitchen!

I learned from a friend that the director of the unit had made a statement to the press which had been printed in a previous day's national
paper. It appeared that Frank could well be the twenty-fourth liver transplant patient mentioned. I found it a little bit distressing for I dreaded
controversy at this time.

The article, dated March 28th 1990, was centred on the front page of
the *Daily Telegraph* and headed *Livers on the NHS for Drinkers*. It was
written by David Fletcher, Health Services Correspondent.

'Alcoholics who develop cirrhosis of the liver are being offered life-saving
transplants on the NHS despite the prejudice that they have brought
the fatal disease on themselves.

'A total of 24 alcoholics with end-stage cirrhosis have been given new
livers at Addenbrooke's Hospital, Cambridge, and at King's College
Hospital, London, and 66%, are alive a year after the operation. Dr
Roger Williams, director of the liver unit at King's, said: 'If they survive
for another 12 months after the operation they have a very good chance
of going on for at least another five years.

'The only stipulation made by the doctors is that patients must give
up alcohol for at least 6 months before the operation. Dr Williams said
yesterday that only one patient had returned to alcohol abuse.

'Alcoholics were not delaying liver transplants for other people because
there was no shortage of donor livers, he said.'

Sister had said that although the hospital could not tell families what to
do, it was certainly advisable to refrain from speaking to the media for it
was only too easy to get out of your depth and be unable to cope with the
intrusion into your privacy.

Only a few stories had yet been printed as liver transplants were comparatively rare but the true and marvellous miracles were normally left
unreported.

We had seen one or two appeals for donors on television over the previous two years by desperate relatives at the eleventh hour in the battle against death, including that of Colin Barnett to keep the mother of his new daughter alive.

I had decided that I would not appeal for a donor organ for Frank if the occasion had arisen for there is a great deal of difference between prolonging a useful and healthy life with a good quality and prolonging the life of a dying person, which is what I had always believed would be the case for Frank. As an alcoholic, his whole body had been abused and damaged, not just his liver.

I could not understand how placing one very important organ in a worn out and diseased body would create a life with a better quality than before. I was terrified of a future in which I watched him continue a battle against the demon drink, for I knew that he believed that with a new liver he would be able to control and enjoy his drink. What I found more horrifying was that when he asked the Bart's consultant whether, with a new liver, he would be able to drink alcohol again, the answer had been that the odd glass of wine, etc., would be alright.

Having lived with an alcoholic for a few years, I knew that the first drink was one too many. Unless I was mistaken, the transplanted organ would not take away the craving of an addict. My feeling was that Frank had tried so hard and so bravely in his battle to give up alcohol that he would feel that life was not worth living unless he could live it his way. I was now to pray that not only would Frank live and have a decent quality of life, but mainly that he would find the courage to continue his biggest battle and not let everyone down by becoming the second transplant to return to his addiction. Even thinking this way made me take on another burden of guilt. What hope had he of success if I didn't trust or have faith in him? I was so aware of his need in me, his need to be believed, trusted and loved by me more than anything else in the world. We both needed to face the future head on, without fear or shame.

19. On the Move

Later that day, Wednesday March 28th 1990, Frank was moved from isolation into intensive care, the first major step in his recovery. He was soon bravely sitting out of bed although still strung up with a multitude of tubes, wires and equipment restricting any movement. He was obviously very pleased with himself. After all on the previous Sunday he had thought he was going to die during the transplant operation, and here he was with his tremendous effort, courage, stubbornness, determination and bravery beginning to show. So was his sense of humour.

Instead of a team of nurses and doctors with him at all times, he was now reduced to the first-class care of one specially trained nurse. She radiated kindness and was chatty and friendly. It seemed a strain to be returning to the near normal world with noises being very noticeable. Aprons still had to be worn by those visiting Frank with only two people at any time, but these two people could be any members of the family. The only way to get privacy now was when the curtain was pulled around the bed, for the bed in intensive care could be seen at all times by the sisters and doctors on the desk and by patients and visitors entering the rest of the liver wards.

It seemed a dreadful shame that Claire had not seen her stepfather when she visited a few hours earlier for I am sure she would have gone home with a more settled mind; and Frank would have loved to see her, with her medical background, always a reason for his pride in her.

Colin Barnett, a frequent visitor to the hospital, was astounded to see Frank and waved delightedly to him from the corridor, his face aglow with delight at Frank's progress. He had been totally unaware that the transplant had actually taken place in time to save his hospital aquaintance, who was fast becoming a friend. What recent memories this sight must have stirred in him. Perhaps this transplant would end more happily than that of his late wife.

There were three beds in the intensive care unit at the time and fortunately all was unusually quiet and calm, the lull before the storm. We learned that another lady had been rushed to the hospital in a helicopter when her liver failed. As Frank had now vacated the isolation unit, it was able to accommodate her, the bed being free for another transplant should a suitable donor organ be found in time to save her waning life.

I continued to follow my daily and lonely routine, sleeping in my damp and dreary room, eating alone in the staff canteen amongst the doctors, nurses and administration staff, all now recognising me with encouraging smiles. When I noticed the irrational diet of the overworked and tired doctors I really thought that this was a case of 'do as I say and not as I do.' They loved chips with just about everything, gulping the food down between their bleeps and phone calls. There were many frequent puffs of cigarettes too, but lots of rather long stubs left in the ashtrays as there never seemed enough time for the smoker to finish the cigarette. I tried not to sit near any of the team who were caring for Frank as it seemed unkind of me to intrude in their breaks, but if they saw me first I was often invited to join them at their table. I suppose that I was becoming hospitalised too.

Thursday dawned and suddenly life became busier and harder to cope with. The feed lines and catheter were removed from Frank's body. Frank was again informed by the doctors that his spleen had been removed and it would mean that he would have to take an additional tablet of penicillin daily for the rest of his life. This in itself was no problem but it was confusing for us both to learn from the surgeon that the spleen was intact when he visited Frank later. Frank was aided by a nurse and it appeared to be a trial and certainly an error when he was clothed in his pyjamas for the first time since the transplant, for within minutes these pyjamas were covered in blood from the very messy and oozing 'mercedes benz' logo shaped wound.

Now the horrific extent of his operation and wounds became more visible. He had many stitches and clips under his left arm, across his armpit and in his groin as well as those across and down his body, making him look like a 'Hot cross bun'. There were other scattered incisions over his body too. The surgeon informed us that there were thousands of internal stitches as he had used well over a hundred needles during the lengthy and complex operation; during this time the whole blood supply had been diverted and 'cut into two', with one circulation at the top of the body and the other at the bottom end of the patient. There were drains removing fluid from the body and when Frank moved in the slightest in his bed these drains leaked everywhere. This was to continue for many more days but we were informed that there was no need to worry about this as *Better out than in* was their motto.

The physicians also told Frank that he had fluid accumulating around the lungs, a problem we had been dreading, but this fluid could be drained if it became too uncomfortable for him to bear. Fortunately this wasn't necessary, which seemed incredible to me as Frank had been such a heavy smoker until the last few weeks, as it is a very common problem for transplant patients. Frank co-operated by taking painful deep breaths to keep the lungs active, in turn keeping the fluid down. He wore an oxygen mask for most of the day and later was given a nebuliser as well to keep his lungs free from congestion. He was to use this throughout his life. He was living in a dream and was becoming more and more exhilarated to be alive. His confidence in himself was growing in leaps and bounds but I was told not to get too optimistic as there were still many possibilities of complications ahead. However, his progress was truly remarkable and later that day he was moved out of the intensive care unit to a six-bed ward one step further away from the sisters and doctors' desk.

It was fantastic progress and physically he was ready for the move, but mentally this move was premature for both the patient and even for myself. He had been moved rather earlier than anticipated because of the attempted and failed suicide of a young girl who had fallen out with a boyfriend in the north of England. She had been rushed here as the local hospital had done all they could for her and her only hope of a future was now with the experts of this liver ward. The stress and strain being felt by her brother and his girlfriend was apparent to all, as also was her total lack of co-operation with all those who were caring for her. She was enjoying being the centre of attention and looked like the cat who had just had the cream.

Frank's new ward was noisy. The beds appeared very close after the spaciousness and peace of intensive care. On the table near the bed beside him was a television with the sound volume turned up far too loud; all the ward had to listen whether they wanted to or not. It would have been a little bit more reasonable if the patient had stayed by his bed to watch the programme but he often disappeared into the cloudy smoke-filled day room for one of his multitude of daily sneaked smokes.

In the evening he had eight loud visitors at one time even though the rules allowed only two adult visitors at any time. I could not adjust to the fact that only a few hours ago Frank was to be kept in 'cotton wool' away from any source of infection and yet the visitors at the bed nearly on top of him were either questionably too young to be admitted, were obviously just in from the pub with the coughs and splutters of a winter outside and were certainly far too rowdy to visit any sick person.

Frank was tired and weak. He had tried hard to please the physiotherapist after being wheeled to the toilet along with his drips and drains and had even taken a few steps on his way back to the ward, four days after his massive operation, but now he could not tolerate this unreasonable hustle, bustle and noise. I reported the fact to the staff nurse who really seemed oblivious of the recent events which had taken place in Frank's presence in her ward. Whether it was because I had complained or not, the patient in the next bed was moved the following morning. That day Frank had his first light food which he had to struggle to keep down.

I began to feel very guilty and was struggling mentally with the fact that it now looked more likely that Frank was going to live after all. Because I had never dared believe that this could be possible, I had subconsciously begun to grieve for him and had prepared myself for a life alone without him, thinking that his passing would then not shatter me. Now I had to adjust to the fact that he might survive. It seemed impossible to talk about this feeling to anyone who could even be expected to understand or who would not judge and wrongly believe that I really wanted my husband to die. I had also been warned so often by the medical teams that Frank's death had been 'On the cards' during the last six years.

The suddenness of the normal hospital ward routine and noise shook us both. It was hard to accept so many people around Frank when only a few hours before no one had been allowed near him. I felt that a little more time for us to be alone together when Frank was conscious and able to communicate with me in privacy would have reduced pressure and strain for us both. The last time we had any degree of privacy had been in the bathroom prior to the transplant in an unreal atmosphere. How we needed that quiet moment alone together now! How we needed to be close at this time and open our hearts to each other. Every moment was so precious and so unsure. It seemed unbelievable that there was not a small room where a patient could sit quietly and discuss the situation with a relative or a member of staff, away from the noisiness of other people.

Over the next few days we were concerned at the lack of continuity of the nurses and their apparent disregard for instructions and respect for the medical teams. Although there were three sisters for the ward, they did not seem to care sufficiently over routine details and certainly did not inspect the wards often enough or make sure that the nurses coming on duty had sufficient information from the nurses going off duty. Frequently the agency nurse had no training on equipment in use and they seemed to bluff their way through their duty, never to return again.

The surgeon told Frank to 'Steady down and take life easily and not to walk to the toilet or around alone yet'. However, the nurses tended to disregard this and push him too hard. They seemed to think that his transplant was weeks ago and not just days, until they were told otherwise, as Frank was putting on a brave act and was 'running before he could walk.'

The ward was unpopular and rather difficult to staff. I was glad that I was with Frank most of the time for I could only feel that otherwise he would not have received as much attention as he required. It is difficult to judge the matter fairly as it could also have been that because I was present, the nurses felt they could ignore him. As Frank grew stronger I was made aware that quite soon I would have to return home and vacate the nurses' room, but on the two occasions that I brought the subject up with Frank, his face fell and he grew despondent. I continued to stay in the hospital.

I had been informed by the cleaner that the room I should have been sleeping in had been occupied by a mother and father (who left the hospital daily to go to business) for much longer than was normal because of their social standing. Snobbery certainly counted for something if this had been allowed to happen. The father returned every evening carrying his briefcase, attired in an immaculate business suit and clean well-pressed shirt which was being laundered and ironed by his wife in the hospital, using facilities which would have benefited us all. She spent hours telling other patients' visitors that the family were great friends of their GP and that she was a teacher. She always managed to look fresh, rested and happy, which must have given a great amount of comfort to her recovering teenage daughter.

Most patients and their families kept their stories to themselves, remaining private individuals.

There was a very high percentage of foreign patients, mainly from Italy and Ireland, and rules and regulations were written in many languages wherever they were displayed.

Frank was nearly a 'local' and I could have travelled from home daily to visit him but our need to be together at this critical time after the transplant was made no less than those same feelings of folk who lived further afield. Many of the Irish relatives of patients were staying in bed-and-breakfast accommodation in the Croydon area with nearly all family (close and distant relatives) using this as a means of combining the hospital drama with the business of visiting the well-known London sites and sponging off the rather over-generous state in some cases.

I felt that because the river Thames flowed between the hospital and home and because I would have to drive either under it through the Rotherhithe Tunnel, or over it on Tower Bridge, the hospital was much further away than it actually was.

Frank's recovery was fantastic. His attitude showed great courage, pride and positiveness. He was beginning to be a wonderful example to other apprehensive and doubtful possible future transplant patients.

Four days after the transplant Frank had painfully walked to the toilet from his bed with the aid of the physiotherapist.

The porter was amazed to find Frank waiting for a chair to take him to the X-ray department on the fourth day. He had expected to wheel a sickly-looking man lying on his back in bed to the radiographer. Instead, Frank was wrapped in blankets and pushed in the heavy wheelchair looking for all the world like a day patient.

I tried to keep up with the porter as we traversed the wide corridors. It seemed incredible that it was only Thursday and that a similar journey had been made by the three of us on the previous Sunday.

The lights appeared very much brighter than on that Sunday night. The department was buzzing with business and the waiting room which had previously been closed was now in use.

The radiographer greeted Frank with surprise and obvious delight. Congratulations were in order. Today was so different from our last visit when all had been so quiet and urgent. However, transplant patients are not kept waiting and Frank was rapidly whisked away from me and the 'pictures' were taken.

He was in considerable discomfort, which he tried to keep to himself. It crossed my mind that the waiting patients hadn't any idea what he had suffered or how serious was his condition.

He looked so determined to live now and was very happy to be alive. The other mere mortals were feeling sorry for themselves in their plight and sickness.

It seemed incongruous and disturbing that Frank was sitting in the waiting room with coughing and spluttering patients spreading their germs like spectators at a snooker match! Frank was by now feeling the cost of his efforts and returned to his bed in an exhausted state.

Frank continued to progress towards recovery. He had both good and bad days, as expected. He always retained his wicked sense of humour and became the life and soul of the ward.

Patients came and went. Those who had damaged themselves with alcohol abuse listened to his advice respectfully and kept in touch with him. He was determined to get home as soon as possible for two main reasons: first, to make medical history by being the shortest-stay liver transplant patient to date; second, he absolutely hated this particular hospital and loved his home.

He had built a good rapport with the doctors, calling them by their first names and being really cheeky but not disrespectful towards them.

'If they keep calling me Frank and not Mr, I can do the same,' he said, laughingly.

'My God, that is a bastard tie you have got on, Andes,' he said to the Australian doctor. 'Who has got the bet on that you dare wear it?'

Cards were now arriving daily from friends and business associates, many who had not been in touch for a long time. I was comforted by the cards and letters which were sent to me from my close friend, Nancy. I'd never heard of a patient's relative receiving mail whilst staying in a hospital and it was wonderful to know someone cared about me too.

Cards and signed photographs arrived from the famous as well, all boosting Frank's confidence and pride in himself. These were hung by Blu-tack and drawing pins on the wall behind and beside his bed, becoming a talking point and an additional way of making new friends and meeting new people.

Frank did not think that a man should receive flowers and when the flower arrangements started to arrive I was ordered to place the beautiful flowers anywhere other than near his bed. 'I'm not a sissy,' he said. We all knew that to be true. Even telling him that it is alright for men to receive yellow flowers fell on deaf and uncompromising ears. The reception area to the ward certainly benefited by his attitude and was frequently more cheerful with his floral displays.

The fruit was more successful and Frank delighted in making sure that the nurses and doctors never left his bedside without an item of fruit from his overcrowded bowl. Of course he had not been allowed any of these items in intensive care.

The first Sunday after the operation is one which I wish I could forget. It caused both of us and our visitors much distress.

Sunday was the most difficult day to find staff, or so it appeared to the visitors who, like me, were most concerned over the obvious slackness. After all we are all most concerned that our loved ones are cared for in the best possible way.

However, the day started without the normal newspaper delivery to the wards and many of the patients were lost without their football news of yesterday. I took an order from those patients who wanted me to try to get them a paper and went down the three floors in the massive lift only to find that the W. H. Smith shop was closed.

I was attracted by the spring sunshine outside the main entrance. The weather had been so wintry when I had arrived for my brief hospital stay. Somehow the spring sun, like snowdrops, gives the feeling of new birth, freshness and hope.

I noticed that there were bundles of the larger Sunday newspapers and colour supplements on the steps to the hospital but no one around to sell them. One rather senior doctor arrived and we decided to remove the papers we wanted from the bundles without untying them. It was a diffi-cult task as the papers were tightly tied to make them secure. Struggling, tugging and breaking finger nails, we eventually loosened the first few papers which in turn made it slightly easier for us to remove the rest that we needed.

It was then that we noticed the irate and disgusted looks of people making their way in and out of the hospital.

'Comes to something when a senior doctor stoops to steal papers,' were whispered remarks made by mouths hidden by cupped hands.

'Tut-tut' is a polite way of expressing what they were really thinking of us.

The doctor and I looked at each other properly for the first time as we stood up, stretching our aching backs, for we had been bent over for some time and the bundles had been rather heavy to move. We both burst out laughing as, clutching the small denomination coins collected from the waiting patients, I joined him at the reception desk where we asked the receptionist to give the newspaper vendor the money when he arrived.

This fiasco had only occurred because the day before had seen a massive demonstration in central London against the 'poll tax' and a militant group from the area had been ringleaders and actively involved in the mass destruction of shops, property and cars. Somehow this damage had caused a problem for the delivery of papers which had arrived much later than normal and the vendor had given up waiting. Apparently, travel in the normal world, of which I was still not a part, was totally disrupted although it did seem odd that the permanent staff were able to get from areas the temporary staff could not leave.

There had been a previous occasion during the week when a group of anti-poll tax activists had been allowed to canvass in the staff canteen. I watched as many people signed the petition they carried just to get rid of them so that they could get on with their meal uninterrupted. I had told the activists that in no way would I sign the petition and got in a slightly heated argument with them about the docks and the borough of Tower Hamlets of which they had a sketchy and incorrect knowledge, mixing the responsibilities of the local council with that of the London Docklands Development Corporation.

The patients were waiting impatiently for my return.

'Where the hell have you been?' shouted one liverish and crotchety man.

'I could have printed it in the time it has taken you to get to the shop,' said another ungrateful person, and when it was found that I had muddled the order and bought the wrong papers for one or two people my popularity was not as great as I had expected. Nevertheless, I believe that it was for the best as later in the day the newspapers were being swapped by patients who, up till then, had not said a word to one another.

Frank was taking many different drugs on which his life depended. He was continually monitored so that every little change in his body was noticed. Blood tests were taken every few hours and sent to the laboratory for analysis. There were usually a few doctors in the vicinity of the ward and three sisters in charge of the nurses, with a minimum of one nurse in each section of the ward.

It was difficult to find any of these staff on a Sunday and the visitors were left to tend the neglected loved ones.

Cyclosporine is one of the anti-rejection drugs administered to transplant patients. The body would reject the organ as a foreign body if anti-rejection drugs were not given in the right doses and regularly at the right time.

Frank was still taking cyclosporine in a drip and not in tablet form. It would take up to two hours for the drip to feed his dose into his blood vessels. On this day the drip was set up at midday but there seemed to be a problem for his arm was swelling; it was getting heavy and painful and the drip did not appear to be emptying fast enough.

I hunted everywhere to get attention but there was no medical staff to be found. I knew that the drip was 'tissuing' and that the vital drug was not entering his body as it should yet I could do nothing about it. There were no alarm bells at the beds, no strings to pull or buttons to press to summon help. Strictly speaking there would have been no need for these if the ward had been covered by staff at all times as it should have been.

Added to this problem was the fact that Frank would do everything in his power not to use the bedpan. I am certain that this was because of a lack of dignity and that his enormous backside dwarfed the largest of pans, unsteady on a mattress. Curtains around the bed do not hide the sound of the bowel or bladder emptying nor camouflage any smells, therefore Frank preferred to struggle to the lavatory at the end of the corridor when answering the call of nature.

As he now had the additional drip attached to his left arm, he was holding his buttocks tight and probably crossing his legs to delay his visit to the toilet until this drip had emptied rather than allow me to get him his bedpan.

I found that the sister had returned to her desk and I reported the drip problem to her at 2 p.m. as soon as I knew she was back.

Just as I returned to Frank, my cousin and his wife peeped around the entrance not expecting to see Frank at all. They lived close by and had kindly offered me help with washing clothes if I required it. Amazement showed on their faces at the sight of Frank who defied our somewhat pessimistic expectations by looking better than he had done for years.

'We didn't expect to be allowed in to see Frank because of the risk of infection,' they said, as they sat on the edge of his bed, something so frowned on in many a hospital.

I continued to look for help with the offending drip but to no avail and

Frank was now in a desperate state with the visit to the toilet of paramount importance. Visitors or not, we were going to have to move him off the bed into a wheelchair ourselves and get him to the lavatory. I knew that he would not consider a bedpan whilst there were people present under any circumstances.

I found a wheelchair with a mind of its own – one which managed to knock everything I tried to push it past. I lined it up beside the bed, working out how not to get tangled in the drip when we moved the chair again with Frank as a passenger. He weighed well over 16 stone and was heavy to move from the bed and also to wheel around, as he clutched the pole supporting the drip with its own set of wheels on its tripod base, beside the wheelchair.

Worse worry was still to come.

The stench of stale urine hit me as we reached the toilets. There were half emptied and dirty bedpans complete with wet used and unused toilet paper clinging to the sides of the pans near the autoclave awaiting sterilisation.

I had to step carefully to avoid treading on faeces; some were already trodden on and spread around the floor, as I wheeled Frank to the *Ladies* door, for the *Men* was so dirty that I could not bear to let Frank attempt to use it.

Frank would not let me clean the seat with paper from the toilet roll but struggled to wipe it clean himself, flushing the paper away before sitting on more paper which he had used to cover the offending lavatory seat. I closed the door to give him the privacy he craved and stood near the entrance in case any lady wanted to enter.

With tears in my eyes at this disgrace, I thought of the thousands of pounds spent on the operation to save a life, while this area which could promote or endanger personal hygiene was a nightmare of neglect. I do not believe there could have been any acceptable reason for this state of affairs. Neither the National Health Service nor the lack of any funds could be the cause of this filth. I can only say that I felt it was neglect of supervision of the far end of the ward by the staff. It is no use spending thousands of pounds on well-equipped laboratories only to neglect the basic yet so essential details.

My sense of equilibrium and beauty was recovered when glancing through my tears at the outside from the open door on to the fire escape, I watched a grey squirrel jump and play on the fire escape steps.

Frank called me for he was ready to return to the ward. I brushed away the telltale tears. Stepping carefully, I helped him into the chair which I had previously turned to face the opposite direction and wheeled him to the open door so that he could see the squirrel. He held my hand as he smiled at the perky little creature. All three of us, including the animal, knew that it was good to be alive.

The chair was heavy to manoeuvre along with Frank's weight but with a little trial and error I managed to get him back into his bed. My cousin and wife had been waiting for the *warriors'* return and said their farewells, knowing that Frank had exhausted himself.

At 5.30 p.m. interest was shown in Frank's cyclosporine drip by a nurse who then called a doctor. He removed the drip completely and inserted a new venn flow for future use in the other arm. The drip was reinserted, around six hours late.

I took care not to discuss my concern with Frank but in the evening when his daughter and son-in-law visited him, I took David to one side and asked him to inspect the toilets. He came back horrified and disgusted.

'If the toilets were in a public house, the premises would be closed down immediately as being insanitary,' was his comment.

I pondered over what action I should take but didn't actually do anything other than report the matter to the staff nurse. I did not want Frank to be ostracised, but I did notice a distinct cooling off by some of the nurses towards me.

Frank appeared to be out of immediate danger and I was building him up to realise that I should be returning to live at home and drive to the hospital daily, which he dreaded, as he wanted me by his side all the time while he was dependent on others. He did not think that he could rely on someone being near enough to him if he needed help urgently. I was worried about this too due to our experiences so far.

However, I found it tactless that Sister should talk to Frank's daughter and not me about the fact that it was nearly time for me to return home. She was rightly concerned that I had lived in the hovel of a room for too long, but I would have preferred that she had spoken to me directly as I had built a good relationship with the doctors who told me truthfully all the details, whether good or bad, so that a sense of mutual trust had been formed. I did not like this secondhand message and immediately felt like a guest who had overstayed a welcome or a child who was a nuisance.

That evening Sister came and sat on Frank's bed and asked him what the problem had been.

'My life depends on drugs and no one took any notice of the drip not working. There was no one here when I needed them,' he said.

She made fun of this as if it was not that important.

I had to break the news to him later that I would be going home on the next day and he was obviously upset.

'Look at it like this,' I said: 'You must be getting better and this will be the first step to your following me out of here.'

I spent eight days and nights in the hospital constantly by his side to boost his morale and to care for him as only a wife can. In his weakest moments he had me to talk to and calm his fears. When things looked better, we had each other to celebrate with. Life is about sharing, and we certainly did a lot of that.

I was very worried about what would happen to Frank with some of the nursing staff looking after him, not knowing that we would eventually find out in a rather dramatic way.

I gathered my belongings together in my room with the peeling walls which had become home to me of late. I was going home alone today. My family were worried that I should return to an empty house and had organised that my ageing mother would stay with me and be in the house ready to greet me. Nancy had greeted her and made her familiar with the area by going to the shops with her and calling in daily until I returned.

I wondered who would be the next occupant of this dreadful room and decided to try to lessen the initial impact of horror by leaving some fresh flowers in a glass on the bookcase with a note saying simply, 'Good luck, God bless.' I hope these flowers gave someone some comfort and masked the musky smell.

I stripped the bed and folded the sheets and blankets, leaving them on top of the mattress. I left the window slightly ajar for some fresh air to circulate.

I still had the torch and flower vase lent to me by Sister. The lighting remained exactly the same in the communal area of the nurses' quarters, still being virtually nonexistent. But Sister's intervention over the heating had brought results and the room was now warm, if not cosy. I walked past the doors with *Do not disturb* notices hanging outside and assumed that the occupants had been on night duty. A couple of electric kettles were bubbling away on the floor outside other rooms, which like mine had no power point, the nearest point being that used for the vacuum cleaner.

Although I had been resident for eight days, I had never seen any cleaning being done but the bins along the wall of the corridor were emptied each day so the oriental lady at the far end of the corridor did actually move and do something. There had been many moments when I thought she might have been a permanent fixture rooted to the spot with superglue, or possibly just a figment of my imagination.

I returned the vase and torch to Sister with my gratitude. She had forgotten that I had them both.

I went to Frank and sat by his side, holding his white hand. He looked sad and drawn. I knew that his bravado image had all been an act to help me not to worry and to show the people caring for him that he was co-operating without moaning. He had been incredible till now. It would be harder to maintain his morale now that the pretence was beginning to slip. I had always been with him during any crisis. I could feel his fear. We were so close, I was under his skin and he was under mine. Words were not needed for us to communicate. Each knew what the other was thinking.

We talked of the donor and wondered if he had any family. Neither of us felt that we could cope with knowing who they were and certainly could never meet them. Our gratitude was being overtaken by our sorrow for them in their loss and a guilt complex was developing in us both. Frank felt that the donor should be alive instead of him for he had been a young man with more years ahead of him. I felt guilty that I still had my man whereas someone else had been bereaved. I got an illogical feeling that his wife, if there was one, shared Frank with me and certainly knew that I must never meet her, face to face. I had joked with the surgeon and Frank when he had been by Frank's bed.

'What a fantastic change there has been in Frank,' he said. 'Although the kidneys are struggling with the anti-rejection drugs and we have a few problems, the replacement and younger liver is doing splendidly. I told you I'd make a new man of him!' Frank glowed with pride.

'I always fancied a toy boy and now I've got one,' was my reply.

'I'm looking forward to celebrating my first birthday,' said Frank, 'and no one will keep up with me.'

He was not as buoyant now that I was to go home and I left him with mixed feelings. I secretly still wondered if he would ever leave the hospital. He managed to walk to the ward door with me to say goodbye. As I left him I did not want to turn back to look at him, but as I did, he was walking with his shoulders hunched over and not with the confident straight back he had normally. I wanted to go back to him and cuddle him and tell him how much I loved him.

He always said 'I am my own man' and I knew that shortly he would be standing upright on his own feet and tackling this problem in his own way. He had small change so he could telephone me when he wanted if the trolley was wheeled into the ward for him to use. He must have been very fit as a young man, for it was his strength that was helping him in his battle now.

I walked past the phones that had gobbled up my change during my daily calls to the office and family. I would not walk past them again until tomorrow.

Alan, our friendly and reliable minicab driver, was waiting outside. He collected the camp bed used by Lydia, our blankets and all other items originally brought in during our emergency dash on Mothering Sunday, except Frank's belongings.

The sun was shining but it felt cold. I handed the key to my room to the receptionist. As I stood at the top of the steps I was overcome with emotion. This was *déjà vu*; 'I'm reliving my nightmare,' I felt, 'only there is something wrong.'

I did not believe that I would ever leave Frank alive in the hospital. I had done this before in my sleep, but my loneliness then was because he was dead. My loneliness now was one I would experience because he was alive and not with me.

I now moved as if I were a robot. I answered Alan's questions and knew that I had to remain cool and calm until I got home. I felt as if I wanted to cry and cry until all the pent-up emotion and strain were released. It would be luxury to have someone cradle me in their arms and let me cry until I could cry no more.

I was unaware of the journey home but it did seem to take an eternity. I paid Alan his fare and he put the luggage into the house for me. My mother was waiting for me and gave me her customary kiss on the cheek. As Alan left me, I closed the back door and burst into uncontrollable tears. The tears streamed down my face washing my make-up away. My mother took one look at me, not knowing what to do.

'Now, now. We don't want any of that,' she said firmly. 'Pull yourself together.'

I did precisely that, clamming shut like a shellfish, becoming hardened and cold in my aloofness and not wanting to communicate with her.

It was a very long time before I was able to cry or release stress again. I was exhausted. Home is not always where the heart is when your man is away. My heart was in the hospital. But home is also a place where you can relax, let your hair down, drop the mask of pretence and be yourself. I could no longer do this for there was an unsympathetic atmosphere at home. My mother was kind in her own way but did not begin to understand the situation and she was probably doing the only thing she thought right.

'I found this packet of cigarettes on the floor when I was cleaning,' she said. This jolted me back to the time that the call had come regarding the donation of the liver and of Frank's reaction as he had thrown these into the air.

'I think we will put them back on the table beside the phone where Frank normally left his cigarettes,' was my reply. I knew that Frank should be the person to throw them out if he returned home. It would not have been good to take the matter of throwing them out into my own hands for it could have been interpreted as my having no faith in the person addicted. What pleasure it would give him to perform that small and simple act.

The house was spotlessly clean and the Mothering Sunday cards from the family which had been on display when I left the house were now neatly piled on the table. So much had happened since they had arrived. These little things were bringing me back to normality but it was hard to adjust into any sort of routine.

Priority for me was a hot bubble bath where I could luxuriate in the warm silky water. I ran the water but there was no steam. I was so tired I could hardly move myself into the water which hit my body with shock and woke me up. It was cold.

'I had a bath just before you came home,' my mother said, 'and I've not turned the central heating on.'

Everything seemed to be stacked against me. I turned on the immersion heater for this would heat the water quicker than the gas boiler, and thought of food.

I could hardly believe that the only goods my mother had purchased were a newspaper and fruit. She had found some potatoes which she had peeled but she'd not planned our lunch. I had some food in the deep freezer but this would need to be thawed, all taking time. Perhaps I was expecting too much, but I understood that I only had a visitor in my home at this difficult time to help me. I was not in a mood to entertain or look after visitors and it did appear that my mother was expecting to be treated like a house guest. I felt her a responsibility that I could not cope with in addition to my troubles and I would not be able to worry how she was filling her time in my absence for I would be spending most of my time in the hospital, being aware that an emergency call could come at any time. I found two fish pies which could be cooked from frozen which I heated and we ate off trays in the lounge later.

I was desperate for peace and quiet but my mother who was lonely and eager to chat, kept talking and I found that I was not listening. I hope that I was giving the right answers in the correct places during her brief pauses. I longed to sleep in my own bed again. I asked to be left alone until I awoke naturally.

'Please do not wake me in the morning,' I said. I needed time to gather myself and recharge my batteries.

The door bell rang early next day and my mother went downstairs to see who was there. Although I heard the bell, I chose to ignore it. The next noise I could not ignore for the burglar alarm had been set off and an unholy row was wailing from our box on the wall on both sides of the house. My patience was exhausted, and I stormed from my bedroom to deal with my mother and visiting Nancy, the two panicking women, and stop the noise downstairs.

'Jinxed again,' I thought.

It seemed unreal to be doing normal things like shopping. The news of

Frank's transplant was travelling fast and everywhere I went I was greeted warmly. I learned that he was known by everyone and loved by so many. This was comforting.

'We are including him in our prayers,' I was told over and over again by members of different church denominations.

The neighbours had been kind and helpful to my mother in my absence, but I found it an increase in my responsibility to keep her with me.

'It does seem silly you being here to just look after the house as I'm at the hospital nearly all the time, when your own house is left empty in Dorset,' I said, trying to be kind. 'It must be lonely for you.'

We agreed that she would go home on the Thursday coach and be met by a friend at the other end of the journey, but that I would take her to see Frank first.

Her return lightened the pressure for me and I'm certain that she was happier in her own familiar surroundings.

In the meantime Frank was progressing better than we could ever have believed possible. He was proud of the fact that the director of the unit had asked if he would talk to a gathering of eminent professors in London for a conference.

Early in the afternoon, the doors of the liver ward were opened by a junior doctor; a group of very important people swept past him like minders around the famous, tall and distinguished director whose face was well known to television viewers for he was often in the news. The surrounding professors were from all parts of the world and a stir was caused by their presence. They made their way to Frank's bed and, as he said later, 'It felt like being visited by God and the disciples.'

He felt pleased and proud as he was congratulated on his progress. Apparently the visitors could hardly believe that the transplant had only been carried out during the week previous to their visit.

'I've got Roger to thank for making me give up smoking,' said Frank, cheekily calling the director by his first name, a thing never done before, as he talked to the professors. 'I could not have the transplant unless I did that, but I told Roger that I had to do it in my way or not at all,' he continued. 'When I make a promise I always keep it,' he chatted on, 'and I will not smoke again.'

I remembered only too well the occasions when he had said to our local doctor, 'I cannot promise that I will never drink again but I will promise to give it a good try,' for he knew that it was too difficult a promise to make and keep.

It was a face-saver to be able to say, 'I never did promise that I would never drink again,' and still be seen as an honourable man.

I was acutely aware that I had a hard time ahead for if Frank did come home, and this was seeming more and more likely; I would need my strength and health. It would have been easy to live off bread and cheese or in moments of exhaustion not bother to eat at all. I therefore purchased complete frozen meals which would only need to be put in the microwave and tried to look after myself. I was losing my appetite so these small meals helped me to continue to eat because my plate never looked overloaded.

I developed a routine which involved visiting the hospital each afternoon and returning home in the early evening so that both Frank and I could get some rest. I was spoken to by the doctors every day, being given all the facts, and I was still being told that we had a long way to go yet.

I felt much brighter after a visit to the hairdresser's and much more peaceful after I had quietly spent some time alone in St Mary-le-Bow, watching the flicker of the candle I had lit.

I visited my business but really was unable to concentrate properly and absorb all the facts. Where had all my efficiency and business acumen gone?

The first time I returned to the hospital, I drove around the locality for an hour to find somewhere to park the car. In desperation I went to the security men on the gate and told them of my plight. They found me the small space that I needed.

'You want to go to the admin department and get a pass. You see that lady over there?' – they pointed to a young woman about to get into her car – 'Well, she has to visit her son every day and she got a pass to park.'

Eventually I was admitted to the administration office by two young girls who didn't seem to understand what a temporary parking permit could be. They went to a more senior lady who then came out of her office to speak to me.

'I am no longer resident in the hospital but I am visiting a liver transplant patient who is my husband daily. I would appreciate it if you can let me have a temporary pass for my car?' I respectfully asked her.

She was rude and totally unsympathetic. 'You're not the only person with a seriously ill relative,' she barked. 'If we give you a permit everyone else in the liver ward with a transplant will want one.'

'I did not say that I am the only person with a seriously ill relative and I am not aware that I even implied that,' I stunningly replied. 'But I can say that I am the only liver transplant relative likely to ask for a pass.'

There was only one other transplant patient on the ward at the time and the family were not local and did not have a car in London. I also felt that I would not have needed to let anyone know. Of course the medical staff were rightfully being given priority.

We did not live in the catchment area of the hospital and my daily journey had to be made by car and not public transport. I was not to get my pass. The woman who blocked it was the person who dealt with the bereaved when a person died in the hospital. There wasn't an ounce of humanity in the department and their uncaring attitude hurt me deeply. It felt like the straw that broke the camel's back.

I spoke to the surgeon about it in one of our chats about Frank and he was far from pleased. I explained that it seemed to be petty things that were the hardest to cope with during this time of stress.

I've always got on well with people, trying to treat them as I would like to be treated myself. I think the security men on the gate realised that I was not exaggerating my problem, for when I returned to my car and thanked them for trying to help me out of a fix, they asked me if I had done anything about the pass. I told them that it had been refused which they felt had been totally unreasonable.

'Each day as you come here, make sure that we know that it is you and we will always find you a space,' they said. Not only did they keep their word but they sent Frank various cards of best wishes during the rest of his hospitalisation and always asked me for an update on his condition, giving me a daily smile and welcome that restored my faith in people.

I learned of every lump and bump in the road between my home and the hospital on my many journeys. Sometimes I would go home happy and hopeful and on other occasions I would be sorry and sad.

I preferred to bring Frank's bloodstained pyjamas home each day to wash. His wounds were still leaking every time he moved, and occasionally there would be dark bile stains from the drain leading into the bag which had to be emptied frequently.

I was encouraged by Frank's spirit and his light-hearted attitude to other patients with most of whom he got on well. He seemed to inspire others to take a positive attitude towards their problems which in view of the past negative attitude he had displayed when he had wanted to finish his own life was in itself a miracle. He could not tolerate any patient who did not try to get better and one in particular, in the bed beside him, really irritated him.

This young boy had no fight in him and when he turned his television on at five o'clock in the morning Frank shouted at him: 'Turn that ... television off or I'll personally throw it through the window,' to the loud cheers of the rest of the woken patients.

Television is company for a patient who is well enough to watch it but sheer hell for those who are not. When there are six televisions in a small six-bed ward, each capable of showing four channels, it is bedlam.

What was more amazing was the way that the televisions, once turned on, were hardly ever watched. The sounds competed with one another from every angle and were only turned down when a doctor could not hear himself think.

We learned that it was an Italian patient's 52nd birthday, and that he had been away from his bambinos for many weeks, having had a liver transplant and the complication of cancer. He had to have one final operation before he could go home and he spoke very little English. He was extremely brave but obviously very lonely. The nurses gave him a pot plant and we all sang 'Happy Birthday' to him. Occasionally he had a visit from a translator to explain what was happening to him, but otherwise he kept himself isolated in his corner.

There was another Italian in another ward who resembled a puppet from the *Thunderbirds* programme who would turn up uninvited and talk loudly to *our* Italian for hours on end. This irritated the rest of the ward but he was eventually stopped from coming without permission for he would wake the sick man and had tried to shake him out of his anaesthetised state.

On one Saturday night a young separated husband went on a drinking binge to drown his sorrow. He didn't normally drink heavily but this night was an exception and was to change his life for instead of going home afterwards, he was rushed into the liver unit in a critical state, having badly damaged this organ. He was jaundiced and looked rather yellow. He also felt very ashamed. He idolised his baby son whose photograph took pride of place beside his bed. Frank chatted to him about his foolishness and was listened to with respect and understanding. This man kept in touch with Frank after the incident but was sent to a local hospital quickly after his admission.

Frank was talking to one of the doctors when Colin Barnett walked down the corridor. Frank excused himself as he went to greet his friend. The doctor seemed pleased that they were getting on so well.

'You unfortunately lost your wife but I am going to make it. Together we can help each other,' he said, to the agreement of both Colin and the doctor who left them to talk for a while.

Frank was now finding much to amuse him and it was a relief to find him laughing. He was not the easiest man to understand but the medical team had got to understand his caustic sense of humour and often rather crude approach, appearing to be on the same wavelength.

Frank continued to gain confidence during each of his bonus days. It was a sobering thought to know that by now he would have been dead if the transplant had not taken place. He was appreciating each day far more than those of us who have grown to take each day for granted.

I tried to find something to take in to him each day for by now he was rather fed up with hospital food, although he was given a menu daily with a choice of three different main courses. I purchased some strawberries which were out of season and his eyes lit up as he noticed them. Typical of his generosity, he asked me to offer them around to those in the rest of the ward who were allowed to eat them. This broke the ice with the Italian who was delighted to be included and later always offered Frank anything that he had received from the interpreter after her visits. I am sure that he felt less isolated and every time I arrived in the ward I was given a beaming smile from him. I decided that the next time I went into the city I would try to get him an Italian newspaper and magazine. These strawberries were eaten as if they were nectar from the gods and I knew that I had to try to get more for the ward.

The 'television fanatic' returned to his bed from his dialysis and when he noticed the small delectable fruit asked longingly for one. I will never forget the joy that this small sweet fruit gave to someone so ill.

'I'll get my mum to bring some into the hospital when she comes from Bristol,' he said, but he never asked for these, she said.

I could no longer have a cup of tea with Frank in the ward for I was no longer resident. I found that I flagged at tea time, noticing that the daily routine was tiring. I decided to bring a small vacuum flask of coffee for myself into the hospital on each visit. It seemed to give me strength to overcome my weariness.

I had already been told of the serious aortic aneurysm found in Frank during the operation. The doctors were rather concerned about this and felt that Frank should know about it.

I was unhappy for him to be told now as his recovery had been nothing short of a miracle and he was appearing happy and relieved. It seemed a cruel blow to tell him while he was 'riding high'.

The medical team knew that he would experience considerable pain from the aneurysm and that it was also dangerous to keep him ignorant of the facts in case he ever collapsed and needed emergency treatment.

'It will help him to understand what is happening and he will know the cause of his pain,' they said. 'He will have to adjust his way of life if he is to live with it.'

I could only agree that ignorance creates more fear and I could also see that I would be overruled if I continued to object to his being told the facts. My heart ached for him.

'Leave it to us. We know the best way to tell him,' I was reassured.

20. Painful Truth

When I arrived on the following day, the medical team came to Frank's bed and drew the curtains around the bed for privacy although we were somewhat cramped inside.

'You have both furred arteries and weakened ones that stretch like a balloon, carrying too much blood. This is not an immediate problem but in a few months' time we want you to see the heart surgeon,' he heard.

Frank took the news calmly but the problem was not to wait as long as the medical team had hoped. Later that week Frank looked very white and was getting considerable pain around his kidneys every time he moved. He asked for, but did not always receive, adequate painkillers from the nurses. He was totally convinced that they thought that he was making a fuss about nothing and got angry when one nurse said, 'One of these tablets will control the pain just as well as two of the same.'

An annoyed Frank told me, 'I won't be taken for a fool. Surely they realise that I didn't cause a fuss when I was in dreadful pain after the transplant and that I would not ask for relief now if I didn't need it.'

When I was sound asleep in my bed that night, Frank was taken to the X-ray department for an emergency scan of both the liver and kidneys. It was very unusual for Dr Cohen to be in the ward on a Saturday, but he joined my son, daughter-in-law and me at Frank's bedside unexpectedly. He was concerned at this latest turn of events and assured Frank that he would be given the necessary painkillers and that he would take this matter in hand immediately. The cause of the pain was still a mystery but it could possibly be due to muscles and bones, in particular the spine, being affected by such a long operation.

Frank still aimed to be at home as quickly as possible and told the doctor that he still wanted to break the record. The doctor smiled at him warmly.

'We will get you out of here as soon as possible.'

Frank was exhausted from the strain of the pain and because he had no sleep at night. We left him earlier than we had anticipated and were greatly concerned.

I could see that my son Alan was very worried. I was greatly comforted when Alan said that he was full of admiration for his stepfather and praised him for his 'guts and courage'. Alan had always been critical of Frank's drinking and had not tried to understand the addiction. The fact that Alan now admired him and was praising him broke down my barrier and as we were walking out of the hospital along the main corridor my composure began to crack.

Surrounded by visitors making their way to the wards, he encircled me in his arms and with my head on his shoulder softly said, 'Let it out, Mum.'

I did not want to make a fuss or cause a disturbance.

'It doesn't matter a damn where you are, just let it come.'

My tears flowed for Frank, who was fighting so hard to come home to me. He was suffering so much. Warnings had been given to me not to get too optimistic or excited as his general health was not very good.

'Your husband is a very sick man,' had been said to me more than once, the last time being after the transplant by the surgeon.

Yet he had appeared to be doing better than most of the other patients in the ward and was the only one who had been given a transplant.

Alan was a great help to me at that time and I gathered myself together, saying that I would drive home for I knew that I would need to concentrate and that it would help to take my mind off my worry.

The next day was Palm Sunday. Once again there was an acute shortage of nurses. Frank now had a prisoner in the bed next to him who was causing no trouble and was being treated like the rest of the patients except that he was constantly watched by two prison warders. I was led to believe that the prisoner was a drug addict and the family who were due to visit later had to be watched carefully for they were most likely his suppliers.

These warders had been very helpful to Frank, often doing tasks for him because of the absence of the nurses, and I was relieved to know that someone was keeping a caring eye on him now that I could not be by his bedside when he needed me. I learned that the warders were actually in the ward near the sister's desk when Frank had been admitted, and had been aware of the drama as it unfolded from the transplant of the organ up to date.

Today was to be the last time that the family were going to be able to visit the prisoner, so although the warders looked comfortable and discreet in the two armchairs (which also had to be their beds), they were not missing any movement.

The prisoner's mother arrived at the hospital with two younger women and as they approached they were discreetly led outside by a warder for searching and/or instructions. They looked as ordinary as anyone else and certainly I would not have suspected them of passing drugs. I mused that no criminal walks around with *criminal* plastered on his forehead. This would take away the fun of detection! The mother did not look stupid enough to jeopardise the life of her son. A very careful search was made of his fruit and Easter egg gifts. His cigarettes were opened by the warders, who checked that the seal was normal. They were then passed to him. He had to eat as much chocolate as he could for the remaining eggs and fruit had to be left behind when he returned to jail. As soon as his visitors left he started to stuff himself full of his goodies.

One of the warders had taken it upon himself to comfort a lonely girl who had tried to take her own life by drinking bleach and who was in another part of the ward, promising to visit her after he had left the hospital. He was making her see that life is too precious to throw away because of falling out with a boyfriend. It must have helped in her recovery that a man was showing interest in her as a friend and I often wonder if anything ever became of that relationship.

It was interesting to see that both the staff and patients treated the prisoner the same as anyone else.

During the last two weeks I had been interested in the transplant patients as they returned for their check-ups. Frank swapped experiences with them. I thought they all seemed a little disillusioned after their great struggles. Two of them said that they would not have gone through it all if they had known of the future difficulties in the big outside world. They felt that people in general were not ready to receive them and were not able to accept them as normal any more. There were many questions regarding their ability to return to work. Both men had to litigate to keep their jobs and in one case the job content had been altered, making it impossible for the man to continue.

The wife of one of the recent patients, who was herself a nurse, would not return to visit the hospital as she was having a difficult time in coming to terms with her recent trauma and found it difficult to accept normal life again.

There was a notice on the noticeboard in the corridor with the telephone number of a woman who had had two transplant operations, the first one failing, who was acting as a co-ordinator for people who wanted to talk to another transplant patient in their area. I felt that this impersonal approach was totally insufficient. A voice on the end of a telephone who also might not be able to handle the situation correctly would in no way be a help. I felt that the lack of counselling was the biggest drawback of the whole set-up.

Sunday came and went in the standard hospital way. Monday was the beginning of a new week, Holy Week. Life was going on normally but to the patients in the ward and their relatives, very little of their lives was normal. We had the sensation that we were existing on the edge of life and were outside it all. A sensation of remoteness.

One patient went for his usual dialysis. He had damaged his liver and kidneys by excessive drinking of 'scrumpy', Somerset cider.

Irish Patrick was admitted to a bed prepared by the orthopaedic staff so that he had a pulley to use to pull himself into a sitting position to get in and out of bed. His wife was with him most of the time. He was here for liver transplant assessment.

A tremendous struggle to hang on to life had been waged in the intensive care unit by a haemorrhaging man looking old beyond his years. He had been moved into the bed beside Frank.

I had watched his wife go through hell during the struggle. She had not left his side but last night she had managed to get a few hours' sleep. She had also been ravaged by the tragedy and trauma that drinking alcohol had on her husband and she too looked many years older than she should. She was always clad in flat fur boots and fur-collared coat, irrespective of the heat of the ward, and these made her look dumpy. I felt pity for her. It was obvious that she could not accept that the problem was self-inflicted with drink.

I had overheard her on the telephone to a relative when she tried to explain it all away as just being a blood vessel bursting and not drink at all. I knew exactly how she felt and remembered the time I did the same thing in Bart's hospital.

As she walked down the corridor she realised that the bed in intensive care was empty, with folded covers on top of the bare mattress. I could feel her distress but knew that instead of the worst happening the patient was out of immediate danger. She was near to collapsing as I went to her, holding her up by her arm.

'Your husband is out of intensive care and in the bed next to my husband,' I gently told her. 'You have just had a nasty fright, haven't you?' I asked.

Too shattered to reply, she just nodded her head, breathing fast with short breaths and crying quietly. I got her to a chair and went to the kitchen to ask for a cup of tea for her, explaining the problem to the sister, sharing her distress.

She was soon in a fit state to visit her husband, who was off the ventilator but had an oxygen mask on and a drip into his arm.

All people who live with a terminal illness are subconsciously expecting the end but do not like to admit it even to themselves for it makes them feel guilty, as if wishing it to happen.

I know that at this stage I became an introvert and believed that the whole world revolved around me and my problems. Living in a hospital day and night waiting for death makes you get everything out of proportion. The Italian in the corner was at a low ebb. He desperately wanted to leave the hospital and couldn't understand why the final operation had not yet been performed. He was withdrawing into himself.

I had been into the office for a couple of hours in the morning but had not been able to concentrate nor eat my lunch. I decided to take it to the hospital to eat and thought that Frank might share the sandwich with me. I walked into the ward carrying the sandwich in its own designer carrier bag. It had cost me an arm and a leg. I felt like a monkey in the zoo with an audience as I tried to eat and was pleased when Frank said that he fancied half of the delicious poached salmon in granary bread.

'Ugh,' he said loudly at his first bite. 'There are pips in my bread. Bread should not have pips. Damn this health kick.' Everyone started to laugh and I had to go to the kitchen to get some ordinary bread and butter for him so that he could remove the salmon from the pips and place it in the new bread. I think he then felt that this was cordon bleu in comparison to hospital food.

Frank was far from well. It was now time to start clamping the bile bag each day, necessitating a clip to stop the bile flow into the bag. It had been clamped for two hours today. This was a positive step nearer home for he could not leave the hospital until the bag was removed even though the bile tube would remain in his body for some time afterwards. The pain in his back persisted. He was finding it hard to be pleasant and to keep his sense of humour. None of the tablets seemed to provide sufficient pain control and I became apprehensive. I could see fear developing in my husband.

Frank was no better on the next day. His bile bag was not clamped again for he was in too much pain. Frank's pain, although very real, remained a mystery. The usual crocodile of white-coated, stethoscope-swinging doctors visited him, and many additional tests were carried out.

'It's rare to sail through a transplant without some complications,' and similar comments were being thrown at him but Frank was sure that they would prefer to know what the complications were.

I had anticipated that Frank's morale was going to be low and knew that he needed a laugh or at least cheering up. I was glad that his friend Freddie had visited him for a short time. Frank had received signed photographs from the cast of *London's Burning*. Glen Murphy had signed his photograph under his comment, 'Hurry up, get out of bed, you lazy bastard.'

Frank loved this and was greatly cheered.

I was reading in bed at 11.30 p.m. that night, in the hope that the reading would help me to sleep, when an extremely agitated Frank phoned me. He was very angry.

'I asked Patrick's wife to telephone you to say that I had collapsed in the toilet but the nurses stopped her,' he said. 'But I am phoning now because I can't go to sleep until I have spoken to you. The doctors have all been to me and they have given me an injection to ease the pain, so don't worry now. Always remember that I love you,' he said.

I knew that he was very frightened and had wanted me there by his side. I could not sleep. I was grateful that the nurses had asked Patrick's wife not to ring me. I do not know how I would have reacted to a call from a hospital visitor but I was extremely worried that Frank had phoned and that he was obviously giving cause for more concern.

I moved my phone on to my pillow in case it rang in the night and I couldn't feel it in the dark. I could not sleep and the night was long. Eventually dawn broke in a chorus of melodious birds on the guttering outside my window.

21. Two hours to Eternity

Birds were not heard in the hospital.

Frank had indeed collapsed in late evening. He had gone to the toilet and locked the door. He had removed his paisley dressing gown and hung it on the door while he sat on the toilet seat, hoping to empty his bowels – so often a problem after surgery. No one is sure exactly what happened but he lost consciousness for a time because of excruciating pain in his abdomen, the pain coming from his aorta and not his bowels. When he regained consciousness he pressed the alarm bell repeatedly but no one came. Frank struggled with himself. Could he control his pain, his body and his brain so that he could reach the door of the cubicle?

Somehow he reached the lock and released the catch, put the lid on the lavatory and sat on it. Then he shouted and shouted for help. Medical staff did not hear him. The cleaner heard him as she approached the bathroom.

In the next cubicle was an invalided Vietnamese, also sitting on the toilet, his wheelchair left outside the door. The cleaner got help and the nurses managed to get Frank into the vacated wheelchair and back into his bed. They had summoned the doctors.

The Vietnamese was aghast and confused by the situation and decided that he was going home. Once he had his chair back he would do precisely that. Have wheels, will travel! He was eventually caught in the lift after belting hell-for-leather down the corridor on his way to freedom and drink. It was also at this moment that the young man in the bed beside Frank haemorrhaged and spewed masses of blood. He had to be moved into intensive care immediately and his relatives were summoned to the hospital. They were also told to remove his clothes and belongings.

It was now that Frank wanted me. He thought that if I got a call I could be with him. He thought that he might never see me again.

Frank's blood pressure was perilously low and his condition was deteriorating fast. The cardiovascular team were called to him. His aorta was leaking. In the early hours of the morning of April 11th he had another body scan and I received an official call from the hospital.

'The doctors want to see you straight away to explain to you what happened last night.'

I called a minicab for I was not going to drive, and left the house immediately. Initially I thought the doctors were going to apologise for the panic and the delay in treating Frank on the previous night. As I neared the hospital I felt fear begin to grip me. I had been cautiously optimistic after the transplant but now realised that Frank might well be losing his battle for life after all. I was mentally talking to myself.

'Don't trouble *trouble* until *trouble* troubles you.'

My outward appearance was calm but inside I was desperately worried. I arrived at the ward and was told that the doctors would be with me in a minute. I sat on the bench outside the blue door, waiting.

There was much coming and going and it was obvious that there was a crisis. Doctors I did not know were in a desperate discussion with one familiar doctor. 'Could we do this?' 'Can we try that?' But it was a negative answer in each case.

Frank was wheeled by me, hardly knowing what was going on. He looked dreadfully ill. He was returned to his bed.

Frank had been through the body scan and had very little chance of living. He was lying calmly in bed and was having an injection every few minutes. He was having a blood transfusion and another unit of blood was ready when the current one ran out. The Australian doctor spoke to both of us together.

'A visit will be made to you in the next few minutes by the professor and doctor of the cardiovascular unit. If they decide not to operate there is nothing that we can do. Let's take it an hour at a time.' Frank was given only two hours to live.

We were used to taking life one day at a time . . . but one hour at a time . . .? Time was so precious and never more so than when it is running out. I moved closer to Frank and took his hand in both of mine. The doctor moved to let me pass him, his eyes meeting mine; he felt frustrated and sad that there was no more that he could do at present. I was speaking to give myself confidence as much as to Frank.

'Darling, we have got through so much together when everything seemed impossible. This is only another hurdle which we have to get over together, and with God's help all will be well. You are not alone; I won't leave you.'

I had to leave him with the doctor, who would shortly be going off duty, for a few moments as I telephoned for our priest and also left a message for Julia at her place of work as she was at lunch. The message was to tell her to get to the hospital at once.

There were no telephones free and in desperation I asked a relative of one of the patients if he would mind hurrying his call so that I could summon the priest. He understood immediately and handed the phone to me.

'Good luck,' he said. He knew the chips were down.

It was the Wednesday before Easter and the Revd Victor Stock was offering the Eucharist at a midweek service to a congregation of 90 people.

Prayers were said for us both and we found this comforting. I would have been in the church myself, making my Easter confession, if things had been different. Immediately the service was over he jumped into a taxi, something he did rarely, and commenced his journey to the hospital, carrying the Eucharist for Frank and me and anointing oil for Frank.

Meanwhile the patients were subdued and the ward was hushed. Everyone felt that we were going to lose a high-spirited man who had been able to joke and make fun of life: a man who had often set an example to the others in their moments of doubt. He had determinedly persevered to get this far. Everyone seemed to know him.

The ward was getting busier for the visitors were arriving, but all were extremely quiet. There were a few tears in their eyes. Nurses now seemed to be everywhere.

We were not left alone for a moment with so many medical matters to deal with.

I stood at the foot of Frank's bed when the transplant surgeon arrived and stood beside me with his arms around me.

Quietly he whispered into my ear, 'You are doing very well.' He obviously knew exactly what I was going through. What a wonderful, kind and sympathetic manner he had. He didn't raise my hopes but was supportive. Human contact such as his arms holding me is so important at a time of crisis.

We all turned to look as a stranger rapidly walked into our lives. Dressed ready for theatre, he looked like a miniature green giant for he was wearing a green hat and gown, was slim and of medium height. Very gently but straight to the point he told Frank and myself that Frank was dying for there was no chance of saving him. The operation would hardly improve his chance of living. It is a dangerous and major operation without a newly transplanted liver. Nothing could be done.

It seemed Frank would die within two hours. I was numb as I looked at my calm husband lying still in the bed as he was propped up on pillows. Frank looked at me and our eyes showed each other how much we hurt. He turned to the surgeon, whose healing hands had saved so many lives.

'You have the skill,' he stated with a hint of a question.

'Yes,' replied a hesitant surgeon.

'Well, I've got the fight,' replied Frank, as his life was ebbing away.

The surgeon stared back at Frank and their eyes and thoughts locked into one. The decision was made in that moment.

'I'll scrub up,' Mr Pain said, 'and I will see you in the theatre in ten minutes,' and with that he left the ward.

Elsewhere there was great activity as an alert went out for blood, units and units of it. The hospital was buzzing with the news.

'Don't give much for Frank Craddock's chances,' was a comment repeated by many people. This news had already reached the City via a contact in my office and the laboratories.

Frank had received his new liver only 15 days earlier. The complications were numerous.

The patients in the ward were fighting back their tears as their visitors joined them.

Patrick handed me a note which said simply that he would be praying for us. I was allowed to be with Frank for a few moments whilst the commotion was going on. I closed the curtains. In our closeness, little needed to be said, for we knew each other's thoughts.

'You are my life, my love, and I love you for ever. If I had my life to live again I would do the same with you. No regrets,' he stated.

'No regrets,' I said. 'I love you.'

'Tell Julia I love her.' Frank said, as the priest peered around the curtain. He had managed to get there in time.

I was asked to leave the two men alone together for a moment so that Frank could make his confession and be anointed with the holy oil. I was trying to be brave for Frank but I felt desolate.

The beds were being moved to enable the nurses and porter to move Frank on his bed. He was not to move his body at all. So much was happening but I could only twiddle my thumbs, feeling totally lost and useless.

Father Stock asked me to join him and Frank behind the curtain.

Sitting on the side of the bed holding Frank's hand tightly, we took the Eucharist privately together. At one point Frank said quietly into my ear 'I'm going', and he seemed to lose his balance. I was unsure whether he meant that he was dizzy from the injections or that he was dying.

We prayed for strength for each other. Father Stock was not only our priest but was also a friend and he was the best person to be with us both at this critical time. He gave us courage and faith to cope.

Frank was brave but pale and suffering in silence.

The theatre porter arrived and Frank was being moved out of the small ward. It did not seem possible that I had walked this way before only a few days ago as I held his hand. This time everything was stacked against him except prayers, very much love, a brilliant surgeon, God and Frank's attitude.

Father Stock was walking behind me. He remained calm and cheerful.

'Well Frank, have you got all you need for your trip,' he jovially asked. 'Got your passport?'

'You've just given me that,' was the quick reply, for he had been anointed for his entry into heaven. We continued to walk, getting nearer and nearer the lift which once again was lit, with the doors open and waiting. I realised that I had been through this before. Sister's voice cut into my thoughts.

'Only go as far as the lift this time,' she ordered.

Frank turned to me and, with determination showing on his face, said: 'I wish I had my Samurai sword with me.' He repeated, 'I need my Samurai sword now.'

The sword had been a Christmas gift from me of which he was very proud. It was one of his most treasured possessions but I would not have thought that he would think of it now.

Events were moving too fast and taking over. I've been through this so recently; life can be so cruel. I had him back for such a short time. Please don't take him now. He has been through so much pain and trouble; can I expect him to be spared a second time? It felt as if I was asking God for too much.

I felt an emptiness as Frank was wheeled into the lift. He had said no more.

'God bless. I love you,' I said.

The lift door closed and he was gone.

There was a great pause in my life. I was in a sort of vacuum. Father Stock was still with me for a short time before he returned to his Holy Week pastoral duties. We both believed that we would never see Frank alive again.

I knew that if he had not been able to get to Frank in time, I would have made the sign of the cross on Frank's forehead and blessed him myself. Now Frank was in the theatre fighting to survive.

'Remove all Frank's belongings,' Sister said to me as I still stood with Father Stock in the corridor. 'I'll give you some hospital bags to put them all in.'

'Is he already dead?' were both Father Stock and my thoughts. It seemed a cruel way to get me to clear his belongings from the ward, for if he came out of theatre Frank would be in intensive care on a life support machine again.

I felt as if a knife had been thrown in my back and twisted. Father Stock left me with a hug and kiss on each cheek. 'Phone me if you need me or have any news,' he said. I do not understand how people without faith can get through times such as this. Standing in the corridor (for the bedside locker had been moved out of the ward) I packed pyjamas, dressing gown, toiletries, cards, soft drink and fruit. Frank had lost a pair of spectacles when he had collapsed and these were still missing.

I felt at a loss and was worried that Julia would bump into someone who would give her the news before I had been able to tell her myself. I would stay in the corridor until she came.

Julia had been out to lunch when I had made the call with the frightening news. When she returned to her desk she immediately rang David and got the first taxi she saw to bring her to the hospital. The taxi was caught in a traffic jam before it went over London Bridge out of the City, and there was worse to come. She had to sit in the back knowing that they were not moving fast enough. When she was about a mile from the hospital she jumped out, paid the fare and started to walk the remaining distance as quickly as possible.

I saw her just as she saw me. We greeted each other with a hug. I tried to explain what had happened without drama or detail.

We sat outside the blue door on the padded bench for there was nowhere else to go. The three grey bags containing Frank's belongings were pushed under the bench beside our feet for there was nowhere to leave them either.

I had left home that morning after my first and only drink of the day. Nothing had passed my lips since then and it was now mid-afternoon. A nurse looked out from behind the blue door.

'The operation is proceeding; Frank is still alive,' we were told.

Within a short time we were joined by David, who promptly got me a cup of tea. It was hot and welcome and warmed not only my inside but my hands as well as I held the plastic cup for as long as it would stay hot.

There is so little that one can do in a crisis and with this in mind Sister did not allow the beds to be made in the family room allocated to us. This was left for us to do.

Julia had already decided that she would not sleep in the hospital but nevertheless the two beds were covered with sheets and blankets. I did not want to stay in the hospital alone but it looked as if I would have to cope by myself again.

This little room was like a palace in comparison to the room in the nurses' quarters. It was close to the day room and only a short walk from the intensive care unit. There was a small fridge with milk, soft drink and butter left by the last inhabitants, but I understand that much of the food etc., and certain items of equipment had actually been provided by the sister. She had tried (and succeeded) to make the room cheerful. There was a similar room next door.

We made more tea and sat and waited for more news. I sat on the bed that was to be mine and with my head down, dared not say what I was thinking. We were all sombre and worried. I had not thought when I left the house that morning that I would be resident in the hospital again.

Someone must have told my family the news for Chris, my son-in-law, arrived to join us. I was so pleased and surprised to see him. He immediately drove to my home to collect a change of clothes, my night attire, toiletries and make-up. It was a problem for him as he did not really know where anything was kept, nor what was actually essential for a woman. He also emptied my fridge, bringing the food to the hospital. He remembered to inform the milkman of another absence and spoke to my neighbours and friends.

Things looked very bleak. Five times during the operation it looked as if the surgeon had lost Frank. Frank was fighting so hard in his unconscious state that at times he made it more difficult for the surgeon to work. Unit after unit of blood was used. Drip after drip of sweat was wiped from the surgeon's brows.

There was a knock on our door, a sound that I dreaded to hear. I could not tell by the look on Sister's face whether the news was good or bad and probably she did not know either.

'The operation is over and at the moment looks successful but we have a long way to go and many complications to overcome. Please stay in your room until we come to get you. Please keep away from intensive care at the moment. Frank is unconscious but extremely agitated.'

The operation had lasted over six hours. A marathon fight had taken place whilst I had sat on the bed with my head in my hands in a nail-biting atmosphere.

I had been as brave as I could. There had been no tears from me and I had tried to be supportive of Frank's daughter, creating the idea that I was alright. I was upset that not one of the family was going to stay with me during the following crucial hours, for once they had seen Frank, they were all going home. It had been hard staying in the hospital alone. Eating alone in a crowd made me more aware of my loneliness and I longed for someone to care for me for just a moment or two.

Julia and I went to see Frank first, with David and Chris waiting their turn. Frank was fighting his ventilator and his eyes kept opening and looking around, although he wasn't aware of anything. He had drips, drains and mainline feeds as before but he was not as white. When we spoke to him he appeared to know us and respond. I was dreadfully upset to see him like this again. I turned to the sister and choked on my words.

'It does seem so unfair that he is like this after doing so well.' I fought my tears.

Sister put her arms around me, trying to give me some comfort. 'He doesn't look as bad as he did after the transplant, does he?' She did not expect an answer. 'His colour is better. But once again you must not get excited for many problems are likely to occur. He is very agitated and although he is fighting to live, he won't stop fighting us too. We're worried over his circulation, in particular his right toe.' (His legs were wrapped in cotton wool.) 'His kidneys are in serious trouble and there is the likelihood of serious fluid retention. His heart is also suffering and we nearly lost him five times in the theatre. We must not forget that the new liver is being put under stress too soon with all the drugs and strain. It could reject. There is now a plastic graft repairing the aorta in the abdomen.'

David and Julia left with their arms around each other, Julia's head on her husband's shoulder. They had not spoken. They were too stunned to speak to me.

I walked back to my room, softly crying to myself. Once again I was feeling very alone and although I was shattered I dared not be relieved that Frank was still alive.

Chris noticed this. He had a a very long drive ahead of him and would telephone everyone who needed to know of the events on his carphone. He wanted to get home but needed to be sure that I was alright. He could remember the time that I had sat in a hospital through the night with him when his first son had been stillborn.

I settled myself into my temporary home. An hour later I walked past the intensive care unit from the phone. It was very late. The curtain hid Frank from my view but, as it did not touch the floor, I could see many pairs of feet moving around his bed and some of these were at the end of theatre-green trousered legs. It was obvious that the large team were still working hard to keep him alive.

I went to bed but did not sleep for I was really listening for the knock on the door to summon me to Frank's bedside. It did not come.

During the following day Frank continued to fight the ventilator but he was now conscious although far too agitated still. This was affecting his heart and causing concern to the medical team. He was still determined to win his battle. He tried to say something to me but could not talk because of the tube down his throat. He gesticulated but I could not understand him. Try as I might, I could not work out what it was and the more I tried the more cross he became with me. I gave him some paper and a pencil. He struggled to write his message. In big capital letters which he underlined, he wrote NOW. What on earth did that mean? By this time he was really irate with me but I refused to allow myself to get upset for I felt it was excusable under the circumstances.

A long time afterwards I learned that he wanted his spectacles, the ones which were lost.

He had a half-framed pair of glasses, too, but when these were put on his face he promptly ripped them off, nearly pulling the drips out around his ears. Frank became obsessed with the loss of his other pair of glasses, even though the transplant surgeon had told him that he could claim a new pair from the hospital. He was obviously worried and far too active mentally. Julia and I hunted everywhere for his glasses and we asked everyone else to do the same. We could not find them.

Later on that day when we were shopping in the hospital shop we were joined by the transplant surgeon. We had seemed to be following each other around but this had been sheer coincidence and we all laughed and joked about it. I mentioned that I was really in the doghouse because I had been unable to understand Frank.

'You are worried that you are in the doghouse?' he laughed: 'Frank was fighting so hard and was so agitated, he was subconsciously fighting everyone including himself during the operation and hasn't stopped since. He dares not stop his battle in case he can't then win.'

Reassuringly he then smiled at me and added, 'He won't have any more goes at you now. I've put paid to that for his own good. I've calmed him down and told him off too. He is now off the ventilator but has an oxygen mask instead. Unfortunately he keeps forgetting to breathe but this should correct in time.' Frank knew that he was his own worst enemy.

We all returned to intensive care together and true to the surgeon's word, Frank appeared to be calmer and more comfortable. He was trying to breathe normally with the oxygen mask which he was allowed to move enough to say a few laboured and croaky words to us.

'I'm still with you.'

'He doesn't want you up there yet. He knows that my need for you is greater than His own,' I replied, referring to 'The great architect in the sky', as Frank often called God.

Although Frank's head was now raised a little on the pillow, it was apparent that he was still very seriously ill. He could only see ahead for he was not able to move his head due to all the tubes and drips. He was not aware of what was going on around him.

The view would have been extremely disturbing as his dying neighbour had swallowed his tongue and the nurses were stopping him choking. The tongue looked black and swollen as it was held in place with a chain-like contraption. Masses of fluid was being flushed through his inactive body from large clear bags hung at the side of his bed. It was a horrifying sight.

The other occupier was the one person with whom Frank could not relate: the one who had been in the next bed to him before the drama of the collapse in the toilet. He was being kept alive on a machine and was, to all intents and purposes, dead. He had no will to live and was drifting away. Although he knew nothing of this, his relatives were to suffer for days waiting for the inevitable and were in great distress. They were frequently moved away from the unit as he was checked to see if he was brain-stem dead.

'One more chance to see if he will fight,' said the second doctor to the one who had asked for another opinion. This patient did not fight even when he could for there was no fight in him and he was left for the next few days to drift into the world beyond.

Frank's circulation was causing great concern. His feet were resting on rubber gloves which had been filled with water to resemble cows' udders. He was lying on a sheepskin and his legs were wrapped in thick cotton wool.

'I've heard of people being kept in cotton wool,' I joked, 'but I've never actually seen it.'

I was secretly worried by the colour of his extremities, his toes having turned black.

Frank's belongings still remained in the polythene bags in my room. He was not allowed personal possessions in the unit but a concession was made when the post arrived, for amongst it was a large envelope addressed to him and marked *Do not bend. Photographs.*

I found him struggling to unseal the envelope for it was too great a task for him to manage yet.

I went to his aid. His face shone with surprise and joy as he removed a signed photograph of his hero, Steve Davis.

'What a fabulous surprise! How did he know I was here? How was this arranged?' he asked, through his oxygen mask, like a small excited child on his birthday. Frank had been snooker champion of the Stock Exchange on many occasions and adored the sport. We had spent many happy hours watching snooker on television, being constantly irritated, however, by the dreary and uninformative commentary. I had thought of writing to the BBC's *Jim'll Fix It* programme in the hope that Frank would give the commentary on one programme, for he was knowledgeable on the subject and made the sport amusing and fun to watch. (I'm sure that many of his *terms* for shots and actions would have been appreciated and understood by the dedicated fans but would have resulted in a 'bleeped out' programme.) This was never achieved, but my action in contacting *Matchroom* when I knew that Frank was going to be in more trouble after the transplant had resulted in his receiving the best boost for his morale at the best possible time.

There were further signed photographs to be removed from the envelope, including those of Jimmy White and Dennis Taylor. How I wished they could have seen his reaction.

Another liver was harvested during that evening because of the generosity of a grieving family. The whole area became active.

Behind the blue door lay a young theology student on a ventilator with only a few hours to live.

I was mistaken for the mother of the student by one of the doctors who needed to speak to her urgently at a time when she had gone, I thought, to make a telephone call. These parents were staying in the room next to me. It could have only been about an hour later when they vacated the room for another family to move in. The student had been found to be brain-stem dead when he was moved to the theatre for the transplant. So near to being given a new life, he died in dignity and out of pain.

The donor organ was not to be wasted. Another match had been made. The organ was compatible with a young Irish girl who was living in the south of England. Her life had been saved with the use of superglue to temporarily seal a leaking vessel, I was informed by her mother at a later date.

Her mother and family were being flown from Ireland to be in the hospital at the critical time. The doctor who was organising the travel was heard to express concern that there would be a problem with moving so many relatives, but they all wished to be near, in spite of the fact that only two of them would be allowed to see the patient for a few days after the transplant. The hospitality of the hospital was being stretched and, in this case, the tolerance of the other patients and their relatives was also pushed to the limit.

The little room next to mine had only two single beds but there were to be two people in each bed and three more sleeping in sleeping bags which took up every inch of the remaining space. Every time one person moved the radiator creaked under the weight. This did disturb me in the room which had become my temporary home. I had taken to resting for the odd hour during the day for it helped to relax when I could. I did not know what was ahead and wanted to have the stamina to cope well.

The family in the crowded room went rapidly to the nearest Department of Social Security on the first morning in England and returned rubbing their hands with glee at their new-found wealth. They were quick to tell other people to do the same.

Some of the family went out on the town in the West End of London during the evening, but I felt that I should not criticise them for possibly this was how they could relieve their tension. I did find their laughter and jollity too much to endure in my own worry and wished that they realised that there were other people to be thought of in their troubles.

Frank was being given the best attention possible in the intensive care unit by both doctors and nurses. They were compassionate and caring. I sat for hours on end at Frank's bedside, often helping the sister by separating dressings and placing them in the correct place in their box. I tried to keep out of the way. Frank was still being drip-fed and he was still ravelled in wires and tubes. He was fighting every inch of the way. I moved frequently from the area for X-rays to be taken of the three inmates, both for my own safety and to make room for the heavy and bulky equipment. Visitors to the ward looked straight at Frank in bed as they entered the corridor if his curtains were not drawn. As Holy Week was nearing its end, there were more visitors than usual.

It was noticeable that many of them were upset to see that the cheerful patient who had been doing so well had taken a step for the worse, yet those of us who had been with him on the day of the second operation could see that he was holding his own.

It was alarming to see that some of the visitors to other patients walked straight up to him, crossing a dividing line marking the area of intensive care where they were not allowed. I was still having to dress in an apron when I entered the area, removing the apron as I left.

Frank was being sent flowers again which I had to keep from him. He was not allowed flowers in the unit, nor anything else for that matter.

'Sissy,' he called men who received flowers. 'Not normal to send flowers to a man,' and 'Not normal to accept them,' he felt.

His flowers were placed just inside the entrance to the ward to help make it look more cheerful during the holiday period.

I was surprised and delighted to see Nancy walking towards us as I sat by Frank. She had been driven to the hospital by Richard, a friendly neighbour, who wouldn't let her travel all the way by public transport.

They were laden with clothes, smoked salmon sandwiches, a salad and other gifts for me. My neighbours had taken pity on me because I had been in the hospital for so long and were trying to help.

Just seeing them was a joy in itself, and of course they were delighted to be able to see Frank even if not allowed to speak to him. This was something that they least expected although they were shocked to see how he was. I took Richard and Nancy to my little room and was able to make them a mug of steaming hot coffee. It was pleasant to learn that the world was revolving as normal and that life was continuing as if we were at home. Nancy was a wonderful friend to me. She wrote to me most days and sent lovely postcards to let me know that I wasn't alone in my troubles.

Richard and Nancy were not impressed by my accommodation and I had to laugh for they would not have believed how much better it was than the hovel that had housed me before. Now Nancy had brought me fresh flowers for this room too. 'Better than an Easter egg for you,' she said kindly, for she knew that I was finding it hard to eat much in my worry.

Nancy took my dirty clothes home to wash. It was a holiday for it was Good Friday. Poor Frank's body really did resemble a hot cross bun now, with his additional wound. He had been cut open right across and completely down his front. Part of the wound was to leak for some time but as soon as he was messy and the drains or bags were removed and replaced we knew that we would all chant, 'Better out than in!' He had got to rid himself of any impurity.

This was the day that he would bravely co-operate in getting out of bed and sitting in a chair for a little while. He was in considerable pain but was beginning to think of getting home as soon as possible again. He was still unable to eat any solids but was allowed to take a few sips of water. He felt uncomfortable as he sat in the chair for he realised that he was wearing only a white hospital gown and, although he was covered with a blanket as he sat on the chair, when he was moved back into bed he was virtually naked at the back, for the draw strings on these gowns always have a mind of their own and are for ever untied. 'Mooning' for a man of 59 years, and an overweight one at that, was not his nor my idea of fun. Frank felt decidedly queasy and was very weak.

A couple of discharged patients arrived at the hospital to visit Frank. They were only allowed to talk to him from outside the intensive care area and did not stay long. They exchanged telephone numbers with me and left the hospital feeling forlorn.

'Please keep us informed of Frank's progress,' they said. 'Let us know if we can help him in any way. He was so helpful to us when we were in the ward. He really made us see how foolish we are to risk our own lives with drinking. He really understands what we are up against.'

'Try to do what I say and not what I did,' Frank had said. 'Look at this silly old fool here – he was refering to himself – 'You don't want to turn out like me.'

22. One Day at a Time

He knew that he could really only cope with 'One day at a time'. I knew that we had given up a day of our lives for it and tried to make it a day we had not wasted.

Frank's kidneys were in a dire state. It was now a case of touch and go regarding them. The kidneys were as near to failure as 'damn it' is to swearing and all that could be done for him was being tried. He was extremely weak and his drips were replaced with new ones.

A doctor called me to the desk to speak to me. 'We are now experiencing great difficulties with Frank's renal. The problem is that the renal has hardened and clogged. There is great difficulty in the blood getting in and out of the kidney. We do not think there is much chance of the problem getting better but if he doesn't get worse we may be able to come through it all still. We do have the added problem that the kidney is being bombarded with massive amounts of drugs and hasn't had time to recover from the first operation. His kidneys do not like the anti-rejection drug, cyclosporine.'

I was grateful to be kept so honestly in the picture but I said nothing of this to Frank. Frank would not have liked me to know more about his health than he did himself even though most of the time he was not taking in what was actually being said.

It was decided to move Frank from intensive care. At least I would now sit beside a bed in a less distressing area and he was still to be kept very close to the doctors' and sister's desk in case of an emergency. The patients had all worked out that the further down the corridor they were sleeping, the nearer they were to going home. Psychologically this was a good move for us both.

Frank was still using an oxygen mask and nebuliser. He had a timed drip that had to let a measured quantity of a drug (to 'kick' the kidneys into action) into Frank's vein every hour. If this faltered it let out a loud alarm signal, warning the staff to take immediate action. He still had a mainline drip.

All the patients had been watching me on my way to and from my bedroom and intensive care. Sometimes my face told them what was happening and they did not like to ask questions, fearing the worst. Other times, when they caught my attention, they would ask, 'What news?' Now Frank was back among them. They were relieved and amazed to see him.

'My God, you must have been really strong in your youth to survive what you have been through,' said one man.

'No, it's not that,' Frank replied, breathlessly. 'I was just too bloody bad in my youth for Him to want me up there. I'm too flaming stubborn to give in yet.'

However, on the next day he experienced a lot of pain in the kidneys and was leaking blood everywhere from his drainage tubes. It had to happen on a Sunday when the worst agency staff were on duty. It was Easter. The doctors decided that they could not give Frank his anti-rejection drug due to the kidney problem.

The staff were no better on Easter Monday and the pain was not diminishing. Frank was uncomfortable. I was pleased to be in the hospital to look after my husband's needs for there was no one to deal with the bed-pan when required. I was happy to see that the toilet was cleaner than of late.

I spent most of that Easter carrying a clean and empty bedpan from the toilet, closing curtains around the bed, helping to ease a 'Sumo wrestler' on to the comparatively small pan either on the bed or the seat beside the bed, finding toilet paper, easing the heavyweight off and walking, with what dignity I could summon, to the toilet with a covered and full bedpan, trying to ignore the staring visitors. Ah, what it is to be a nurse!

At night I had settled Frank on to the bedpan on the chair when I noticed that he was sitting in a pool of blood.

'Nurse, we need your help, please,' I said, as a nurse was walking past the closed curtain.

'I'm just off duty,' was the cheerful reply, as she carried on to her break.

I placated a frightened Frank and went to the desk.

'Frank is sitting in a pool of blood,' I told Sister, in as calm a manner as I could muster.

Sister went immediately to Frank who was now sitting with hunched shoulders and drooping head as he was feeling dizzy.

Fortunately it was not as serious as it looked. It was just a leaking drainage tube. Frank was made comfortable in bed but a little later his drip alarm let out a loud scream which appeared to be ignored for too long. The reason why the staff had tried to ignore it soon became apparent: none of the nurses knew how to reset it and each of them hoped that someone else would be able to deal with it.

Eventually one of the more senior temporary nurses dealt with the drip but within a few minutes the alarm woke everyone up. The drip was reset again but repeated its squeal three more times before a nurse from another ward was called to put it right. The agency nurse had connected the wrong drip (there were two bags suspended on the pole) but nothing was actually getting through the closed tap. I was made to feel worried and uncomfortable that agency staff were provided and taken on by the sister without checking that they were capable and familiar with the equipment and their duties.

Once again Frank knew that I could not always be with him when problems of this type arose for at some time I would have to return home. This was a worry to us.

Tuesday was the day on which the director of the unit visited all the patients. He was aloof to most people, including me, but was on slightly more relaxed terms with Frank. A host of doctors hovered around him as he looked at Frank's laboratory report. Blood tests were still taken at least once a day.

They all left Frank and me with reserved smiles. Shortly afterwards two of the doctors returned to sit with us both. This was the moment when Frank was to learn of his kidney problem, but it was to be minimised so as to cause the least possible worry and panic.

'Your kidney has the same disease as your aorta and we are very concerned,' Frank was told. He took the news very calmly but was remarkably quiet. Who knows what thoughts went through his head.

'How long will it be before I can go home?' he asked. 'I could still break the record and be out quicker than anyone else who has had a transplant.'

His bile bag was no longer being clamped so he shouldn't even have been thinking of home for some time, that is if he would ever get home.

During the morning of the next day Frank was too tired to speak to a friend who had called in to see him from the Stock Exchange. He was extremely weary and two more doctors expressed their concern to me over his kidneys, saying that the matter was very grave. Neither of them believed that there was any chance of the kidneys improving. Indeed, one of the doctors was surprised that Frank was still alive when he had returned from Cambridge. Frank had been two hours from death and had not been operated on for the aortic aneurysm when he had last seen him.

The young man in intensive care would not survive the day and his life support machine would soon cease functioning. The family had said that they would not need to be with him, but now that the moment was imminent they changed their minds for they felt that he should not die alone. I vacated my room for them. I had been reassured that it was unlikely that anything could happen so quickly to terminate Frank's life that I would not have time to get to him.

The family had spent many moments in conversation with me and came to speak to both Frank and myself. The brother of the dying man seemed to take charge but his son was fighting his emotions. Julia took him into the corridor and he was able to cry on her shoulder without the rest of the family knowing. The father had been in the Red Berets – tough and highly trained assault parachutists – but unfortunately the younger son had not inherited his fight for life. His son sadly drifted away as his mother sat by his side. She had given birth to him and now she had seen him die. His love of scrumpy had cost him dearly.

I returned home. I had been given a bunch of beautiful red roses by my neighbours on the day before the crisis. Now they remained in the vase, drooping, dark and shrivelled. Everything was as I had left it after my unexpected further eight days away from home. It was good to be home again. I was feeling exhausted. Nothing felt real. It was as if I was living a dreadful nightmare.

I luxuriated in a warm bubble bath, lounged in my dressing gown and curled my toes in my soft carpet. I could speak privately on my telephone and didn't have to search around for the right change for the payphone. I did, however, miss the families of grey squirrels which I had watched as they jumped and played on the roof of the hospital. I turned on the television and tried to feel normal again. I appreciated that I could stretch my body across the width of our double bed and fell into a deep and untroubled sleep – the first time I had had a break from worry for a long time.

I had brought Frank's dirty pyjamas home to wash and took clean ones into the hospital with me late on the following morning.

Frank was off cyclosporine temporarily to help his kidney. His new liver was still coping well but it would reject if totally without the anti-rejection drugs. The results of his recent tests had been slightly better and Frank now appeared to be walking well. He was still sleepy and he was unable to eat. He was nauseous and had vomited but he did look a little better than he had during the previous day.

There is always an advantage when the family are not in the hospital for the patients tend to mix more and help each other. The company can be good for them if kept under control and Frank's room-mates did appreciate how ill he was and did not over-tire him.

Frank was now surrounded by masses of get-well cards; some were beautiful and moving, but many were funny or even rude. He had lots of signed photographs of the well-known and loved TV stars hung on the wall. These all became a talking point for both the patients and staff. I was totally shocked and surprised that he also kept some of the magnificent flower arrangements near the bed but really believed that this was because there were so many flowers everywhere else and nowhere could be found for them.

The friendly parking attendants had allowed me a parking space so I could drive to and from the hospital daily. Today they gave me a 'Get well' card for Frank. He was becoming a bit of a celebrity himself. Although he did not feel well, Frank's a sense of humour was returning although I knew – and he later admitted – that he was putting on a brave act to cover his real fear.

One of the nurses was sitting on his bed with us. She was an attractive woman with beautiful auburn hair and a great personality to go with it.

'I'll be leaving you tomorrow to go on holiday,' she said, 'and I don't expect you to be here when I return.'

'That's it. Just when I've got used to your ugly mug you leave me in the lurch. Where are you off to?' Frank teased.

'Antigua, where there is a beach for every day of the year. Think of me lounging in the sun, swimming in the sea or lying in the Jacuzzi.'

'Jacuzzi, Jacuzzi,' replied a saucy Frank. 'The only Jacuzzi I've known is a good fart in the bath.'

'Really, Mr Craddock,' she feigned horror and disgust: 'Nurse, Mr Craddock has just told me that a Jacuzzi is a fart in the bath.'

At that the whole ward was in fits of laughter and they were joined in this hilarity by the nurses and medical team.

Frank's temperature rose on the next day. His kidneys were no worse but were not going to get any better. Now there was the possibility of infection from his venn flow in his arm and this infection could fly to the grafting in his aorta. His wounds were weeping badly and he could not keep his pyjamas clean for more than an hour. This meant that I was washing his clothes every day but the blood did come out better when I washed them at home.

Frank remained weary during the following weekend but his kidneys did not deteriorate further. He tried to walk on Sunday but his feet were now very swollen, so much so that he could not put his slippers on. His venn flow was removed for he would hopefully now take the cyclosporine orally, another step nearer getting home. I would try to buy slippers that I could cut to open the sides for him to wear.

Frank was now eating small meals but not really enjoying his food for he still felt sick.

Monday was St George's Day and also the anniversary of my father's death. I went into the office in the morning and lit two candles in the church sitting quietly alone with my thoughts and prayers. I was going to need strength to manage when Frank came home for it would be a long time before he would be well.

I wore my red rose for England and my father. I had another with me for Frank and I knew that this was one flower he would not refuse for he always wore a red rose in his buttonhole on St George's Day. How he teased everyone who was not English during the afternoon. He was still calling all the doctors by their Christian names, still saying that if they could call him Frank he was only returning the compliment.

I sat at his bed drinking my cup of coffee from my vacuum flask. Frank now had a new Vietnamese neighbour who could not speak English. His son was allowed to be with him most of the time to act as an interpreter and he hardly ever turned his small portable colour television set off. During my visit the patient's wife arrived and cooked a Vietnamese meal at the bedside for the patient. I was fascinated and understand that this is quite usual abroad when the whole family will also descend on the hospital to eat together.

My staff visited Frank and were pleased to see that he was recovering. Frank was over-excited on the next day for he had been told that he might be allowed home on Saturday but would have to return after the one night away, being back in the hospital on Sunday afternoon. His bile bag was being re-clamped and he had been able to walk along the corridor to telephone me, dragging his swollen feet.

The director and his 'minions' had seen Frank again in the afternoon. It was never known for the director to joke but today he was going to break the habit of a lifetime.

'Well, what is it to be next time?' he asked Frank. 'How about a hernia?'

The next day one of the doctors approached a very white Frank and his swollen feet. He examined his patient, noting the problematical feet.

'Well, now, how about this hernia?' he asked seriously, believing that Frank had yet another condition needing attention. 'Causing you trouble?' Frank did not know how to stop laughing.

The bile bag was clamped for ten hours before being released. There was great drama in the ward during the following evening when the Vietnamese patient who had been in the toilet when Frank had collapsed was readmitted.

He had been wheeled into the ward and left in his wheelchair beside a vacated bed on which was placed his luggage. Seeing that there was another Vietnamese in the ward he craftily asked to be wheeled to the lift in Vietnamese.

No one could understand what he had said. Trying to be helpful, the youth pushed the chair into the corridor and was well on the way to the lift with the edgy patient who was looking rapidly around to see if he had been seen. He was clutching his case to his lap as if it contained the crown jewels.

They were spotted by a nurse who immediately called for assistance and rushed to the pair telling them to come back. At this, the patient tried to take control of the chair and, using his hands on the wheels, struggled to wrench the chair out of the hands of the youth. A mini-battle ensued which was joined by the nurse and a doctor helping the youth get control of the chair again. It was, by this time, half in the open lift which was obviously now stuck at the third floor.

The chair was eventually wheeled back to the ward with a frustrated passenger.

Sister searched the man's coat pockets and his case. A miniature bottle of whisky was found in the pocket and money from a cashed giro cheque was in the case. The alcoholic, as it now appeared he was, was hell bent on spending this money on drink.

He was strapped into this chair but shouted and struggled for freedom. He was upsetting all the patients and visitors alike. Eventually the patient turned the chair over and landed on the floor with the chair on top of him. We called for help and a doctor settled both patient and chair in an upright position and left the ward. A very young and petite nurse was left to look after the patient who continued to struggle and shout at the top of his voice for someone to get the police.

Conversation was rife among both the patients and visitors as to the power that the hospital had to hold a man against his will. No one called the police.

Suddenly the chair was turned over again but this time it landed on top of the frail nurse and the patient. It was obvious that the nurse had been hurt but she tried to carry out her duties without making a fuss. A doctor, hearing the shouts from the ward, came hurrying into the ward to take charge again. He calmed the patient who was put into a bed and restrained. The wheelchair and whisky had been removed. It appeared that the patient had been staying in a halfway house where he had been too much of a handful. The halfway house was provided for patients undergoing this type of surgery or who suffered from addiction; it eased them into the real world again after hospitalisation; they were still under the care of the hospital but receiving little or no medical treatment. It was also easier to keep people here in case of organ rejection, for the ongoing tests and after care than to send them home, which was usually very far away. (I understand that there are about 60 technicians in the laboratory caring for transplant patients both during and after hospitalisation.)

Frank was greatly concerned over the young nurse and called her to his side.

'Go and have a hot sweet cup of tea. We will be OK for a little while,' he sympathetically said to her.

'I can't do that. I cannot leave this ward unattended,' she replied. She was bravely fighting back her tears. Frank put his arm around her and gave her a gentle kiss on her cheek, feeling concern. The tears started to trickle down her cheeks just as another nurse walked past in the corridor.

'Nurse, please come and take over here for a moment,' Frank shouted, as if he had authority. The nurse stopped in her tracks and joined us. She seemed to assess the situation quickly.

'Take your break now. I'll cover for you.' She then kept an eye on this six-bed ward and the similar one next door until the bruised but now more composed nurse returned.

'Thank you,' she smiled at Frank. He had seen someone else behave as if alcohol was the elixir of life.

Frank had developed a cold sore which might become serious if the infection spread and this was both watched carefully and treated with yet another drug.

The transplant surgeon had sat and talked to Frank during the day and I was told that the subject of the conversation had been me. I was gratified to learn that they both considered that I was coping well with the ongoing trauma.

I had tried to uplift my morale during the day by going to the hair-dresser. I had prepared the wages in the office and bought a scrumptious custard slice for Frank. He was now allowed to have food taken in from elsewhere to eat. I understand that a couple of patients who were not bed-bound had been outside for a meal without the staff's knowledge and that it was not unknown for the occasional visit to a pub. There were some 'take away' restaurants in the vicinity and some of the patients would telephone for pizzas which they smuggled into the smoky mist of the day room.

Frank was moved further away from the desk on the following day and his bile bag was clamped for the whole day. The tube would remain for a few more weeks but was wound around and stuck to a dressing on his body.

The kidneys were remaining the same but his liver was reportedly a little lazy today.

Frank was grumpy and found fault with petty things. He complained that he did not have enough room around his new bed. He was finding it difficult to move easily.

One of his friends from the Stock Exchange visited him and I was concerned because the main subject of discussion was drink. I would have thought that his friends would have learned a lesson from the last few years of Frank's life and tried to cut down their own alcoholic consumption. I noticed both the puffiness of the face and stale smell of 'booze' on his breath.

Frank was exhilarated and over-excited. He was putting pressure on the staff to let him come home now that his bile bag was clamped.

23. Triumphant Return

Early on Saturday April 28th I received a phone call from the hospital telling me that I could collect Frank but I must return him on the following day. I was filled with emotion, both joy and apprehension. I was going to be responsible for my husband's care and attention. I was greatly worried over the stairs in our town house and how I would be able to help Frank, who was so heavy. Nevertheless I set off to collect him as early as I could for I did not want him to be getting tense and irate as he waited to come home.

The parking attendants waved me into a space and were overjoyed to hear the good news. They moved me to the hospital exit so that there would be no distance between my car and the steps.

Frank was eager to get out but had to wait as I was given dressings for his wounds and instructions on his care. I was told of symptoms that would require an emergency return to the hospital. It had been a massive struggle for him to get into his day clothes and it was a blessing that I had found soft slippers and cut them open, for he could could not get anything else on to his grossly swollen feet. I was given his drugs, which seemed enough for an army let alone one day's supply for one man. Certain life-maintaining steroids were no longer being manufactured by the body and would have to be supplemented as well as the anti-rejection drugs for the rest of his life. We had to get used to administering these more than once daily. The porter could not be found so I pushed the heavy old wheelchair to the lift. I had not learned that I needed to pull and not push it into the lift but after a struggle I worked that out. I was puffing and panting by the time we reached the exit. My back felt as if it would break in two. I noticed two smiling faces outside on the steps. The parking attendants were waiting to help me to get Frank into the car. No one cheered but it felt as if the whole world was shouting and singing for joy. Frank was coming home and he was alive.

I drove very carefully trying to avoid any bumps in the road. I did not speed but Frank was critical of my driving.

'For God's sake, slow down,' he mumbled, as he clung to his seat.

I was driving at 30 miles per hour. I slowed down further but I could tell that his brain was unable to accept the speed of any moving object and that he was finding it difficult to adjust to the noise and movement in the real world. I hoped that there would not be people around the house when we got home and as we turned into the square I was crestfallen to see a few neighbours near our garage. Frank immediately put on his typical act and was waving and talking to them as he savoured the moment of glory. He insisted on getting out of the car, which meant that he had a slight incline to tackle to walk the distance of the drive into the house. He hadn't bargained for the fact that it would be harder to walk on uneven and hilly ground.

It was an enormous struggle to get him into the house and up the stairs to the lounge. He found it hard to breathe and was gasping for breath. How I wished that we had oxygen in the house. He had a nebuliser with him and a few puffs of that periodically helped his breathing. Frank sank into the comfort of his leather chair.

'I'm home, I've made it,' he said, emotionally, as his weary and sad eyes told me of his courage and bravery. It had been an uphill struggle and still one that he could never really win. Home was the nearest place to paradise for him at that moment.

'Every day I live is a bonus,' he added.

We hugged each other, taking care not to hug too tightly, for that would have hurt his body. We looked at each other and knew that we had suffered so much together.

'I couldn't have done this without you. I would not have done it if I did not have you to live for,' he said to me.

I was filled with sadness for it felt as if this struggle had only been made because of my husband's great love for me and not because he really had wanted to live. This made me humble and sad. It felt a very heavy burden to carry and I vowed to myself that whatever life he still had to live should be made worthwhile and enjoyable.

I was more aware of the struggle, skill and dedication of the hospital surgical team as I cared for him while he rested on the bed at home.

'They have really buggered up my modelling prospects,' were humorous comments from Frank as I changed the messy dressings. I thought of the many people who had given blood for the transfusions and of the donor of the liver. I prayed that Frank would have the strength and willpower to stay off alcohol and knew that it would be impossible to share the shame if he lost that fight.

'Frank, do you remember asking for your Samurai sword before your operation?' I asked.

He nodded his head.

'Why?'

'I was going into battle,' was his reply.

The weekend was a tremendous strain. He was unfit to be home and I was worried and scared that I would not be able to cope. I could not understand why he was allowed to come home at that time. We had bypassed the halfway house where we might have gone to acclimatise to normality because our home was within reasonable distance of the liver unit. We were filled with emotion and felt tearful.

Frank's legs and feet were swollen and he had to wear surgical stockings. He could not move around the house for he was not able to do so without becoming weak and having great breathing problems. I was terrified in case he collapsed on the floor for I would not be able to move him by myself. At least we still had the Homelink to activate for help in a crisis.

I was exhausted. It was during this weekend that I learned how much the strain had taken from me.

I could not sleep on the Saturday night for Frank could not breathe. He had to sit, leaning into pillows for the whole night, and when he dozed off his breathing was so laboured that I was frightened.

Before he dressed himself on Sunday, I had found him standing naked in front of the full-length mirror as he looked at his body. He was crying. He turned to me and his eyes were showing so much pain.

He noticed the cigarette packet by his chair on that Sunday and remembered throwing it into the air when we learned of the organ donation.

He picked it up and went slowly into the kitchen and deposited it into the waste bin.

'I've no need of them in the future. I'll never smoke again,' he proudly and confidently said. 'Dictum meum pactum' (My word is my bond.) I was sure that I had done the right thing in leaving them for him to throw out himself and knew that he really had won that battle.

It was as much a struggle to return Frank to the hospital and I could not find any help when we arrived at the deserted entrance. I left him sitting on a chair near the door as I hunted for a wheelchair. It was equally heavy and difficult to push and pull as before. I'm sure that it had been used in a supermarket for it kept pulling to the right.

I know that he was relieved when he arrived in the ward. I spoke to the staff and told one of the doctors how weak Frank was and of the difficulties we had experienced.

I knew that Frank would minimise these so that he could come home quickly but I really would not be able to manage to care for him properly without help.

I went to Oxford to lecture to a group of college students on the following day, hoping that my tiredness was not apparent. It wasn't until evening that I could visit the hospital, and I found Frank receiving a blood transfusion. He had to have two units of blood because he was anaemic. I was told that it would help him to climb stairs without being as breathless. He was probably going to be allowed home on Wednesday. Julia, David

and I were worried about this. I wanted him to come home but I was very
worried and tired. I also felt that if he only had a short lifespan it was
better for him to be in his own surroundings at home.

Julia asked, 'What about a birthday party?' Frank would be home in
time for his 60th birthday. His face fell. He knew that he would not be
well enough to celebrate and he did not want to share it with anyone
other than me. We left the matter in abeyance.

The doctors spoke to me on my next visit to the hospital. They gave me
an update on his condition which was still grim. It did seem that the liver
transplant in itself had been successful but the other problems were still
causing trouble and there was no likelihood of these every changing. Frank
had new blood now. He had put on a stone in three days so his weight
was increasing rapidly through the malfunction of the kidneys. He looked
puffy and swollen. I was to return him to the hospital if he ever had a
temperature rise or if he was jaundiced or in pain.

A few people who looked on Frank as a friend took photographs of him,
knowing that he would soon be on his way home and out of their lives.
We were not going to stay at the halfway house and I am quite convinced
that Frank had been telling the doctors that our facilities were easier at
home than they were in actuality. He had been hospitalised for nearly six
weeks. It seemed like an eternity.

Thursday May 2nd was bright and sunny. I rose early to shop, for Frank
wanted, 'The biggest box of chocolates I could find for the staff of the
ward.'

Sister telephoned the local surgery to arrange for a district nurse to
deal with Frank's dressings on a daily basis. I was given a huge amount
of sterile dressings and instructions as Frank was moved onto the wheelchair. He seemed to have collected a mass of luggage. I smiled as I emptied
his locker for there were small bottles of Branston pickle, mustard, mint
sauce, tartare sauce and salad cream as well as his own tea bags and
coffee. I had received instructions to bring them to him to make it seem
more like home. He had also asked for hard boiled eggs and tomatoes
which he always ate for breakfast when he was allowed. Other patients
had started to copy him. I'm sure that the refrigerator in the kitchen must
have been bulging now. There had been moments when Frank was given
predigested food in the form of a drink.

I left his fruit behind with the Italian for he had no relatives in the
country to shop for him. He was due to return to Italy after a short
rehabilitation in the halfway house.

Frank was sitting in the wheelchair in the corridor getting a little
impatient, for he could not get home fast enough. His feet looked so
painfully swollen, his stomach enormous and his face podgy. I had not

expected him to recover and then be in the same (if not worse) state as before the transplant. We had assumed that he would either die or that everything would be 'hunky-dory' again. Here was a very sick man who had no real hope of getting any better. Had his life been prolonged or was it that his death had been prolonged instead?

Frank was given a hero's send-off by the staff and patients. We were euphoric as we left the building. Even the squirrels on the roof in the sunshine appeared to be jumping for joy. Everyone smiled at us as we walked down the corridor for our smiles were infectious.

Standing outside were the carparking attendants who had grins on their faces which matched our own. They applauded Frank who by this time was showing signs of emotion. He was helped into the car and we travelled slowly and carefully towards home. I was going to have him back for his birthday. It had to be made a very special one for him but he would not be able to cope with the strain of a party.

The square where we lived looked beautiful as we drove into it. Everything looked different for we were looking at the world as if we had never seen it before.

It was extremely difficult to get Frank up the stairs into our town house and I wished that I had a wheelchair and oxygen at home. This had been thought unnecessary by the hospital whose judgement I had to respect.

Frank went directly to bed. I had scattered seeds on the window boxes earlier in the year and the colour of the early marigolds made a splash of glorious colour on the balcony outside. The sun was streaming in through the patio door as he lay down and went into a deep and natural sleep.

Our local newspaper sent a reporter and photographer to the house in the early evening. I only allowed them to come in if they undertook not to tire Frank and would go away if he did not want to see them. They were made welcome by Frank and did not stay long.

The district nurse arrived next day and was intrigued by her charge for she had not nursed a liver transplant case before. She had a cheerful scrubbed face which broke into a smile as she giggled every few minutes. Frank's wounds were still messy. The area of the bile drainage tube had to be carefully cleaned and sealed frequently. Frank had not been in a bath for six weeks and would not be able to bathe for a long while yet for it would be weeks before the bile tube could be removed.

'Dizzy Dope' (our affectionate name for the nurse) or I would blanket-bath him. Frank preferred me to blanket-bath him more than anyone else for his pride was left intact and he liked the way I 'talced his bottom' and 'tickled his fancy'.

The nurse had not taken her driving test and had to cycle everywhere. Eventually she would pass this test and buy my white Peugeot 205 from me which she immediately named 'Daisy.' Poor Daisy spent more time in hospital, as she called the garage, than on the road for she was always getting 'pranged'.

I found it difficult to get into a normal routine again and was disorganised. I tackled the chores of washing and shopping and planned a couple of surprises for his birthday. Frank had a bad night through his laboured breathing. He was filling with fluid. Could it be that he was drowning inside? I felt frustrated and useless as I could not think how I could help him.

I found a lambswool underblanket and placed it on his bed for he was so heavy and seemed to lie in the same position. This would help to prevent more bedsores.

Nancy came to us first thing on Friday morning with a copy of the *East London Advertiser*. Frank had made headline news. There was a photograph of him sitting in his armchair with me on the arm of the chair snuggling up to him. The story carried the banner heading: *Doctors amazed at liver swap Frank*, and was subheaded *Dad beats death at the double*. It was an 'exclusive' story, by Jonathon Pimm:

A man who twice looked death in the face during two major operations has miraculously returned home just days before his 60th birthday. Fighter Frank Craddock of Capstan Square on the Isle of Dogs underwent an eight-hour liver operation six weeks ago, having spent five nail-biting months on the waiting list.

Kindly cops from Limehouse Police Station rushed Frank by high-speed squad car to King's College Hospital – where Hackney woman Aisling Barnett had her operation – immediately the donor organ became available. Retired stock jobber, Frank, was making an amazing recovery when suddenly on April 11th a large blood vessel in his stomach burst and began leaking. The team of top doctors looking after Frank held an emergency meeting to decide what they should do.

After much agonising they told Frank he was not well enough to face a second major operation and added that there was nothing more they could do. But fearless Frank pleaded with surgeons, saying 'if they had the skill then he would do the rest' to survive.

'I virtually had to talk them into it; they did not think that anybody could take so much in such a short time,' said Frank. But for 16 days after his second brush with death Frank was on the critical list before he gradually began to get better.

Loving wife Ann, 52, said: 'Not only did he look death in the face once with the first operation but he had to go through the whole thing a second time.' She added: 'Frank has a tremendous power to fight and this is what got him through the terrible ordeal.'

Now the courageous couple, who have five children and three grand-children, are regarding every moment as a bonus.

Frank, who has to take nine different tablets to stop his body rejecting the new liver, plans to spend his birthday tomorrow (Saturday) very quietly.

Dr Cohen from the hospital was keeping in continual telephone contact with us. He told Frank to keep his fluid intake down as this would help a little regarding the fluid retention. We were so used to measuring a litre a day for him. This was a bitter blow, for it was something we had hoped would be in the past after the transplant. It was already noticeable that there would not be much difference in the quality of life before and after the operation. We were to visit Outpatients at least twice a week for a time.

We had not used the 'Homelink' so I activated it in a test situation, not knowing whether we would need to use it in a possible crisis. It was functioning normally.

Frank had a visit from our young neighbours who had decided to bring him a bowl of fresh fruit salad instead of the curry previously promised to him. Frank loved Indian food and the two girls, being Asian, would have been expert curry producers. I'm sure they did the right thing at the time. Frank had always suffered with wind and frequently embarrassed me as he held a motto: 'Wherever you be, let the wind blow free.'

A curry at this time might well have meant a truly windy night. Frank achieved the 60th anniversary of his birthday. There were many beautiful cards conveying congratulations and love. Dizzy Dope pinned a badge on his pyjamas: 60 TODAY, AND I STILL HAVE MY OWN TEETH. I turned on the radio on to Radio 2 in the bedroom at midday.

'Do we have to have that on?' Frank asked me, for he enjoyed the peace and quiet more. He turned the radio off.

'Please Frank, can I leave it for a short while?' I said, as I turned it on again. He looked at me and nodded. I was relieved for I knew that shortly he would have the first of his birthday surprises.

Gerald Harper was presenting his weekly programme. The music stopped. Over the radio we heard Gerald Harper say, 'Happy birthday, Frank. Frank Craddock. My word there are a lot of reasons why you shouldn't have had a happy birthday.' He then mentioned the two oper-ations. 'But you have a lovely wife, Ann, who loves you very much, so Frank for you here is Sarah Brightman with something which sums up your wife, *Something to believe in.'*

I do not know who was the more moved, Frank or myself. Gerald Harper had also said that he would send Frank a bottle of champagne if I telephoned in with our address on the Isle of Dogs. 'I'm sure the doctors will let you have a teaspoonful to celebrate,' he said over the air to Frank.

We listened to the clear voice of the beautiful and talented singer with tears in our eyes. Frank put his arm around me.

'How did you arrange that?' he asked me. I did not tell him that I had managed to telephone the producer in the studio but I now had to make another call to them with our address.

I thanked them most profusely whilst the news was being read. I also explained that we would not drink the champagne ourselves but would take it to the hospital for the surgeons to drink for they were the people who had done all the work in saving Frank's life. There was no way that Frank could even sip the alcohol.

Imagine our surprise when Gerald Harper started the second half of his programme by thanking me for our address and saying that I had said we would give the champagne to the doctors.

'In that case I will send you two bottles so that you get a sip yourselves.' We eventually took the two bottles of champagne to the hospital so that each of the surgeons could have a bottle. One was wrapped in pink paper and the other in blue with signed photographs of our benefactor enclosed in the box.

The second surprise was that I had ordered a blue and white iced cake from the local baker. It was lovely to look at and also to eat. Nancy and Richard joined us. We watched Frank in his sweater and pyjama bottoms cut the cake with his unsheathed Samurai sword. He had never removed it from its scabbard before. The cork from the champagne bottle hit the ceiling with the bubbling liquid following to leave a stain on the surface.

Frank had been unable to get into any of his trousers because of his massive girth and was upset by this. However, it did not spoil his enjoyment as he sipped his soft drink.

'Just because I cannot drink does not mean that I do not want anyone else to drink and enjoy themselves,' he said. 'In fact it makes it easier for me if I can see that I am not stopping anyone else drinking.'

Nancy and Richard did not stay long. Frank tired very quickly and today had been one he would remember.

No nurse came to look after him the next day so I had to deal with the dressings. He had a badly weeping wound. I changed the dressing twice. He was breathless and could not sleep. Everything was a struggle. We were both feeling the strain.

The nurse found Frank to be the same on the following day. We were beginning to be disillusioned. There was no noticeable progress. We had both given up a day of our life for this day but apart from having each other it appeared to be pointless.

Next day I had to drive Frank to the liver clinic. Once again I did not have difficulty in parking because of our friendly attendants who were pleased to see us again. I still found it difficult to wheel Frank and this time we were lucky for we sat and waited inside the door for a porter and actually found one. The clinic was on the ground floor and there was no waiting about. We were expected and seen by the familiar team immediately. I was able to tell them my worries in an unhurried way. My report on Frank seemed to be important.

There was concern over Frank's heart disease. He was drowning in his fluid retention which was making it difficult for his lungs to work properly. The usual seven blood tests were taken by the doctor which meant that we did not have to go to the laboratory, but we did have to go to radiography for a further X-ray of Frank's chest.

It was decided that Frank had better have an injection of frusemide to speed the fluid on its way from his body so we went to the ward for the injection to be given. I was given a 'bottle' for Frank to use in the car in an emergency on our way home for we could not stop in the London streets for him to relieve himself. We carried a mottled grey cardboard bottle in a black rubbish bag in the car for ever after.

I noticed that the ward had been stripped and alterations were about to commence in intensive care. There were going to be three intensive care beds in future for transplants and I felt that the other alterations were long overdue.

Frank had the injection and we were told not to lose any time in making our way home. And sure enough, the bottle was soon put to use. Frank sat in the car during the rush hour emptying his bladder, pretending to the world outside that all was normal.

There were no telephone calls from the hospital that day so nothing had shown yet in the tests or X-ray.

We had one day of grace but then had to return to the liver clinic on the following day where Frank was given another injection and a week's supply of diuretic tablets.

I was delighted to see how well the other patients looked. They were returning for their scheduled check-ups. Perhaps in time Frank would improve too but at present he was unable to walk around like them. I had total confidence in the doctors.

My accountant visited me that evening for I was gravely concerned over the state of my business. It was showing signs of neglect and a fall-off in business within the City of London. He did not advise closing down so I knew that I had to inject capital into the business in order to continue. I took out a mortgage of £60,000 on my house which at that date I owned 100%. Frank would not be able to help by earning a living again and would be dependent on any money I could make in the future. Indeed it had been like this for the last few years for he had not been fit enough to work for a long time. I was desperately worried over our financial future but had to put it out of my mind or else I would not have been able to cope with my priority in life, that being my sick husband and our immediate future.

I was angry that my landlord had spent too much money in the office building on new and, in my opinion, extravagant toilet fitments and carpeting. I had to find £4000 in addition to my normal rent and pressure was being put on me to pay it immediately.

At last the fluid in Frank's body was beginning to decrease and his wound appeared to be healing better. The nurse found the first of many stitches that had been left in the wound which had caused part of the trouble. However, after she left, the wound around the bile bag poured and I had to re-dress the area.

So we continued with the frequent visits to the liver clinic and the days between at home. Some days were good but there were still the odd bad days. I was now feeling the strain and Frank was much quieter and more thoughtful than normal. Although we were together and it was wonderful to have him at home, I felt very isolated and alone. Somehow I knew that I was still living with death. I was not negative and remained cheerful on the surface and supportive and encouraging to Frank.

One morning Dizzy Dope cut into the bile drainage tube as she was removing the dirty dressing. The strong bitter smell of the bile and the dark yellow-green liquid trickled out. I held the tube at an angle so that the bile would not continue to run out as she went to speak to the liver unit on the telephone. She received her instructions to clamp it nearer to the body. The panic was over and no great damage was done. Apparently there were feet of this tube in the body.

Frank was walking more and more. I could leave him for longer periods but apart from reading a newspaper he had very few interests and hobbies, and little company. He did not feel well enough to join others.

My birthday came and went without anyone really knowing about it. Frank was upset that he had not been able to buy a card or present but I told him that I had the best present he could give me, that he was at home with me.

I missed physical contact with him for although he had never been very demonstrative, now he did not appear to want to touch anyone.

He did tell me that he noticed that his body odour had changed and that he never felt really clean. He always maintained that this had changed with his transplant and often questioned whether the donor had been a coloured man. We were never to learn the answer and did not press the question for it was right that the anonymity of the donor should be kept for all our sakes.

I drove Frank to the barber's and he strutted in like a proud peacock, putting on an act that belied the difficulty he was really experiencing on his first outing since the operation. This obviously boosted his morale and from then on he tried to walk a little more outside each day.

His kidneys were continuing to rebel against the massive amount of drugs they had had to cope with during the last few weeks and there were many calls from the liver unit to change his dose of cyclosporine when the results of the most recent blood tests were shown. He had to have the odd day without the drug.

I was trying very hard to get back to normal but when I nearly burst into tears as I was driving away from the house one day, leaving Frank with a friendly visitor who was in the police force, the visitor stopped my car and as I wound down my window he held my hand and said,

'Don't rush it Ann.' This was the first kindly concern that I had received and it made me more emotional and weepy, but it did relieve some of the tension.

Frank did not complain much. He enjoyed the attention which I felt he deserved. His eyes looked pained to me and I knew that he was struggling with himself mentally.

I am sure he was already once again in a battle against drink. His conversation always seemed to revolve around the subject and he often said that he'd found it much harder to give up drink than cigarettes. He often had bad headaches and complained of his deteriorating eyesight.

I had eventually found the missing glasses in the hospital on an empty locker in another ward so he had both pairs of glasses to wear now. I was spending more time in the office and was unhappy with the way in which it had been run. I was also chairing the festival committee meetings.

24. One Step Forward – Two Steps Back

On June 6th 1990 Frank returned to the hospital to have the bile tube removed. He suffered considerable pain afterwards but was in the right place for the correct attention. He obviously enjoyed being with other people with drink problems and when he returned home the next day, he had many stories to tell of them all sitting together with a doctor as they swapped stories and advice. Frank had been angry with one patient – a journalist – who was being given cans of drink by his girlfriend in the hospital, for he felt that the journalist was making a mockery of the doctors. Frank told him that he would be the only one to suffer. However, the journalist was not fooling the doctors who were well aware of what was going on, and that journalist was not given the opportunity of a liver transplant.

The district nurse made her last official visit but continued to visit us as a friend. She knew a boy who was going to have a heart and lung transplant and wanted Frank to meet him. They met on many an occasion for chats in our home, hopefully helping each other. It did appear that more counselling and mental care was given to the heart transplant patients and their families, but of course heart transplants were no longer in their infancy, having been carried out for a longer time than liver transplants.

Frank was still in pain a few days after the removal of the bile tube. He became withdrawn and quiet and started to snap at me. I was upset by him when he told me to 'toughen up' for I felt that it was totally unjustified. I learned that I could no longer talk to him about business for he was unsympathetic, lacked understanding and was not mentally capable of reasoning over it. Frank's comment was made after I had received notice from one of my staff – a resignation which was going to make life even more complicated for me. Life seemed to be demanding all that I could give.

Frank's blood pressure had rocketed to 190 over 120 on June 18th when he visited the liver clinic. He was given new drugs after having an ECG, X-rays and blood tests. He was once again told that his kidneys were only just working and were threatening failure. His heart was fluttering and his arteries were very badly furred. He was still very ill. Now his eyes seemed to puff up and he did not feel as well. He knew that in spite of his tremendous fight he would not last much longer but we both knew how to come to terms with our eventual parting. Frank now had to go to the local doctor every week to have his blood pressure taken as well as keeping his appointments in the liver clinic. The blood pressure remained high.

Occasionally Frank had to spend a day in bed for he was too tired to get up. He did not look well but I was always surprised at people's reactions when they saw him on his better days for they would say how well he looked.

'You can't judge a sausage by its skin!' he would say, the comment usually bringing laughter. People did not realise that this was his way of trying not to raise their hopes for his future and telling them that he felt awful.

We were not able to talk of death and his passing as we had been before the transplant, for it made us feel guilty of being negative and pessimistic. It also seemed ungrateful to all the people who had given us these extra few weeks together. Slowly we began to overcome this.

Frank told me that he would not have had a liver transplant if he had known that there would be no improvement in his health. He felt that he had been misled by the consultant who had recommended him for assessment. I also believed that this man had glossed over the truth for I had been present when Frank had asked if he would be able to drink again and how it would affect our lives. Frank had honestly believed that he would die in hospital and that they would learn something from his death. This made his dying have a purpose in his eyes. Alternatively, he believed that if he lived he would be really fit again and would be able to help others with similar problems. The dreadful fact was that he also only had the operation and fight to live because he felt that he had let me down and that I deserved a better life than we had had together. He hoped for more time with me to make up for it all. There was never a doubt in my mind that he really loved me.

In desperation he decided that he would drink again for it was his life and if he was dying he might as well go in his own way. This binge lasted one day. He drank a bottle of whisky and was ill enough to stay in bed. Nancy came in to see him not knowing of this problem.

'Nancy,' he said, 'I'm dying.'

'Now my love,' she sadly replied.

'But Nancy, what makes it worse is that I want to die,' he gasped. She put her arms around him for a moment and left minutes later in tears.

'You poor dears,' she said as she left me. We were both crying. Frank was both honest with the medical staff in the hospital and the local doctor over his action. He was not proud of himself. They were understanding and explained to him what he was doing to the delicate chemical balance in his body. They did not pontificate nor really lecture him, which is one of the reasons I believe that he did not attempt this again. He was also terrified that I would not get his life assurance money if he killed himself with alcohol.

'I could always stop taking my drugs,' he had also said, in a depressed moment. He always took his correct dosage of drugs.

We had many moments that were beautiful together but we never made love again. His manhood had gone. His organ would not work and his pride was shattered by aborted attempts. Somehow I turned off so that I did not crave sex.

When he held me in his arms the earth could move for me. He was warm and alive because of his love for me. What more could I have asked of him than that which he had given me.

Frank spent most of that summer sitting on our balcony in the East End of London. He had to tolerate the noise and dirt of the redevelopment of the docks. He was upset by his enormous pot belly and the uninformed jokes made about it when we went out. We went to eat on a boat in the docks on our fourth wedding anniversary. Frank had written in my card: 'Let's make each year worth ten. No regrets. My love, Frank.'

He was getting more and more weary but he did keep his sense of humour most of the time. And he was not short of courage.

October saw the three-day festival to raise money for local charities and I was extremely busy co-ordinating, organising and taking part. It was a tremendous success. Frank was only able to attend the evening function with the transplant surgeon and his wife amongst our guests. He needed medical help in getting him home for the effort had cost him dearly. Julia had been very concerned that her father had been successful in bidding for the special bottle of port, port and wine glasses in the auction. I knew that he wanted me to have them as a souvenir of the occasion.

I was very honoured to receive the Freedom of the City of London in November. Frank could not get into his clothes so he had a jacket and trousers made for the occasion. He was so proud and was not only able to attend but gave me a champagne party and dinner afterwards. This was to be our last public occasion together. He never wore the jacket again. We had not spent a Christmas with my grandchildren and he felt guilty over this. He insisted that we went to Lydia for the festive season in spite of the effort it would cost him. He knew that this would be our last Christmas together and it would be easier to enjoy in their company than alone with our thoughts.

He was delighted that I had a buyer for the business for I would now be able to spend the rest of his life with him. He would have been horrified if he had known of the troubles that this would give me later for the deal was never completed and I was left with the rent and rates to pay and no business in which to raise the money.

We were beginning to live in an artificial world. We saw in 1991 together in our home. As Big Ben struck midnight we hugged each other in tears.

'You don't need to tell me what you are thinking,' he said, as his eyes devoured mine. I knew that he knew.

'Somewhere a family are together tonight but they are one very special person short and are missing him dreadfully. I'm dreadfully sorry for his wife.' I choked as I said this, assuming that the donor was married. Frank nodded. We had this magic moment together now and were eternally grateful.

'But darling, next year you will be alone, too,' he replied, the tears streaming down his cheeks as we thought and felt as one.

I had never expected the luxury of not working and filling my time with things that I wanted to do. Frank and I had 6 weeks of unadulterated pleasure in each other's company. It was as if we were getting to know each other all over again. I was able to show my love for him in the care I was able to give to him. Cooking was a creative pastime in which I could express my feelings of 'doing it all for him' and the normal chores of housework actually became a complete satisfaction.

We were both shattered by recent events and I had never felt as tired in my life. I did have to go into the City as a consultant to the proposed purchasers of my business but most of the contacts were dealt with at home. Frank always went to the Island Gardens overlooked by Greenwich on the opposite side of the Thames for a walk in the afternoon. He needed to get out every day and provided he drove to this park, he was able to walk from bench to bench and sit when he felt he needed a 'breather'. There was a café in the park too but I do not think it was open at this time. He liked to be alone on this walk and I stayed at home. He should be given time to himself.

People were very important to Frank and he was known by everyone in the area. He knew everyone by name and loved his cheerful gossips and teasing with them. He was always eager to help anyone in distress but had been quick to react when about to be mugged himself in an earlier incident; he had swung round and laid the two youths out.

He had a quick wit and an answer for everything. The informal atmosphere in a pub appealed to him and I wondered if that was one place where he had made friends when I was at work.

He could never be on time for an appointment. I pulled his leg and told him that he would be late for his own funeral.

We tried to look at what we had got rather than at what we had not. It helped us to keep a sense of balance.

The weather was typical of winter and in late January and early February the ground was covered with thick snow, even in our part of London. Frank became restless and wanted to go out. He had to stay indoors because it was impossible to get the car out of the garage for a few days and I would have been greatly worried if he was out in the cold. One of the neighbours got us shopping and dug a pathway to the door. Soon the snow cleared and Frank was free again.

He seemed to be tiring. He was sleeping more and more during the day. The fire of his personality was burning out and he was quietly taking everything in his stride, calmly and complacently, which was alien to him.

He seemed to be getting a little remote and forgetful.

Normally, he would get up first in the morning and make us both a cup of tea. He always gave me mine in bed but had his in his special mug downstairs. He then drove to the newsagent for the daily newspaper and returned home where he wearily shaved, always rubbing his hand down his cheek to check that he was smooth and unstubbled. He loved to cook his own breakfast of eggs, bacon, sausages and tomatoes or something similar. Now, instead of sitting and reading his newspaper he returned to bed, rising at about two o'clock in the afternoon. He would leave the house at around three o'clock for his trip to Island Gardens in the car.

Frank was getting heavier and putting on inches all over. Even his pyjamas were uncomfortable for him to wear now. His new clothes would not stretch for him to wear. He wasn't drinking alcohol but treated himself to a can of non-alcoholic lager every evening which did not help his weight or fluid retention problems. This was his only pleasure of the day.

On February 18th I had to go back to the hairdresser and attend a short charity meeting . . . In the morning Frank made a point:

'Ann, you won't let them operate on me again, will you?'

I told him that I thought it was highly unlikely that further surgery on him would be considered. 'Unless you want to take up the offer of a hernia,' I joked, remembering the laughter in the hospital. Frank looked relieved as he appreciated the joke.

We miscalculated the time and I had to leave the house in a rush so that I didn't miss the riverbus. The dirty lunch plates were left in the sink – something that I never did – and Frank said he would wash them for me before I came home. He drove me to the pier and then went to the doctor during that afternoon for his check-up and to get a repeat prescription from the chemist.

There had been bomb scares in London and all the mainline stations were closed, causing total chaos for commuters. I was advised to get home as early as possible by the riverbus captain as crowds of people were using the river for transport. When I arrived at the Isle of Dogs I phoned home to ask Frank to meet me. He did not answer so I left it for a few moments and then tried to get him again. He answered and duly arrived for me. As I got into the car I was struck by pungent body odour. Frank was scrupulously clean but over the last few days he had seemed to ooze this sour and unsavoury smell, totally unfamiliar to me. It crossed my mind that I must help him bathe the next day for he found it difficult to get in and out of the bath now and he could not reach his extremities over his stomach. Nevertheless he had a very thorough wash every day.

I had 'auto' set the oven so on our arrival home we were greeted by the appetising smell of a nutritious casserole. Frank said that he was not really hungry but tried to eat an average helping of stew. I noticed that the lunch plates had not been touched and indeed the house looked as if nothing had been stirred since I had left it.

I asked Frank what he had done during the afternoon and his reply made me realise that he did not know nor remember.

The evening was spent quietly watching television, both of us nodding off for forty winks occasionally. Frank often sat up after I had gone to bed and he liked to be the last to retire. I used the opportunity to lie in bed reading a good book as he watched one last programme of the day.

However, on this night he decided to go to bed at the same time as me. I went upstairs to use the bathroom. He went downstairs to use the toilet. During the afternoon at the meeting I had been talking to a man who was distressed by the recent death of his sister. I knew that I had a copy of the Scott-Holland reading which I had read at my Father's funeral and that it had given me comfort when I had needed it. I cut out the words from the funeral service sheet and had them in my hand as a dull knocking sound came from downstairs.

'Death is nothing at all ... I have only slipped away into the next room ... I am I and you are you ... whatever we were to each other, that we are still. Call me by my old familiar name, speak to me in the easy way which you always used. Put no difference into your tone; wear no forced air of solemnity or sorrow. Laugh as we always laughed at the little jokes we enjoyed together. Play, smile, think of me, pray for me. Let my name be for ever the household word that it always was. Let it be spoken without effect, without the ghost of a shadow on it. Life means all that it ever meant. It is the same as it ever was; there is absolutely unbroken continuity. What is this death but a negligible accident? Why should I be out of mind because I am out of sight? I am but waiting for

you, for an interval, somewhere very near, just around the corner ...
All is well.

25. Till Death Do Us Part

The gentle tapping which I had thought was next door had stopped when I realised that Frank was weakly shouting.

'Ann, Ann, I need you.' I placed the reading by the side of the bed and hurried to him.

'It's OK Frank. I'm on the way,' I called. I quite expected that Frank had been unable to control his bowel movement and had more than 'skid marked', his pants as he would have embarrassedly said.

Frank was sitting on the toilet with his trousers around his ankles and his underpants stretched tightly over his knees.

He must have pulled the towel rail off the wall and had probably been using it to tap the wall for my attention. It had now been dropped on the floor. He was limp.

'I'm dying,' he said, 'I didn't think it would be like this.' He wasn't complaining but making a very weak statement.

I did not immediately realise that he was right, for we had thought so often that he had been dying before. I tried to comfort him.

'I don't think you are dying, darling. You are just having a nasty turn. Are you in pain?'

He nodded slightly with a head that looked too heavy to hold.

'My shoulder blade hurts and my poor old ticker is working like the clappers. I've lost the use of my arms.'

I gently tried to move his arms and it was true that the arms were limp and useless. However, as I put my hand under his fingers in his hand, they curled around it.

'Darling, you can still grip me, see?' I said. There seemed to be an aura around me, not allowing me to accept the harsh fact that this was going to be the end of our life together. I hadn't thought it would be like this either.

I tried to lean him against the wall so that he would not fall off the seat but his head fell onto the tap in the basin. If he would just stay balanced for enough time for me to get a cushion I might be able to lean him against that, I thought.

'You'll have to try to help me to help you,' I said. 'Try to get your arms around my neck so that I can try to lay you on the floor.' I raised his arms around my neck but they immediately fell to his sides. He vomited slightly and his eyes closed as his head lolled against me. I was hugging him to my body with his head pressing on my breasts.

He said something in a growl in his throat but I could not understand what it was. This was repeated; I pray that he said,

'I love you. No regrets,' as he had said before.

He lost all control of his reflex actions. His nose ran and he emptied his bowels, an action accompanied by the most enormous fart.

'Anyone would have been proud of that,' he would have said, if he had been able to acknowledge it.

I listened to his breathing with my ear against his back as I leant over him. It had stopped and started again. It stopped and did not start again.

I was hugging him to my body. His head was leaning on me, facing down. I could not see his face. I leaned over his shoulder to listen to his heart through his back but I could only hear my own heart racing.

A few minutes must have felt like a lifetime, or did I really hold this man in my arms for an eternity? I hugged him, supporting his body so that it did not crash to the floor. I noticed that his ears had turned blue. He was feeling cold to my touch.

I had lost my treasure. God had finally and mercifully called him. I licked my finger without understanding why I did it. I had no anointing oil or holy water. I made the sign of the cross on his neck, the only part of his body that I could reach while my arms were still around him.

'God forgive you. God bless you. Sleep tight.'

Why, oh why, hadn't I realised that this time he really was dying? Why hadn't I told him that I loved him while he was dying? Why hadn't I comforted him more?

I knew that he was now at peace and his soul had left the troublesome body behind. Frank had died in my arms at home, just as he had prayed, for God had finally been merciful to him.

I wanted to lay the heavy body onto the floor and worked out that if I walked backwards his body would fall forward with me. I knelt on the floor slowly so as to lower the body to the ground. I levered him gently but it fell the last few inches with a horrifying thud. I found an old garden coat close by and covered him as if he were still alive. It was cold. I was stunned.

'Ambulances are for the living,' I thought, as I slowly went to the telephone. I called the doctor. The telephonist seemed remote as she asked,

'Which doctor?' I told her the name of our GP. She seemed to pause for too long. I was agitated. 'Please hurry, I think my husband has just died,' I coolly stated.

'I'm getting the doctor now dear. Are you alright? Are you alone? Is there someone who could be with you?'

Frank had been a proud man in life and I was going to allow him that pride in death. No one was to be allowed to visit the house to see his semi-naked body lying on the floor, for his trousers were still around his ankles and his pants were only a little higher up. His naked bottom and legs were sticking in the air under the coat. I wanted no one in the house until the doctor and undertakers had been.

The doctor took nearly an hour. I spent the time with Frank's body, holding his hand and stroking his hair as I sat on the bottom step of the stairs. I kissed his neck. I did not cry nor feel like doing so.

The doctor was wonderful. He bent over Frank and said gently to me, 'I'm afraid you are right. He is dead.'

The doctor and I walked into the lounge. We had a cup of tea which I made. He was so very kind and very calm. As he wasn't our normal doctor he phoned him up to tell him what had happened.

He had asked, 'How do you feel about a post-mortem examination?'

'I think that we as a family have been through enough without that,' was my calm reply. 'However, if there has to be one, we will have to agree to it.'

The two doctors agreed and did not think that there would be any need. They would talk to the coroner in the morning. The doctor very kindly phoned the undertakers for me.

The doctor stayed with me for two hours, in spite of the fact that I was trying to get him to go home for some rest as he had a surgery in the morning. He did not want to leave me until the undertakers had arrived and made frequent calls to them to find out how long they would be. Eventually he left me, after straightening Frank's body as it upset me to see it in such an unnatural position. The undertakers had said they would only be 20 minutes. In fact six hours elapsed after Frank's death before they arrived. The doctor told me to take my time and not hurry or push myself.

'Have a good rest before you pick up the pieces.'

I had been rambling on about the fact that I would have to get a new job and had tried to sound as if I had the whole of my life planned before me. I did not cry.

I sat with Frank's body. I opened my heart as I talked to it. I stroked his hair again and smoothed his forehead. I touched his hand and his back. I had loved him dearly and knew that love was eternal and that death would not finish that love. I told him how I wished that I had known he was really dying and told him that I was sorry that I had not handled it better. I wished that I had been gentler at his passing. I told him that I knew that he was at peace and that I would continue my life in a way that I hoped would make him proud. I thanked him for all the love he had given to me.

He sighed and expelled air. Just for a moment I wondered if the doctor was right and that he really was dead.

The black van with the extractor swishing on top came into the square looking for the correct address. It drove around a few times and the undertaker even phoned to say that he could not find me.

Looking like crows and sounding like robots, they shook my hand. In a monotone and sounding expressionless they said, 'Condolences Mrs Craddock.' But their eyes did not mean it.

My daughter, Claire, telephoned me as Frank was removed from his home for the last time. She deliberately kept me talking so that I could not see what was happening, and she had been phoning me periodically during the night to make sure that I was alright.

I shampooed the carpet where Frank had been lying. Now family and friends could come but I would not telephone anyone for a couple of hours as I did not want to disturb their sleep.

There were difficulties regarding the funeral arrangements for I wanted the service in the City and we moved Frank to a different funeral director who was far more helpful.

There was no post-mortem.

Prayers were said in St Mary-le-Bow at 7.30 a.m. and prayers were said in St Paul's Cathedral two days later. Our priest came as quickly as possible and prayed for peace in my home which gave us great comfort. He pronounced God's forgiveness for Frank's sins in life and agreed to the service which Frank and I had previously planned.

The house was peaceful and quiet. I kept the curtains drawn and placed a black bow on the door outside. Daylight seemed to intrude and be offensive. I was protected from the harsh reality of the world outside. I had to play Frank's favourite music for I felt that if I did not listen at this time, I might never be able to listen to it again. I blasted *Pie Jesu* through the stereo system for a whole evening. I sat in Frank's chair for I did not want to have a ghost there and I asked others to do the same. I made a point of using his mug and glass for I did not want them to become untouchable objects.

I found it difficult to walk outside the house and wanted to rush back inside. I found it an enormous strain to register Frank's death in spite of having Lydia with me. The registrar was sympathetic and understanding but the aura surrounding me began to let reality in. The receptionist had asked me, 'What relationship with the deceased?'

I know that I thought 'Widow' but couldn't say or admit it. 'I was his wife,' I thought I said, but my daughter believed that she heard me say the first. It hurt.

When the registrar asked me the same question a few moments later, I took a deep breath and replied, 'I am his widow,' then I repeated it over and over again during the day until it stopped hurting me as much.

Frank had died from another aneurysm, this time in his head. His liver had lasted and would probably have continued to function well.

For the first time I realised that I was glad that he had been given a transplant for we had spent a happy six weeks before he died that I will always treasure. We had been able to enjoy each other's company without the pressure of business. If he had not been given this chance his death might have been very different and I could have been feeling bitter and angry.

My brain seemed to switch off if I was put under stress. Lydia filled in most of the innumerable forms for me and my memory did not seem to be good. I could not concentrate nor retain information. I felt empty, numb and emotional. I cried a lot and found it comforting when others cried with me.

26.   No Regrets

Flowers, plants, cards and letters came in batches. The newspaper announcement appeared in *The Times* and *Daily Telegraph*. All this was slowly making me aware that it had really happened.

I brought out his tantalus and put it on display. This was my way of showing that I accepted him as he was, faults and all.

Five days after Frank's death, I went to see him in the chapel of rest. He was lying in his coffin, looking at peace, with a mischievous face, 20 years younger than in life, about to laugh with me. His gown resembled that of an altar boy, which was appropriate for that is what he had once been.

I found that I was lighthearted with him and chatted to him as if he were alive. I was actually heard to laugh by those outside.

I told him that he would be given a send-off of which he would be proud. I fell in love with him all over again. Now, if there had been any lingering doubts, I knew why I had been overjoyed to become his wife. I adored him, his charm, his kindness and generosity, his humour and his teasing, his spirit and determination, his loyalty and his love. Now, in my new role, I knew that I would be proud and honoured to be his widow. I wanted to hug him.

'No regrets,' we had said. 'No regrets,' I said, and I meant it. I never saw Frank again.

That day the 'City Diary' of *The Times* carried an article about Frank by Carol Leonard. He would have been livid at the omission of a *D* in his surname for he went to great lengths to spell his name correctly: C R A *double* D O C K, not as in Fanny. She has only one, he would say. He often affectionately called me 'Fan' and we had laughed when I had some cooking utensils delivered from Selfridges to see the disappointment on the delivery man's face when he found that there was more than one Mrs. F. Craddock in the world – in his eyes – I was the wrong one.

Farewell to Frank.

The City's old guard will be saddened to learn of the death this week of Frank Cradock, one of the more colourful characters to tread the International Stock Exchange trading floor. Cradock was a keen sportsman and, in his day, a member of the Stock Exchange Veterans Football Club. He began a 40-year career in the Square Mile as a broker with

Vickers da Costa before switching to market-making with Denny Brothers and, later, Pinchin Denny.

Known as much for his love of bawdy tales as for his taste for Piccadilly cigarettes – producing them with a flourish from a silver cigarette case and tossing them into his mouth – Cradock was also a connoisseur of fine whisky, and sometimes knocked back four glasses at one go. 'He was a well known raconteur,' says a former colleague, adding that Cradock's tales were often to be taken with a healthy pinch of salt. The funeral is at noon on Monday at Bow Church, Cheapside.

I read it and laughed. It was written with such affection and I knew that he was laughing too. He had so often said that 'The darkest hour is just before the dawn.' Somehow, daylight was just beginning to peep through the dark.

I hugged the coat he had worn on the first occasion that I had met him and when he had first taken me out, burying my head into it in the hope that I would pick up his scent if it lingered on. I sobbed into the coat, alone in the bedroom. My family wisely left me alone for today was his funeral and I needed to compose myself.

The coffin was totally covered, as I had wanted, with masses of white lilies and chrysanthemums on a bed of deep green leaves. My card said simply that God's need of Frank must be very great if it is greater than mine. No regrets Everlasting love, Ann.

The day of the funeral was very sunny but there were difficulties in London as all stations were once again closed because of an IRA bomb scare. The cortège wound its way around the Isle of Dogs, passing Island Gardens where Frank had so frequently strolled. 'Memories,' I thought, as we drove by. The traffic had snarled as we entered the square mile. I remembered that I had always said that Frank would be late for his own funeral, but I had never believed it.

We made good time and were only a fraction late. As we entered Cheapside we were greeted by the solemn and slow 'Bong . . . Bong' of Bow bell in mourning. I expected the church to be rather empty with all the travel problems but it was packed. I'd only ever seen the church this full and that was at the annual carol service.

There were friends and colleagues of both of us, many members of the Stock Exchange and his Masonic Lodge, committee members of mine including police and fire brigade, and City dignitaries including the Lord Mayor elect. The service was moving and beautiful, all of us singing for him. He would have been so proud and honoured. Donations were given, instead of the flowers he would have thought 'sissy', for a new altar frontal.

I know there will always be a little bit of Frank in the church when I worship there.

I stood at the door, thanking the mourners for joining us, and as they left I felt unreal but happy from the warmth and sincerity of the service and secure in the warmth of their friendship.

As we left the city, the City police stopped the traffic in Cheapside and saluted Frank as he went by. The workmen on the building sites downed tools and took off their protective hats, bowing their heads.

We entered the crematorium under the arch and drove slowly behind the hearse along an avenue. It felt as if we were gliding in some American movie towards the chapel, between the trees and birds in an artificial film setting. Other avenues crossed ours and similar funeral processions were gliding soundlessly as if in a dream towards their destinations. There was a holdup and we had to stop and wait for another funeral ahead of us to move on as we were parked in the allotted space.

The recorded music, the glow of tinted artificial lights and the plastic flowers were the exact opposite of the sanctuary of St Mary-le-Bow. I expected an American evangelist to appear at any moment. 'Alleluia' I thought.

With a quiet dignity, the final prayer was said by Father Stock, who had travelled with us from the church. The curtains closed around Frank's coffin.

The wine bar and pubs in Bow Lane in the City were doing a roaring trade as City people were drinking that Frank would not be forgotten.

At home we chatted and laughed at the many humorous moments associated with such a lovable rogue. I was humbled, honoured and upset that Frank had told his closest friends that he only had the liver transplant because of his love for me.

'He believed that you deserved better than him prior to his drying out,' they said. 'He said that you were his life. He only wanted to live because he had you.'

No greater love could any man give any woman . . . no greater heartache. The *East London Advertiser* carried the following report:

Every moment with a loved one is precious. So says grieving widow Ann Craddock, whose husband defied death for nearly 11 months following a heart and liver swap operation.

Fighter Frank, 60, died peacefully and without pain in his wife's arms at their home in Capstan Square, on the Isle of Dogs, last Monday evening.

Said Ann: 'He was standing in the bathroom getting ready for bed when he turned to me and said, "I'm dying." '

'Within five minutes he slipped into a deep sleep from which he never recovered,' she added.

Retired stock jobber Frank had undergone his eight-hour liver transplant operation in March, last year, and was making a good recovery when a large blood vessel in his stomach burst and began leaking.

The team of doctors looking after Frank had decided there was nothing more they could do. But fearless Frank pleaded with the surgeons, saying 'If they had the skill he would do the rest' to survive.

And 16 days after his second brush with death, Frank was on his way to recovery.

Devoted Ann, who was made a Freeman of the City of London in November last year, said that things had been getting 'More and more difficult for Frank over the past few days.

'He had always struggled to stay out of hospital and spend as much time as possible at home,' said Ann, 52.

'I always think how lucky we both were to have had the extra ten and a half months together,' she added.

'We were very, very grateful for that and realise some family had made a difficult decision to donate the liver of a dying loved-one to allow someone to live,' said Ann.

Frank would have celebrated his 61st birthday on May 5th.

Frank had requested that his ashes be interred in the quiet and beautiful churchyard of St Mary Magdalene in Loders, a tiny village in Dorset where my father lies and where our marriage had been blessed four and a half years earlier.

On a lovely sunny March day I walked with his ashes to his final resting place. His casket carries the motto of the International Stock Exchange below his name: *Dictum meum pactum*, my word is my bond, the manner in which he had tried to live his sixty years. There were no crowds and no fuss. Just four generations of my own family who had taken him to their hearts, a family where he belonged. His own daughters were not present. I placed my red roses near the Portland stone.

Chris, my son-in-law, stumbled over the words as he read, through his tears, the passage Frank had asked to be spoken at his grave, which he wanted us all to remember:

> Do not stand at my grave and weep,
> I am not there, I do not sleep;
> I am a thousand winds that blow,
> I am the diamond glint of snow,
> I am the sunlight-ripened grain,

I am the gentle autumn rain.
When you awaken in the morning's hush,
I am the uplifting rush of quiet birds in circled flight.
I am the soft stars that shine at night.
Do not stand at my grave and cry,
I am not there, I did not die.

The battle was over. Frank wanted us to learn from his death in order that his living would not be in vain. He wanted to help those in trouble with the addiction he had suffered, with the trauma and dilemma of transplant surgery and with the acceptance of death itself.

As I stood at the grave a blackbird sang in the tree above.

'Yes, Joey, even you are singing farewell to a warrior. A man whose wings brushed against the angels on so many occasions.'

Frank's fading image stood with me at his grave. In his hand he carried the sword of the Samurai, the sword that he believed to be the soul of the legendary warrior of Japan.

He replaced the sabre-like, curved blade which is as powerful as his spirit, into the imperial blue and gold scabbard. The ceremonial sword was laid on the ground in front of me. He could do no more.

I had the choice of leaving the sword on the ground but his aim to help others with the telling of his story would not have been fulfilled. I put out my hands towards the fading image. Frank smiled and bent to pick the sword up. He passed it with pride and love to me.

A pigeon flew over me, leaving a white mess on my black coat. Frank had joked that he would return as a pigeon and shit on us.

As I looked up, I smiled; Thanks Frank,' I said, Thanks for everything.'